The Property Species

The Property Species

Mine, Yours, and the Human Mind

BART J. WILSON

OXFORD
UNIVERSITY PRESS

OXFORD
UNIVERSITY PRESS

Oxford University Press is a department of the University of Oxford. It furthers
the University's objective of excellence in research, scholarship, and education
by publishing worldwide. Oxford is a registered trade mark of Oxford University
Press in the UK and certain other countries.

Published in the United States of America by Oxford University Press
198 Madison Avenue, New York, NY 10016, United States of America.

© Oxford University Press 2020

CIP data is on file at the Library of Congress
ISBN 978–0–19–093679–2 (pbk.)
ISBN 978–0–19–093678–5 (hbk.)

Hardback printed by Bridgeport National Bindery, Inc., United States of America

To Ryan, love of mine

Nobody ever saw one animal by its gestures and natural cries signify to another, this is mine, that yours.

Adam Smith

Contents

PART II CLAIM AND TITLE: EFFECTS

Acknowledgments

I have accumulated a number of intellectual debts, not all of which I can acknowledge here. The book pays homage to three in particular. Vernon Smith has taught me the meaning of being a scholar, always encouraging me to read broadly and work narrowly. By his example I also learned how to learn from proving myself wrong in the laboratory. In 2008 Matt Ridley gave me a draft of his manuscript that became *The Rational Optimist*. I now realize that it took a biologist to focus my attention on the most important foundational observation in the study of economics, namely that human beings are the only species to routinely truck, barter, and exchange one thing for another thing. Adam Smith clearly understood that, though he punted on explaining why, and we still don't know why. But I anticipate. Deirdre McCloskey's *Bourgeois Era* trilogy opened my mind to the possibility that ideas are what make property possible. I treasure her words of encouragement to treat words as data and evidence.

I am indebted to Joy Buchanan, Peter DeScioli, Taylor Jaworski, Erik Kimbrough, Karl Schurter, Adam C. ("Contemporary") Smith, Vernon Smith, and Andrew Smyth. As my coauthors on several economic experiments on property, our many stimulating and fun conversations prepared me for this undertaking. Brennan McDavid patiently guided me through my Latin translations, but all errors are my own. Sarah Skwire generously helped me read Middle English and asked me the right questions to refine my discussion about prepositions. I hope I've convinced her.

For comments and questions on my arguments, I thank seminar participants and conferees at the Center for Law and Philosophy at the University of Surrey, Nuffield College at the University of Oxford, the University of Alaska Anchorage, the University of Arizona, the University of Wisconsin-LaCrosse, the Risk Management Department at Pennsylvania State University, the University of Alabama, the Fowler School of Law and the Economic Science Institute at Chapman University, the 2018 Southern Economic Association Annual Conference, the 2018 Gruter Institute Annual Squaw Valley Conference, and the Philosophy, Politics, and Economics Society Inaugural Conference. A grant from the Templeton Foundation to the Center for the Study of Governance and Society made a seminar trip to King's College London possible in October 2018. The faculty of the Smith Institute for Political Economy and Philosophy at Chapman University deepened my reading of E. M. Forster's essay entitled "My Wood." Students in Vernon Smith's and my Spring 2019 law school seminar diligently worked through the manuscript and helped me refine it.

Three times I presented portions of the book to accommodating audiences at the Property and Environment Research Center, which generously supported me as a Julian Simon and Lone Mountain Fellow during the summers of 2016–2018. I worked on early versions of the chapters during the spring and summer of 2017 when I visited the Department of Economics at the University of Alaska Anchorage as the Rasmuson Chair in Economics. Approximately forty high school teachers at the Alaska Council on Economic Education Spring Forum provided a fun and lively test of the book's ideas, and a lunch conversation at the Katirvik Cultural Center in Nome heightened my appreciation for the connections people make with their tools. Jonathan Fortier and the Institute for Humane Studies generously organized and hosted a manuscript workshop in April 2019. I thank the attendees for their thoughtful discussions and careful reading.

Many valuable conversations have improved the argument and exposition, for which I heartily thank Terry Anderson, Tom Bell, Dan Benjamin, Danny Bogart, Caroline Breshears, Sarah Brosnan, Tom Campbell, Malte Dold, Gian Marco Farese, Price Fishback, Jonathan Fortier, Josh Hall, Kyle Hampton, Tony Hernandez, Lydia Hopper, Bradley Jackson, Peter Jaworski, Taylor Jaworski, Ryan Johnson, Lynne Kiesling, Erik Kimbrough, Donald Kochan, Mark LeBar, Deirdre McCloskey, Brennan McDavid, Molly McGrath, Roger Meiners, Alec Moss, Jan Osborn (who deserves special mention for generously and meticulously commenting on several drafts over several years of an article and then book), David Pervin, David Rojo Arjona, Ron Rotunda, Eric Schliesser, Sarah Skwire, Henry Smith, Vernon Smith, Ilya Somin, John Thrasher, Wally Thurman, Kevin Vallier, and Bas van der Vossen.

For research support, I gratefully acknowledge the work of Logan Hayward, Heather Joy, Brendan Starkey, and, especially, Trent Gerdeman and Mary Howard, whose conversations helped formulate the experimental design in chapter 8. Sherry Leysen at the Hugh and Hazel Darling Law Library at Chapman graciously gave me extended access to "Library Use Only" copies of Grotius's dusty texts. I am grateful to Jeff Kirchner, whose creative, robust software programming made not only the experiments in chapters 4 and 8 but also nearly all of my research programs in experimental economics possible. He also designed the figures in chapter 9. I must also thank Megan Luetje for recruiting and paying the participants in the experiment, and Brecker Brees, Kat Brown, Nick Callen, Nate Everett, Kyle Joye, Danny Liu, Akash Miharia, and Alexandra Webb for coding the responses to the postexperiment survey.

Finally, I thank my partner, Ryan, for his genuine interest and moral support while working on the project, and for regularly reminding me that Stephen King writes 5,000 words a day. The reference to horror supernatural fiction, I think, is incidental.

Bart J. Wilson
Orange, California
July 2019

Cover Art Note

Sentinels is a 2018 painting (acrylic and spray paint on canvas) by Gus Harper from Santa Monica, California.

Gus Harper
Sentinels, 2018

I met Harper in 2008 at his gallery show when he had been creating and selling art for eight years. Two years later, he painted *Pomscape Grid Painting* for me, a four-by-five-piece grid of one-foot square canvasses.

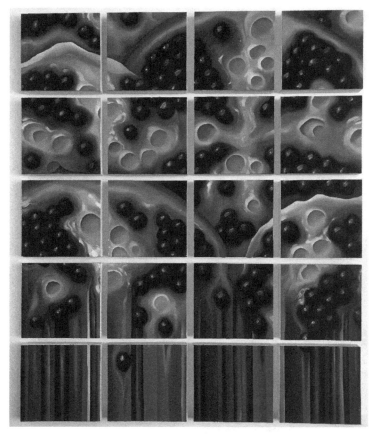

Gus Harper
Pomscape Grid Painting, 2010

Magnifying the organic world into a recognizable abstraction, our minds interpret his early grids of flowers, plants, and fruits as icons reminiscent of works by Georgia O'Keefe (1887–1986). Harper's creations explore, in his words, "the beauty of everyday life by changing the scale and context" of the ordinary world around us.* When our minds impose a force of gravity on the previous image, the pomegranate bleeds vivid colors and melts into a further abstraction of feeling. Such impositions of our minds on the quotidian world of things are key to how property works.

* Personal communication, January 31, 2019.

Sentinels is one of two paintings that Harper created after reading a draft of the first three chapters of the book. Inspired by prehistoric cave paintings in France, which re-present to our minds representations from the minds of human beings who lived 17,000 years ago, the cave wall in Harper's painting connects the minds of its humans to their ancient ancestors' minds whose traditions bequeathed to them 400,000 years' worth of accumulated knowledge on how to create a spear.

Our minds classify the intricately stenciled patterns in the foreground as distinct objects emerging from below a white background that tops the canvas. Lacking a complete shaft, the prominent downward-facing point in the foreground is but a point and not a spear. What makes a point, hafted to a shaft, a spear and not simply a point, a shaft, and some haft collocated in time and space? Our imposing minds.

The human form further in the background is complete, and one with a spear. With proximity, the complete spear in the foreground becomes a distinctly shaded object within the proud hunter's grasp. What happens when he puts the spear down? Is he still one with it? The book explores the significance of such questions for comprehending property and, ultimately, our humanity.

Bibliographic Note

For excerpts in chapter 3, I thank Elsevier for permission to use "Language Games of Reciprocity," *Journal of Economic Behavior and Organization,* 68 (2008), pp. 365–377. I am grateful for permission from Springer Nature to use "Further Towards a Theory of the Emergence of Property," *Public Choice,* 163 (2015), pp. 201–222, as the basis for chapter 4 and the last four paragraphs of chapter 6. The antepenultimate paragraph in chapter 4 is verbatim from "Becoming Just by Eliminating Injustice: The Emergence of Property in Virtual Economies," in *Justice* (2018), edited by Mark LeBar, Oxford University Press, pp. 67–91 (which itself was also drawn, with permission, from the aforementioned *Public Choice* article).

Prologue

Within arm's reach of where I write sit a pen and a cup. Someone made these things for people like me to use, and someone made and used the tools to make the pen and the cup for people like me to use. Both the pen and cup are themselves tools that extend the powers of my hands to do things that I cannot physically do with my body alone. While many animals use tools, and a few animals make and use tools to make a tool, only human beings make and use tools to make and use derivative tools like those that are needed to make pens and cups.[1] From the Machiguenga of the Amazon Basin jungle to the !Kung of the Kalahari Desert, a common characteristic of human tools is that there appears to be an invisible connection between an individual person and the tool.[2] In a legendary tale, such a connection means that only King Arthur could pull Excalibur from the stone. In our unenchanted world, if I leave a pen or cup on the table at a faculty meeting, people tend to ask questions like "Is this someone's pen?" or "Whose cup is that?" Such queries are an attempt to establish some sort of connection between someone in the room and the thing. The answer can be as simple as "It's mine," and its utterance completes the connection sought between a person and the object. Even though professors can always use an altitude-proof pen, and everyone uses some sort of container to help them satisfy their thirst, people, as a general rule, do not seize every fine pen or durable cup they see and could make good use of. In a world filled with things that humans have made, there is an order, a pattern, to how they engage them and one another.

This book is about how human beings perceive the world of useful things, and how and why they act in the orderly way that they do regarding them. To an economist the source of this regularity needs some explanation if we are to tackle the grander question, as it is typically posed to first-year students of economics, of how a society allocates scarce goods to people with inherently unlimited wants. Jurists, and the lawspeakers before them, have been pondering the rules governing the order of people and things for time out of

---

[1] Donald Brown (1991).
[2] Allen Johnson and Timothy Earle (2000).

mind, and philosophers from the ancients to the present have reflected on the justifications for connections between people and things. Comparatively recently, anthropologists and archeologists, and even linguists, have studied the relationships between people and the things they make and use. How does such a connection work, and why do human beings make them? What composes the connection between a person and a thing? The book is a cross-disciplinary synthesis, with a distinctly biological eye, about the ordinary details we take for granted regarding people and the world of things they use.

In the hurly-burly room of a primary school, teachers frequently ask questions like "Whose mittens are these?" and "Whose scarf is this?" For the seven-year-old who shouts "Mine!" and then grabs the Hello Kitty mittens en route to the playground, the ordinary exchange of words makes perfect sense. What more is there to think about? It's time to play in the snow.

Consider what the children and we take for granted in such a scene. While many of the children look at the mittens when the teacher speaks, only one responds, and the teacher expects that only one student will respond to his question. Having spotted the mittens, the girl in the matching Hello Kitty coat also expects to be the only child to respond to the teacher's question. Even the students who have not yet located a pair of mittens do not say anything and do not grab for them. Amid the clamor and scramble for hats and jackets and boots and scarves, there is a semblance of order, a pattern that determines the nature and timing of the children's encounters with a host of inanimate things and with one another.

A closer look at the classroom reveals that the students heed the physical differences of some objects in the classroom and ignore others. A student can tell the difference between a red pencil sitting on a desk and a yellow pencil inside a backpack. But for a student needing to complete a math exam, a pencil on the desk and a pencil in the backpack are both pencils. Both are writing implements, nondistinctively so. Other things in the classroom, like garments for covering hands, are distinctive. A pair of Hello Kitty mittens on a wall hook and a pair lying on the floor are not interchangeable. They may be physically identical in every way, but even if the pair on the floor is closer, a child distinguishes the two so as to grab the pair on the hook before heading out to the playground. Only the child who entered the classroom with the Hello Kitty mittens now on the floor calls the pair on the floor "mine."

The children's minds structure the world of classroom things in a particular way. They perceive distinctive differences in some things but not in others. In other words, the children have different sets of expectations regarding the physical things they perceive in the classroom. From the point of view of the children, their actions adhere to a schedule that constitutes a set of expectations about their actions, and such expectations order what they do, their responses to the external stimuli of sights and sounds in the classroom. If the pair of mittens on the floor is "not mine," the child's schedule calls for leaving them on the floor and walking over to the pair on the wall hook. If the pair of mittens on the floor is "mine," and the teacher asks, "Whose mittens are these?," the scheduling pattern indicates yelling "Mine!" When dealing with mittens at this place, time, and circumstance, the children act in a certain manner. The central question is what composes "a certain manner" of connecting a particular child to a particular thing at this place and time.

The biological-sounding terminology of scheduling, appropriated from the linguist-turned-anthropologist C. F. Hockett, will prove a useful way to organize someone's information about a particular person in a particular community regarding some *thing*. It has the added feature of shaking us out of our comfort zone and giving us a perspective, rather different from our everyday, first-person view of how we human beings deal with one another regarding things. Like a biologist from Mars, we can think of every animal's body, human children's included, as containing a program of actions and events regarding things, a *schedule*. Such a schedule orders the organism's actions as it interfaces with its environment and what the environment offers the organism.

For example, a red-winged blackbird (*Agelaius phoeniceus*) calls out to indicate its presence when perched on a tree. A short and simple vocalization deters nearby birds looking for a limb on which to rest. If a bird nevertheless approaches, the resident prepares to fight the interloper. During courtship and mating, however, the red-winged blackbird's schedule calls for vocalizations that are longer and more complex; that is, the male bird sings to attract a female. If a potential mate approaches, the seduction continues with tail feathers spread and shoulder patches fluffed.

We can think of an organism's body, its nervous system, as running a continuous software program that receives neurophysical inputs from the external world. The software program classifies and organizes these inputs and then gives as output what, if anything, is to be done. If the program classifies the inputs as constituting courtship season, then a male red-winged blackbird produces a long and complex song to attract a mate. If the program classifies the inputs as not constituting courtship season, then the male produces short and simple vocalizations to deter interlopers. The important thing to recognize in this example is that the organism's body contains a *schedule* such that sufficiently similar events in the external world produce a *pattern* of actions to be carried out by the organism. Every April during breeding season male red-winged blackbirds sing to attract mates, and every August after breeding season they vocalize to deter interlopers.

Whether a red-winged blackbird or a first-grader, the timing of an organism's actions adheres to a scheduling pattern that constitutes a set of expectations about what the organism will or will not do, the state of affairs and probable results of the actions, and the appropriate responses to the external events. I use the term *scheduling pattern* to compactly refer to the idea that an organism's body classifies neurophysical inputs of events in the external world to produce a set of expectations regarding an orderly pattern of actions that the organism will undertake in the external world. My goal is to think of a human animal's scheduling pattern as an explanation for why it does what it does in particular circumstances involving certain things.

As an economist, such thinking does not come naturally to me, nor does it, I imagine, come easily to social scientists more generally, philosophers, or legal scholars. It requires us to think of a person's schedule regarding other people and things as being a *physical phenomenon*. Our human scheduling regarding things is located in both the individual animal itself and the animal's environment. The part literally in the animal is, of course, that which is in our genes, our physical bodies, and in the totality of knowledge given by perception and accumulated in our bodies. The part literally in our environment is that which is in other organisms and the physical world of things.

Notice that I do not say that our physical bodies are the sole cause for what humans do. I say much more modestly that, like all animals, our physical bodies supply us with one of two important causes for human scheduling. Our bodies store our accumulated experiences, and all that we know by experience is given to us by our genetically supplied perception. A common genetically scheduled biology means that there are some universal features about humans, including, at least conceivably, how humans perceive and know the connections between people and things. It could also conceivably mean that when it comes to scheduling patterns regarding things, humans are like other primates, or other mammals, or even birds. At this point we do not know if either specifically human genes, or both human and nonhuman genes, or neither explains human behavior regarding things, though the scheduling terminology allows us to put the question marks deeper down.

The second important cause of human scheduling resides in the people and things that surround us. Some birds and many mammals, especially primates, socially transmit practices from one generation to another. Mentors teach the next generation how to attract mates, forage for food, and even make and use tools. Such a cause is physical in that the mechanism resides in things external to the individual organism. It is thus also conceivable that some human communities may pass down different practices regarding people and things, including not having any practices about some things at all. How, then, do we know if it is the first physical cause in our mammalian bodies or the second physical cause in our environment that explains the human scheduling pattern that connects people and things? Or—here's a crazy idea—perhaps the answer lies to some degree in both us and others. As Hockett so wonderfully puts it, "That is not yet known, and the scheduling terminology reminds us of our ignorance."[3]

Up until this point I have purposely avoided using a key term that every reader is surely expecting given the title of the book. Over twelve years ago, almost on a whim but certainly as an afterthought, I started working on "property rights." Except for the subset of economists who specifically work on them, everyone takes property rights for granted, or more precisely, treats them as a given or a constraint in their analysis. In 2006, my colleagues, Sean Crockett and Vernon Smith, and I received comments from a blind review on a project exploring how people discover exchange and specialization in virtual world economies.[4] The reviewers questioned why our undergraduate participants found it difficult to specialize and trade virtual tokens with one another for real cash (as much as $28.00 to $31.50 for a little over an hour's work). They surmised that because our software did not explicitly enforce contracts between the participants, they must have been worried that their counterparts would not fulfill their promises to deliver the goods.

It turned out the chat room transcripts revealed that no one ever complained about such a problem, but the question got us thinking. We had

---

[3] C. F. Hockett (1973, p. 48).
[4] Sean Crockett, Vernon Smith, and Bart Wilson (2009).

taken for granted that our virtual world perfectly enforced property rights. The participants in the original experiment discovered that they could freely move items *to* other people, but they could not move them *from* other people. What would happen if we relaxed that unexamined assumption? What would happen if we changed nothing else in the experiment, not even the instructions, except that people could now discover how to move items both to and from each other?

All hell breaks loose is what happens (virtually speaking, of course, in case members of my institutional review board are reading).[5] Even though all of our participants lived in a Western, educated, industrialized, rich, and democratic society, their first weird impulse was not to give things to other people, but to take them.[6] Items flew around the screen from one person to the next. In their public chat room, they frequently talked about "war." From my view in the monitor room, it certainly looked like chaos. Only about one out of six independent groups established stable possession of the virtual goods and then specialized and exchanged with one another to create the maximum possible wealth. Another one out of six sessions on average would eventually establish stable possession, but it was much slower, and the session ended before they could exploit more than half of the potential gains from trade.

My coauthors, Erik Kimbrough and Vernon Smith, and I were surprised at how easily we could create such a poor and nasty and brutish world with supposedly civilized participants. (They could not virtually kill one another, or their lives would have probably been solitary and short too.) By this time in my career I had conducted a couple hundred laboratory sessions about economics, and Vernon probably several thousand since he started running them in 1956, and we had often seen beautiful, orderly, and prosperous behavior, even when the default expectation of our discipline was for our human subjects to be selfish and inefficient. The sudden vicious appearance of chaotic and poor human societies shocked us.

We first looked for the problems that the different groups faced. Often there would be one bad apple in a group of eight who would prey upon the others without remorse. We wondered what would happen if we gave the participants a way to shun remorseless predators. Some of our colleagues noted that our experiment did not allow people to trade resources with people with the virtual ability to protect them from plunder. Others said that

[5] Erik Kimbrough, Vernon Smith, and Bart Wilson (2010).
[6] Joseph Henrich, Steven Heine, and Ara Norenzayan (2010).

the experiment did not allow people to perfectly commit themselves to refrain from taking things from one another. If we added one of these features, that would solve the problems.

None of it worked. If anything, the externally imposed mechanisms made things worse. Shunning bad apples encouraged isolation from potential trading partners, and the group was thus quite poor; instead of a benevolent protector we observed an unrepentant mafiosa, even though we chose her for the position because she was not inclined to take things before she got her powers; and permanently committing not to take things from others only exposed such community-minded people as suckers to those who scorned such a commitment. In short, we failed in session after session, treatment after treatment, to systematically introduce the means to produce an order regarding people and things. We learned that there is a huge difference between imposed and emergent solutions.

In retrospect, the problem was that we had focused our attention, as is the case in almost every public policy debate, on the ugly failures of the human world, and not on the wonder of its extraordinary and uncommon successes. The scientific failure was an aesthetic one. We had failed to admire the beauty of the rare and orderly way some groups of people acted with regard to things. Notwithstanding the current pessimism at the dawn of the Anthropocene, this book is about the wonder, surprise, and admiration of the human propensity to orderly conduct ourselves with regard to the external things of the world. It is about property, which is, as the eighteenth-century Scottish economist and sociologist Adam Ferguson brilliantly described many human institutions, "indeed the result of human action, but not the execution of any human design."[7]

I postponed introducing the words *property* and *property rights* because familiar words, particularly social and economic ones, come with the baggage of preconceptions. After running my first experiment on "property rights," I started reading John Locke and David Hume for some philosophical insight, and I noticed something curious. They never use the phrase *property rights*, a term pervasive in modern economics, philosophy, and law. They talk about "property" and about "rights," but never the compound "property

---

[7] Adam Ferguson (1767, p. 205).

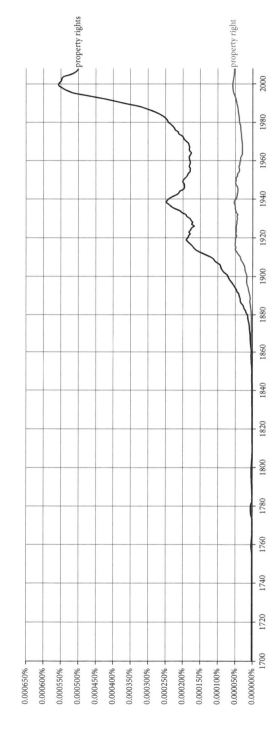

Figure P.1. Google Ngram of *property right* and *property rights*.

Source: Google Books Ngram Viewer (http://books.google.com/ngrams).

rights." Neither do their eminent predecessors Hugo Grotius and Samuel von Pufendorf who wrote in Latin, mostly about *dominium* and sometimes about *proprietas*. Henry of Bracton in thirteenth-century England comes close, but the Roman jurisprudential phrase he uses is always grammatically singular and best translated with the possessive case as the "right of property" (*ius proprietatis*). The earliest use of *property right* that I can find in Google Books is from Lord Gardenston in 1774, and then it is hyphenated and used only once as a conceptual contrast to a copy-right, which isn't the modern usage.[8] At some point late in the nineteenth century the idea of "property rights" takes off, and by the early twentieth century the term is fully entrenched (see Figure P.1).

If property rights are a modern invention, a modern idea, then how old is property? The last few hundred years of Western European history? A couple of thousand years of Western civilization? Several millennia of human agriculturists? A couple hundred millennia of modern humans? A half-million years of hominin hunters? A couple million years of hominin scavengers? Five to ten million years of great apes? Thirty-some million years of primates? Three hundred million years of mammals? All right, I admit it: I am belaboring the question as only a lover of natural history museums would. But the point is, if we are to answer some open questions regarding how property works in the modern world, we also have to be open to exploring why our species happens to have it, which raises the obvious question: So . . . what is property?

---

[8] Lord Gardenston (1774, p. 15): "The great argument, or *ratio dubitandi*, which I own at first almost convinced me, is, that the author has undoubtedly a property-right in the original manuscript composed by himself; why should he lose it by publication, as he intends only to give the instruction or pleasure of reading, not the profit of publication or reprinting? I answer that, certainly the author has a real property in the manuscript of his own work; but, in the nature of the thing, by publication, gives his work to the public, and he gives the same species of property to every individual who buys the book, which he had in the original copy before publication."

PART I
CLAIM AND TITLE: ORIGINS

1

The Meaning of Property in Things

Let me put my cards on the table: Property is a universal and uniquely human custom.

Initial reactions to the claim will differ. Cultural relativists will reflexively cringe at the notion of property being a human universal. Their counterclaim would be that property is a modern, Western European, hegemonic construction, the cause of wars and quarrels in the world. One of their patron saints from the eighteenth century, Jean-Jacques Rousseau, imagined "what miseries and horrors would the human race have been spared" had we not "forg[otten] that the fruits of the earth belong to all and the earth to no one."[1] In the nineteenth century, Pierre-Joseph Proudhon declared what many still believe 180 years later: "Property is theft!"[2]

Biologists will immediately search their mental databanks for a counterexample in the animal kingdom. There must be at least one other species besides *Homo sapiens*—a primate for sure, or perhaps a dolphin or a squirrel—that exhibits, at least on occasion, some behavioral patterns of property. They will be quick to tell you that male baboons appear to own the females in their harems; that red squirrels seem to treat the tree in the backyard as their property; and that rare delicacy of a Spanish mackerel sure looks like it belongs to that bottlenose dolphin holding it with his mouth. Birds also defend their claims on things against interlopers. Western scrub jays, for example, protect their food caches from theft by rehiding them if a potential pilferer is in sight for the initial caching. The biologists' own words to describe such behaviors are *own*, *property*, and *theft*.

Legal centralists, which include most ordinary people and social scientists, will at first take pause at, if not take issue with, the idea of property as mere custom, for governments surely institute and enforce the rules of property.[3] How is custom going to return my stolen bicycle, you ask? Well, report it

---

[1] Jean-Jacques Rousseau (1754, p. 62).
[2] Pierre-Joseph Proudhon (1840, p. 87).
[3] Ordinary people and social scientists are largely exclusive categories.

The Property Species. Bart J. Wilson. Oxford University Press (2020) © Oxford University Press.
DOI: 10.1093/oso/9780190936785.001.0001

to the police and see what happens. Nothing happens. And that nothing happens does not help us explain why millions of bicycles go unstolen each day. But, you continue, don't the police and district attorneys spend more time on the bigger stuff still covered by the local evening news, like department store heists and carjackings caught on surveillance video? Yes, but that's beside the point. Consider that relatively rare exceptions to the rules of property cannot explain the regularity with which people as a rule generally follow the general rules of property. How many people would never seriously consider—even if no one would ever know—taking a misplaced wallet or claiming a rusty box with $52,000 worth of treasure buried in one's own Staten Island backyard?[4] That nonenforcement is the nongovernmental institution in need of a nonlegal centralist explanation. Undeterred, you give it one more shot: Such nonenforcement *is* the shadow of the law extending its reach. Why then, I ask, does the shadow not work the same in all countries? At its core, property is a custom whose practice differs, sometimes radically, from place to place, even though the law's shadow is the same. Laws against crossing the street against the light are the same in Berlin and Rome. Why no same shadow?

Philosophers and lawyers wouldn't first reach for the word *custom* as their substantive of choice. In philosophical and legal treatises, property rests on rights, not custom. Rights, plural, are not as new as an abstract notion as are property rights, but in terms of the human career, a multimillennial old idea is still relatively new. Such a fact by itself doesn't preclude rights as an explanation of property in humans. New abstract concepts are useful, if not necessary, for explaining new phenomena. Quarks, for example, are a relatively new notion in physics, and their indirect validation in experiments in the 1960s subsequently explained the composite particles discovered in cosmic rays in the late 1940s. The old language of protons, neutrons, and electrons was simply inadequate to explain new, more fundamental constituents of matter. But if it is exceedingly difficult, as Auguste Comte put it, to work out "new conceptions in the old language," imagine how much more difficult it is to work out old conceptions in the new language.[5] If the objective is to explain the Rutherford model of the atom and how we came to understand the atom as having a positively charged center orbited by negatively charged electrons, the new lexicon of hadrons, baryons, and mesons, not to mention

---

[4] Google it; it happened.
[5] Quoted in Thomas Dixon (2008, p. 48).

six flavors of quarks, would only bog us down. Even though the modern Standard Model of particle physics explains phenomena unintelligible to physicists a century ago, the Rutherford model does a fine job explaining some practical problems about matter, like why dropping cesium into water is an explosive proposition.

I lay my cards boldly, but hopefully not explosively, on the table because I think it is important to draw the distinctions I wish to make as clearly as I can. Depending on which department you visit at your favorite university, you will hear some rather different perspectives on property. On one side of campus, only some modern human beings have property, but on the other side, all sorts of animals have property in food, mates, and territory. In the buildings in between, home to the law school and the soft but not squishy social sciences, people entertain both views. Social scientists and legal scholars will say that, based on everyday experience, it certainly looks like the family dog has property when he guards his toy, and those same professors will tell you that seventeenth-century Native Americans did not have notions of property like their European conquerors had. As a midmost social scientist and law professor myself, let me propose a sticky compromise: All humans have property in things, and *Homo sapiens* is the only animal to have property in things.

As with most compromises, no one will be happy with this one. Current thinking in biology is that the gap between humans and all other animals is small. (Only human hubris makes humans exceptional in the animal kingdom.) The thinking in humanities departments is that the number and scope of human universals is so small that there are more important cultural things to talk about and social problems to attend to. (Only humans pride themselves on building the world as they imagine they can design it.) Social scientists and legal scholars in the middle blame themselves for not designing a better world (as only an exceptional animal can).

Part of the difficulty in talking about property is that the different disciplines talk past each other in their own languages with different assumptions and different questions. To convince you my compromise has some credence, I need to provide you with a common framework for thinking about property, a few open questions that frame the problem of explaining what property is, and some hard-to-dispute facts that neither the humanities nor the natural sciences—nor the social sciences in the middle unconsciously channeling both colleges—are synthesizing into a meaningful explanation of property.

Property Is a Universal and Uniquely Human Custom

The cultural relativists have a point, but not the one they think. The evidence is clear to the midcentury anthropologist George Murdock: "so far as the author's knowledge goes, [there is property] in every culture known to history or ethnography."[6] Nearly a half century later, in response to widespread denial of and his own doubts about human universals, Donald Brown reiterates the claim that all human groups "have concepts of property, distinguishing what belongs—minimal though it may be—to the individual, or group, from what belongs to others."[7] But these few words are as far as they each go in positing property as a human universal. Ralph Linton is a little more concrete when he says that "all societies recognize personal property in tools, utensils, ornaments, and so forth."[8]

Cultural relativists would challenge the bases for these claims.[9] Sure, all human groups *use* tools, utensils, ornaments, and so forth, and it might appear to modern Western observers that such patterns of use are consistent with modern Western patterns of uses for what we call property. But how do we know that the Ewe in Africa or the Cree in North America or the Longgu in the Solomon Islands think about property like Anglophones do? The word *property*, relativists would claim, is an Anglo concept with roots in Middle French and ancient Latin.

Perhaps, giving it the old college try, there is something in the definition of the word that would help us apply the concept universally. Consider how the *Collins Cobuild English Language Dictionary* (for learners) defines *property*: "Someone's property is all the things that belong to them or something that belongs to them."[10] What does it mean for something to belong to someone? "If something belongs to you, you own it." So what does it mean to own something? "If you own something, it is your property." We're back where we started with an Anglo concept, only now defined circularly in terms of two Anglo-Germanic concepts. The word *own* is a particularly problematic foundation for understanding property as a human universal.[11]

---

6 George Murdock (1945, p. 124).

7 Donald Brown (1991, p. 140).

8 Ralph Linton (1952, p. 655).

9 See, for example, Duran Bell (1998) and Walter Neale (1998).

10 Available at http://www.collinsdictionary.com/dictionary/english-cobuild-learners. Last accessed November 2, 2015. The Collins Dictionary is known for its definitions via the use of the word in simple sentences.

11 Jeremy Waldron (1988, p. 29) also notes "many ambiguities in the term 'ownership'" in different legal systems.

According to the Oxford English Dictionary (OED), the transitive verb *own* is newer than the adjective *own* and has been only in use since the sixteenth century when it began supplanting the use of its relative *owe* in the sense "to possess." To escape such circularity in property terms, we are going to need some semantically atomic concepts to explain the molecular or macromolecular concepts of *property, own,* and *belong.*

The cultural relativists are right then to be concerned if we Anglocentrically interpret tool use by the Ewe, Cree, and Longgu in terms of belonging and owning to assert that they have property like Anglophones have property. Where the relativists go wrong is to leap to the conclusion that whatever is semantically common to *property, own,* and *belong* cannot also be found in every other human language. On the contrary, linguists have identified such a semantic element, so primitive, so basic that two-year-olds parse it from adult conversations and readily adopt it all on their own. That concept is MINE.[12] But I anticipate.

If universally attributing Anglo-Germanic concepts to humans is fraught with Anglocentricism, then attributing the same concepts to other members of the animal kingdom is even more fraught with anthropocentrism, something about which biologists, and primatologists in particular, are reminded every day. Unfortunately, as much as we would like to be more objective and swap out our human-tinted lenses, we can't because we are humans and not DNA changelings. There's no Archimedean point. We must make do with our humanity when interpreting the basics of "property" in nonhumans.[13] Besides, identifying what humans have in common with the rest of the animal kingdom is useful, if for nothing else than to keep us humble.

To preserve our bodies and propagate our species, we must—like all animals—satisfy our basic impulses to ingest, excrete, and avoid pain, heat, and cold, and such preserving and propagating require physical matter external to ourselves. Whether the matter is some food, a potential mate, or shelter from the elements, conflicts among conspecifics (the term in biology

---

[12] Cliff Goddard and Anna Wierzbicka (2016). Small capitals indicate the concept and italics the word.

[13] See, for example, Sarah Brosnan (2011) and Joan Strassman and David Quellar (2014). A key word search for "ownership" in the database for *Animal Behaviour* yields results for 356 different papers.

for members of the same species) are bound to occur when individuals simultaneously desire to satisfy the same impulse with the same rivalrous object. Not every species competes with conspecifics in the same way to satisfy such universal impulses. Conflicts over external objects vary depending on the ecological niche and the patterns by which individuals of the species group together and move around relative to one another, the dwelling and scheduling patterns of the species.[14] For example, yellow pine chipmunks (*Neotamias amoenus*) in western North America and gray squirrels (*Sciurus carolinensis*) in eastern North America scatter-hoard their supply of seeds across their territory, but chipmunks in eastern North America (*Tamias striatus*) and the American red squirrel (*Tamiasciurus hudsonicus*) larder-hoard their winter supply in a single spot. In the event of a conflict over a cache, a single large one must be more aggressively defended than the border of a scatter-hoarding territory.

But why are we (and all animals) not instantly combative with every conspecific with whom we are in immediate direct competition for an external object? Because there are costs as well as benefits to any fight, and any species that does not internalize these individualized costs will not remain a species for very long.[15] As every species evolves, it stumbles upon the many behavioral margins for the conditions under which to fight or not with conspecific competitors over food and mates. Bucks, for example, don't usually kill each other when competing for mates in antler-clashing fights. Through very slow feedback and innovation, species-wide patterns of actions form to govern how individuals engage one another. The rules and order regarding the use of external objects vary by species depending on its ecological niche and its dwelling and scheduling patterns.

One problem with applying human rules to nonhumans is that such concepts are derived from the distinctly human experience of the last 100,000 years. Doing so also leads us to conclude tacitly that there are but minuscule differences between us and the rest of the animal kingdom, because the patterns of actions by which *Homo sapiens* satisfies its animalistic impulses can look like those of other animals. Consider the red squirrel. The biologist Brooker Klugh observes that, like humans, the red squirrel's

---

[14] C. F. Hockett (1973).

[15] Economics 101 and Richard Dawkins (1976, ch. 5). Notice that the answer is not that we are moral beings. Learning not to instantly fight is more the source than the result of our moral insights. See F. A. Hayek (1988, p. 21).

sense of ownership seems to be well developed. Both of the squirrels which have made the maple in my garden their headquarters apparently regarded this tree as their private property, and drove away other squirrels which came into it. It is quite likely that in this case it was not the tree, but the stores that were arranged about it, which they were defending.[16]

So what do biologists' examples of nonhuman property have in common? Whatever nonhuman property might be, the effect of it is that red squirrels, male baboons, and scrub jays defend themselves against dispossession. If another animal attempts to acquire the thing in question, even if the animal is not currently using it, it will aggressively bare its teeth and make some noise. No parent has to teach its young to defend against dispossession. Such a response is inherited, and we can see why. Pushover progeny are less likely to reproduce if they give up their food or mate without at least the appearance of being willing to fight for it. Likewise, no human parents in any community have to teach their child to resist attempts to take things securely within their grasp. Children are natural-born possessors.

Possession, however, is only nine points of the law. The last tenth is important. Nine-tenths of the focus on property is on the *effects* of property. Every nonhuman example of property from biology—squirrels, baboons, dolphins, and scrub jays—is about the possession, exclusive use, and defense of food, mates, or territory in nature.[17] Every human example of the absence of property from the humanities and anthropology—think non-Western European societies—is about the nonexclusive use of certain things by certain peoples. Biology compares like effects across species, and the humanities and anthropologists compare unlike effects within a species. But it is when we consider the last tenth, the *origins* of property in humans, and not simply its like and unlike effects, that we can begin to trace what property is and how it works.

Humans, like many birds and every other kind of mammal, have a home range, an area over which they travel in search of food.[18] A home range typically contains a dwelling within it and its boundaries may be fixed or fluctuating. The subset of the home range, proper or not, that individuals will fight

---

[16] A. Brooker Klugh (1927, p. 28). Notice the use of the terms *ownership* and *private property*.
[17] In his sweeping and penetrating study on property, the historian Richard Pipes (2000) also links universal acquisitiveness in nonhuman animals to the human institution of property. My claims on property in no way detract from his argument that property is a prerequisite for freedom.
[18] William Burt (1943).

to defend against conspecifics is called, we all have heard, the territory of an animal.[19] Territory is usually considered to be a form of property. As Klugh notes, animals fight to defend a territory, not for the sake of the territory itself, but for the food, mates, progeny, or shelter within it. Defending territory is the proximate means for satisfying the ultimate impulses to use the objects within it. Like squirrels, humans fight conspecifics to defend objects within their territories. But we also fight for the sake of the territory itself. Moreover, we do not interlope *for the sake of* not interloping, even if we could use the items in a conspecific's territory. We do not interlope because we do not want to think of ourselves as the kind of person who interlopes. We judge our own motives and other people's motives to be good, fit, and proper. And that is not a minuscule difference between us and the red squirrel. That discontinuity is one crucial item in what makes us human.[20]

The other important point to note in comparing red squirrels and humans is that things like food and mates are logically anterior to territories for all animals, and so things are the focus here. Property in things is temporally and cognitively prior to property in land.[21] Rather than starting with the more difficult cases of land, effluents, and riparian zones, I consider the uncontentious core for how we cognize property in things that gives the more contentious cases the significance they have.

As with territories, there is a gulf between humans and other animals in how we regard the property of things as we go about satisfying our impulses. The source of the gulf is symbolic thought.[22] Symbolic thought is what makes many uniquely human capabilities possible: language, creativity and innovation, art, and trade; and symbolic thought is likewise what makes property a uniquely human custom.[23]

[19] Ibid.

[20] My thinking on this has evolved considerably since my early forays into property in Peter DeScioli and Bart Wilson (2011), but much less so from Erik Kimbrough, Vernon Smith, and Bart Wilson (2010).

[21] David Seipp (1994) contends from reading the Year Books that before 1490 English common lawyers did not use the word *property* to refer to land.

[22] Terrence Deacon (1998). For my purposes, it is sufficient to use symbolic thought and abstract thought interchangeably.

[23] Donald Brown (1991), Derek Bickerton (2009), Matt Ridley (2010), Denis Dutton (2010), and Bart Wilson (2015).

If there is a gulf that separates nonhumans from humans regarding property of things, it need not extend all the way from nonhuman patterns on the one side to government-instituted and government-enforced property on the human other side. Some birds, many mammals, most primates, and all humans pass on patterns of actions to successive generations of progeny.[24] When the patterns of actions are not acquired from the genes of the parent but handed down from teachers who were likewise habituated to the same actions by their teachers, different social groups within a species will have different patterns of actions because the learning of the practices is social and not genetic. The brown-headed cowbird, a brood parasite, passes along different courtship songs that cannot have been transmitted genetically; bottlenose dolphin cows pass along different foraging techniques to their calves; and orangutans in certain locations manufacture and use tools to extract food that orangutans in other locations do not make and use, despite living in the same ecological conditions.[25] The common feature to all nonhuman practices regarding food and mates is that the practice consists in learning how to acquire something. Human beings, though, appear to be the only species to *teach* their progeny how *not* to acquire things. "No!" is how all parents teach their children the rules of how to acquire—or *not* acquire—things in the presence of other members of their species. Thou shalt *not* steal. Play nice, Johnny.

All human groups use the logical concept of NOT; no linguist has ever studied a language that does not contain the grammar to negate.[26] The other side of the symbolic threshold is not simply the capability to negate how we go about acquiring things to use. Our acts to acquire things are also judged, for their own sakes, to be good or bad. Every language can express the simple, indefinable-except-of-themselves concepts of GOOD and BAD.[27] In other words, another discontinuity with nonhumans regarding things is that human practices are moral practices. Thou *shalt* not steal. Tens of millennia before there were governments, humans were teaching each other what not to do regarding the use of things. No human child is born knowing the difference between the good and bad way to acquire things, and even though,

[24] C. F. Hockett (1973).
[25] Dorothy Fragaszy and Susan Perry (2008).
[26] Donald Brown (1991) and Ann Wierzbicka (1996).
[27] Cliff Goddard and Anna Wierzbicka (2002).

as parents will attest, no human child must be taught the word *mine*, all must be taught by their mentors to say, "That is yours," and the customs of when they can and *cannot* say, "This is mine." Every generation of children must be taught the difference between the good and bad ways to acquire things in their community.

Even if a pair of Hello Kitty mittens hanging on a wall hook is identical to a pair lying on the floor, a child distinguishes between the two in such a way as to grab the pair that is "Mine!," regardless of which pair is the closest to them. Property is not the effect of leaving the closer pair of mittens on the floor. Property is not the effect of exclusively using the second pair of mittens on the hook. Property is not resisting the dispossession of the mittens within one's grasp. Property is in the original perception that the two pairs of mittens are distinctly different things in the mind's eye. Property is knowing from experience that one pair of mittens is "mine" and the other is, respectfully, "yours."

Our human minds perceive the world of people and things through a socially transmitted custom of knowing when to say, "This thing is mine," and reciprocally, "That thing is yours." Property is a custom. Property is a custom because it is a practice socially taught and socially learned. Property is a custom because it is a moral practice. And property is a human custom because it is a scheduling pattern of the species. Property resides in our environment—well, partly.

The other part of property, of course, is in our genes. In every human language someone can say, "This (thing) is mine." Every human community distinguishes things that belong to the individual from things that belong to others. Not every human community has property in land, but all human groups have property in tools, utensils, or ornaments. I did say "all." However minimal it may be, there are some things about which only a particular individual can say, "This is mine." Not all spears or ceremonial ornaments are the same. Like lacrosse sticks and Hello Kitty mittens, the custom is such that there is but one individual who can wield or wear it.

If every human community recognizes property in tools, utensils, and ornaments, and if someone in every human community can say, "This is mine!" about something, then it would appear that property is a human universal. And if property involves not taking certain things because they are "yours," and humans are the only species that learns from mentors how not to acquire things, then it would appear that *Homo sapiens* is the only animal to have property in things. A core question is how humans comprehend the meaning of property as a custom regarding things. One consequence of this project is that it dispels the modernocentric myth that "governments must *grant* rights before it can enforce them."[28] If we think of property as a custom a hundred or so millennia in the making, then I think a judge can adjudicate a concrete conflict regarding the content of the custom without a legislature positively granting anything.

If property is a custom about as old as our species itself, then reading into the word the concept of rights to describe property might give us some pause for anachronistic concern. I understand what philosophers, lawyers, and philosopher-lawyers mean when they say, for example, that property is "the right to determine how a particular thing will be used," or "the right to exclude others from a valued resource," or "a right to a thing."[29] I also understand what X means, where X is a thing, excluding others from a valued resource, and determining how particular things will be used. But what is not immediately clear to me is the meaning of "the right to" in "the right to X."

One meaning might be "the freedom to," as in property is the freedom to determine how a thing will be used. In the discriminating language of the early twentieth-century American jurist Wesley Hohfeld, such a species of right is a privilege, or a liberty, for someone to do something with the thing, meaning, formally, that someone has no duty not to do something with the thing.[30] But something is lost in equating a right to use a thing with both a double negative duty and a freedom or liberty or privilege to use a thing. A right connotes something more than being allowed, but having no duty not, to use a thing.

Leif Weinar in the *Stanford Encyclopedia of Philosophy* defines rights as "entitlements (not) to perform certain actions, or (not) to be in certain states; or entitlements that others (not) perform certain actions or (not) be in certain states."[31] Similarly, when the philosophers Douglas Rasmussen and Douglas Den Uyl refer to a right, they say it is "a claim or entitlement that individuals have for how others will treat them."[32] All right, what is a

---

[28] Itai Sened (1997, p. 6).
[29] Respectively, J. E. Penner (1997, p. 5), Thomas Merrill (1998, p. 730), and Henry Smith (2012, p. 1691). See also David Schmidtz (2012).
[30] Wesley Hohfeld (1919).
[31] Leif Weinar (2015).
[32] Douglas Rasmussen and Douglas Den Uyl (2005, p. 77).

claim or an entitlement? Dictionaries like the *Collins Cobuild* are dizzyingly unhelpful:

- "A claim is a demand for something that you think you have a right to."
- "If you have a right to do or to have something, you are morally or legally entitled to do it or have it."
- "If you are entitled to something, you have the right to have it or do it."

Yet there must be more to the meaning of *right* and *entitle* for Sir Edward Coke to say that "every right is a title, but every title is not such a right for which an action lieth."[33] Another clue: The first ten amendments to the U.S. Constitution are not called the Bill of Entitlements. Defining rights via entitlements appears to strip rights of some of their moral force. To escape such a circularity we need some semantically atomic concepts to distinguish the concept of entitlements from the molecular, if not cellular, concept of rights.

Jeremy Waldron says that "the idea [of rights is] that people have certain key interests . . . which they are not to be required to sacrifice, and which therefore may not be overridden, for the sake of the collective welfare or other goals of their society."[34] J. E. Penner's definition contains somewhat simpler constituent concepts: "an interest of sufficient importance to the person who has it to serve as an exclusionary reason guiding the action of others."[35] Both of these are illuminating explanations but also, it should be noted, postaristocratic, bourgeois notions of the rights of individual persons, hoi polloi included.[36] What is the core of property in humans before the Western European world embourgeoisified it with the liberty, dignity, and equality of rights?

According to the OED, the history of *right* as that which is considered consonant with aristocratic justice is much older (and cognate with Old Frisian, Old Dutch, Old Saxon, and Old High German and comparable to Old Icelandic, Old Swedish, and Old Danish) than the word *right* in having the right to do *X*. The right to do *X* is decidedly post–Norman invasion Middle English, which means it does not necessarily include the masses.

---

[33] Sir Edward Coke (1628, i. 345 b).
[34] Jeremy Waldron (1988, p. 13).
[35] J. E. Penner (1997, pp. 13–14).
[36] Deirdre McCloskey (2010, 2016).

The linguist Anna Wierzbicka suggests that since the Enlightenment "it is likely that the semantic equivalents of *rights* in languages other than English (e.g., *les droits* in French, *prava* in Russian) do not have the same passionate moral connotations as the English word *rights*, associated by the speakers of English with 'what is the right thing to do.' "[37] The point of this is to say simply that the concepts of entitlement and the right to do *X*, and the reasons that our species has them, are too modern, too complex, and possibly too Anglo to serve as our species' mass modest foundation for the emergence of property on the Pleistocene savanna. Moreover, it matters for how social scientists theorize, philosophers philosophize, and judges opinionize about property in the twenty-first century that we comprehend its meaning in a way that is consistent with how our species acquires and cognizes, by which I mean perceives and knows, the custom.

Humans Locate the Meaning of Property within a Thing

To ordinary people, property is a dull subject. Big deal, people own stuff. Probably too much stuff, if you ask Thorsten Veblen, John Kenneth Galbraith, or Bernie Sanders. My claim is that property in stuff, whether in too much stuff or not, is extraordinary and uncommon in the animal kingdom. I want to persuade you that biologists and human unexceptionalists are wrong about *Homo sapiens* and property. Once you have become more acquainted with how it works, you will see that property is both evolutionarily new and singular, like human language, creativity, and cumulative culture are new and singular in the natural history of the planet. Property works like language works, with symbolic reference. But more than being uniquely human, I wish to show you the marvels of how we perceive and know the custom of property. The evidence is varied and unexpected to be sure, but it is evidence nonetheless, even if you see the signs of property often, but least of all, in the places I show you.

Our minds have become accustomed, at least since the Enlightenment, to drawing a thick dividing line between our physical body and the environment surrounding it, an impassable border delimiting the "I" in my body and the people and things outside of it. In claiming that property is a human universal I am saying that the long, twentieth-century conflict between genes

[37] Anna Wierzbicka (2006, p. 317). See also Donal Carbaugh (1988).

and the environment is as false when it comes to property as in any nature-nurture debate in both the hard and plastic sciences.[38] Property as part of our common humanity means that we can admire the peace and harmony it brings, and can appreciate the beautiful human things that become possible when property jointly and reciprocally links the minds of individuals to one another, minds of people who do not personally even know each other. I will make the case that the human propensity to orderly conduct ourselves with regard to things is necessary for bettering the social and economic condition of the human race. No other animal has ever extended its own average life expectancy, decreased its own rate of infant mortality, and actualized healthier and more comfortable lives for itself. But *Homo sapiens burgensis* has, and property makes those remarkable feats of nature possible.

You need to be careful here. Not all human conduct done in the name of "Mine!" is beautiful and great, worthy of wonder and admiration. To put it mildly. If you look at the cruel, dark moments of human history, including slavery, colonialism, and violence, more generally, you are going to find people wanting things and doing all sorts of evil things to claim other people's things as their own. I am not claiming that the universal and uniquely human custom of property is absolutely good so that any one of a number of counterexamples of specific rules of property obviously refutes my thesis. To the contrary, the custom of property is not absolute and certainly not absolutely good. Sometimes the bad things that happen are simply the result of human fallibility, of human beings failing in our humanity. And sometimes the bad things that humans do become, when done regularly, a bad customary rule of property. To be able to distinguish a particular bad customary rule of property from a particular instance of someone doing bad things, we must first be able to recognize what it means for property to be a custom, which means seeing the orderly patterns of property in human intercourse. One methodological aim of the book is to establish that property is indeed a custom. It is beyond the scope of the book, in light of such a fact, to evaluate particular rules of property as good or bad, just or unjust, fair or unfair, equitable or inequitable, reasonable or unreasonable, partial or impartial, xenophilic or xenophobic, androcentric or (the purely hypothetical) gynocentric.

---

[38] Matt Ridley (2004).

No single custom stands above all other customs. Property is one of the many customs that humans practice. By embedding property as one piece in the whole of human conduct that regulates our communities, we submit property to the same standards that we submit all customs to. Property, like all other customs, must fit in with the entire scheduling pattern of the community. One benefit of treating property as a custom is that we avoid reifying property as a right, which inevitably puts it into conflict with some other reified right, with the false choice being that one thingy right must trump and displace the other thingy right.[39] Customs of magnanimity or charity might trump the custom of property. Or they might not. If property is about what humans do, about how we orderly conduct ourselves with regard to things, then what we humans do with respect to property is not an either-or proposition. It's a matter of how property fits in with our regularized interactions.

We have traversed some extensive terrain in this opening chapter. If I am guilty of prolixity, it is because I wish to pique the interest of readers from several disparate disciplines about the problem of explaining what property is and why our species happens to have it. There are many open questions in economics, philosophy, and legal scholarship concerning how property works today, and the origins of property in our species might be relevant to understanding them.[40] I aim to show how we might begin answering some such questions.

At the center of property is an individual organism that perceives the physical world through its body. The organism uses its body to see, hear, touch, smell, and taste the world. Seeing, hearing, and touching figure prominently in property. Smelling and tasting, not so much. While the hardware of the brain receives the neurophysical impulses sent from the eyes, ears, and skin, the software of the mind classifies and organizes the impulses as sensations and, according to its schedule, returns as output an instruction to act. The primeval sensations at the heart of property are the harm or injury an organism feels, and the concomitant resentment, when it perceives that a conspecific has severed its connection with an object. Resentment in many

---

[39] The subsidiary assumption, a law of the physical universe, is that two objects cannot occupy the same space at the same time.

[40] Jeffery Stake (2004) discusses how animal behaviors resemble property in humans but not how the custom emerged in our species.

animals' schedules calls for the organism to defend itself by beating back the injury with some injury in return. Such is the micro-foundation of property.

Unlike 80 to 90 percent of all mammals, humans aren't solitary creatures.[41] We cluster beyond mating and raising our young. We live and move and think in a social setting, a community. Our minds do not solipsistically classify and organize our neurophysical impulses. An individual's expectations about what others will do are embedded in the expectations of the other members of the community. The individual's schedule to act shapes the scheduling pattern of the community, and the scheduling pattern of the community shapes the individual's schedule to act. Because injury and resentment at the micro-level can spread like wildfire from individual to individual, quarrels about the connections between people and things run the risk of destroying a community. Third parties with some distance can temper the flames of contention by spelling out for the entire community what the expectations of the disputants should have been regarding individuals and things. Such articulations, arising both from an individual's schedule to act and from the existing customs of the community, simultaneously inform and are informed by the scheduling pattern of the community. At the same time, the articulations update the schedules of people not involved in the dispute. Such is the meso-foundation of the property.

For at least 90 percent of the human career, we lived in small roving bands or tribes of a few hundred people. Then beginning with Jericho and Çatalhöyük some 10,000 years ago, we increasingly began to live in sedentary towns of several thousand people, followed by polities of tens of thousands, hundreds of thousands, millions, tens of millions, hundreds of millions, and now billions of people.[42] In virtue ethical terms, if the micro-level of property is about justice for the individual and the meso-level about temperance from the community regarding justice for the individual, the macro-level is about prudence, the society-wide promotion of economic betterment. The competing institutions that emerge to unite the day-to-day interactions of strangers from different communities are the ones that are comparatively less costly.[43]

Social scientists and legal scholars predominantly think about property at the macro-level and in terms of the modern democratic concept of rights. They pose the fundamental question as, what property rights should the government grant or rescind to support the everyday interactions of its citizens?

---

[41] Peter Jarman and Hans Kruuk (1996).
[42] Christopher Scarre and Brian Fagan (2008).
[43] Oliver Williamson (1993, 1996). See also Douglass North (1992).

Or, what property rights facilitate economic betterment? Such questions frame property rights as being up for grabs and, hence, a source of conflict that pits the majority of the moment against the minority. As the economist Terry Anderson put it to me, might makes rights. A macro-level focus on property rights glosses over the micro- and meso-foundations of property that undergird peace and civil society writ large. Whereas the custom of property is ancient, moral, and universal to all people, property rights are modern, amoral, and majoritarian. Property unites communities and makes civil society, the open society, the great society, possible. The justice and temperance of *mine* and *thine* are necessary conditions for prosperity and human flourishing.

The argument of the book proceeds by integrating nearly every word of this chapter's title into it. Claim and title go hand in hand. Getting to the meaning in a title will take a little time, for it relies on first establishing the universality and uniqueness of the custom in humans.

All animals use things, specifically food, but food is unlikely to be the original object of property in humans. Tools have the potential to be the original objects of property because of how we make and use them. Many nonhuman animals use tools, but there is a gulf between their uses of tools and ours. Symbolic or abstract thought makes meaning possible, and meaning makes composite tools possible. I contend that symbolic thought explains such a discontinuity with the rest of the animal kingdom.

The custom of property emerges out of the social practice of tool use in primates when symbolic thought is applied to it. Primates socially transmit tool practices, but humans share meaning-laden customs. The thingness of property as a custom comes from tools. Tool use is embodied knowledge, and property embodies the claim, "This is mine!" Humans socially transmit property with moral force and jointly shared expectations.

What is the relationship between what is right in a moral claim of "This is mine" and the particular rules that make up the custom of property? What is right regarding things is not derived from the rules of property, but a rule of property arises from our background knowledge of what is right regarding people and things. The spontaneous conversations of participants in two different economic experiments illustrate such a distinction, beginning with what I mean by "what is right." Resentment prompts people to act when other people take things that I claim are mine, and property is the moral scheduling pattern that emerges to protect members of a community from real and positive injury.

The class of words most likely to be overlooked in a title is the preposition. (They're so small we don't even bother to capitalize them.) My working supposition is that language, including the inversely proportional work of the little word *in*, reflects and reveals the unconscious principles of the mind.[44] As Wierzbicka says, "looking into the meaning of a single word, let alone a single sentence, can give one the same feeling of dizziness that can come from thinking about the distances between galaxies or about the impenetrable empty spaces hidden in a single atom."[45] I posit that an English-language convention arose, and now has largely fallen out of use, for dealing with the formidable, yet beautiful, complexity of the meaning of property. The burden of my argument is to show that while this convention lasted for only 500 years, less than 1 percent of the time our modern species has roamed the planet, it provides an insight into how humans universally and uniquely cognize property. And my argument is this: Humans locate the meaning of property within a thing. Property is contained within the thing.

My claims on property reinforce and tie together several legal philosophies of property including Neo-Lockean, Kantian a priorism, exclusive use, and *in rem*. The language of "possession" and "rights" muddies the meaning of property and the conception of possession discards mind and custom. The British lawyer and jurist A. M. Honoré would seem to agree with my claims on property. The Neo-Lockean theory of property invokes custom but doesn't go far enough. Kantian a priorism cannot account for the moral significance and transmission of property, and exclusive use cannot explain property as a scheduling pattern in humans. The *in rem* theory of property has the right idea by returning to the thingness of property, but it is a macro-theory of property rights, not an account of how property works at the micro- and meso-foundations of human sociality.

Several prominent court cases explicate how we cognize property, out of which a clear rule emerges. The custom for created goods is first-in-hand, especially if the thing is your creation, but also if the thing is in the common state placed by nature. The custom may evolve to first-to-work-upon if, as the property law scholar Robert Ellickson clearly explains, the costs are high.[46]

---

[44] Steven Pinker (1999).
[45] Anna Wierzbicka (1996, p. 233).
[46] Robert Ellickson (1994).

Firstness, however, doesn't matter if location priorly matters. Out of the discussion emerges a testable implication of the theory. If you have property in Y and X is in Y, you have property in X in Y. The rule is that simple, and a difficult case indicates how to test the rule. Using my first first-person three-dimensional virtual world experiment, I report a test of the theory. The results of the test are robustly agreeable to the prediction with an unexpected but consistent-with-the-prediction proviso.

One implication of the theory for economics is that the language of "property rights" contains a tacit assumption about how economists think they work. Property rights are the expectations defined by property, not the content of property. In other words, property effects property rights. The micro- and meso-foundations of property make the macro-level of property rights possible. Such a view challenges the felicitousness of the bundle-of-sticks metaphor, which inverts how humans cognize property. It also means legal realists are wrong on the facts to claim that there is no prior normative conception of property.

A second implication is that property, not property rights, is a fundamental principle of economics. The rules of property are not mere external constraints imposed upon an individual, as we are wont to think. Property resides in a bidirectional relationship that extends to and from the minds of individuals and the moral scheduling pattern of their community.

2

All Animals Use Things, Specifically Food

The modern notion of property is closely tied to land or buildings on a piece of land. We synonymously call it "real estate." When we hear the word modified as "private property," the association is even stronger. Keep off the lawn. Beware of the dog. Or, more ominously: Do not trespass. When we think of the origins of property, we naturally, like Jean-Jacque Rousseau, think of land, of "the first man who, having enclosed a piece of ground, bethought himself of saying *This is mine*, and found people simple enough to believe him."[1] With typical pithy flair, the property law scholar Carol Rose poses the problem as "trac[ing] out what seems to be property's quintessential moment of chutzpah: the act of establishing individual property for one's self simply by taking something out of the great commons of unowned resources."[2] The something out of the great commons of unowned resources need not be land. It could be a fox killed on unowned land, but referencing "the great commons" certainly brings to mind the land on which foxes roam. The seventeenth-century Dutch jurist Hugo Grotius frames the origin of property as the successor era to an imagined "golden age" when "in the eyes of nature no distinctions of ownership were discernible."[3] The common supposition is that at some point in time some human beings were the first creatures to declare something to be "Mine!," and that something was a resource lying free for any taker. Who those humans were and what were the original objects of property are questions to which we can only surmise an answer, but my point of departure is that maybe we have been looking in the wrong place. Maybe the quintessential moment of property is not about land or grasping something lying free for any taker. Perhaps the origins of property lie somewhere else, in the very human act of creating something new, something that did not previously exist in the great commons of nature.

---

[1] Jean-Jacques Rousseau (1754, pp. 61–62).
[2] Carol Rose (1994, p. 9).
[3] Hugo Grotius (1604/1995, p. 227). The original Latin for "For in the eyes of nature no distinctions of ownership were discernible" is *Neque enim potuit natura dominos distinguere*, which, for less modern ears, could be translated less ornately as "for nature could not distinguish lords/owners." For the original Latin, see Hugo Grotius (1604/1868, p. 215).

The Property Species. Bart J. Wilson. Oxford University Press (2020) © Oxford University Press.
DOI: 10.1093/oso/9780190936785.001.0001

Food Is Unlikely to Be the Original Object of Property

Because biologists will object, citing evidence from all over the animal kingdom, to starting with the first question of who those humans were, I will focus on the second question: what were the original objects of property for humans? John Locke's famous and influential inquiry on property also begins in a golden age with the earth given in common to all humankind so that nature might support us with "the fruits it naturally produces."[4] Acorns and apples are his illustrative examples of "how men might come to have a property in several parts of that which God gave mankind in common."[5] "When did [the acorns and apples] begin to be his?" Locke leadingly asks. "When he digested? Or when he ate? Or when he boiled? Or when he brought them home? Or when he picked them up?"[6] Food seems like the ideal starting point in the search for the original objects of property in our species. Its rivalrousness indicates its potential as a source of conflict and its absolute necessity indicates an important problem in need of an important solution.

Humans obviously aren't the only animal that needs to solve the problem of food. All animals are heterotrophs; that is, all animals are incapable of using sunlight to convert inorganic carbon into organic compounds, and so all animals must ingest other organisms with organic carbon. Once ingested, the organism containing the organic carbon literally vanishes as an object. That is why food is rivalrous for all animals, and moreover, in the face of scarcity, why it is ubiquitously a potential source of conflict.

While it is certainly possible that food is the original object of property, I suspect it is not. To explain property in humans, unlike in other animals, we ultimately need to have an explanation that gets us from property in food to property in other movable things like tools, utensils, and ornaments, which are things quite unlike food. Because tools are not converted into energy after a single use, they continue to exist and can be used again on another occasion, by the same animal or another conspecific. Property in transient perishable things like food is not sufficient for explaining property in things that persist. It's also one thing to try and take a bone away from your German Shepherd when she is hungrily gnawing on it, but it's quite another when the bone has become a plaything lying around in the yard. Taking food from

---

[4] John Locke (1689, p. 288).
[5] Ibid.
[6] Ibid.

within any animal's grasp when it serves to satisfy an immediate impulse is not the same thing as picking up a hafted spear lying around. While we might similarly shout, "Hey, this apple is mine!" and "Hey, this spear is mine!" to the person who grabs either, the chimpanzee treats quite differently an apple in hand and a discarded pruned twig previously used for termite fishing. Only if you try to take the apple will you lose some fingers. Food satisfies an immediate impulse and impeding it invites aggression for the harm in directly reducing the animal's fitness for survival. Tools can be used to solve immediate impulses too, as they are by a multitude of animals, but only in humans are tools, utensils, and ornaments socially taught to be made and used for purposes with considerable spatiotemporal distance from their manufacture.

Locke concludes his barrage of questions by saying that " 'tis plain, if the first gathering made them not his, nothing else could. That *labour* put a distinction between them and common. That added something to them more than nature, the common mother of all, had done; and so they became his private right."[7] The problem with Locke's examples of acorns and apples as explaining how humans might come to have property in them is that all animals have solved the conflictual problems of food with his labor mixing theory of property. The temptation might be to say that this observation universalizes Locke's labor mixing theory to the entire animal kingdom.[8] If so, then the organizing questions about property would be (1) how is it that humans came to apply these solutional practices to other rather different things—tools, utensils, and ornaments, and (2) how is it that our practices regarding other things became so much more complex than other animals' practices regarding other things? In short, *how did a* genetically *scheduled behavior regarding food or territory or mates in nonhumans become a* socially *taught and learned behavior about how* not *to acquire things—not just food or territory or mates—in humans*? My answer: It didn't.

I find it to be a rather large leap to go from "I'm eating this apple to satisfy my hunger here and now" to "I'll be using this spear on next week's hunt to get the meat that will satisfy my hunger then and there." That's a lot of time and distance over which to stretch the base animalistic impulse to eat. For our purposes, Locke's example conflates the simple use of food in the here and now, a defining characteristic of every organism in the animal kingdom,

[7] Ibid.

[8] Locke's project is to justify why people ought to have property. Universalizing Locke's labor theory would not be a moral justification for property in other animals, but an explanation for observing a common scheduling pattern among all animals.

with the custom of property, which, I shall argue, is cognitively distinct in humans and which stands outside the here and now. So while it is true that solving the conflictual problem of food is vital, I suspect that human tool use is the key to understanding the similar form of the claims (and titles), "Hey, this apple is mine!" and "Hey, this spear is mine!" My contention is that a *genetically* scheduled behavior for food did not somehow, someway become a *socially* taught and learned behavior for *not* acquiring durable things. Rather, property emerged gradually out of the human tradition regarding tools.

Tools Have Potential Because of How We Make and Use Them

Contrary to common thinking, tool use in nonhuman animals isn't cognitively more complex than nontool behaviors. Consider the digger wasp that hammers with a pebble; or the four genera of ants that transport liquid foods by placing drops on carrying containers of leaves, wood, soil, mud, grass, or sand; or the badger that blocks the burrow entrances of ground squirrels with soil, vegetation, or snow.[9] Birds too, especially corvids, have amazed us with their feats of detaching, shaping, combining, and reshaping single tools, but birds are generally limited to using tools in the specific context of extracting food from holes and with but a short delay between the manufacture, use, and acquisition of the food.[10] Wild-caught New Caledonian crows have even constructed a novel compound tool in a captive test.[11] There is, however, no direct evidence that tool use in birds, like the Hawaiian crow, is a socially transmitted scheduling pattern.[12] Even if we do eventually find evidence of a bright bird or two that socially transmits tool use or tool making to conspecifics, our aim is to find the most likely evolutionary roots for property in humans, and a single species of bird would not be the most promising clue for how human beings came to socially teach and learn how not to acquire things.[13]

---

[9] Robert Shumaker, Kristina Walkup, and Benjamin Beck (2011).
[10] Nathan Emery and Nicola Clayton (2004) and Christophe Boesch (2013).
[11] A. M. P. von Bayern, S. Daniel, A. M. I. Auersperg, B. Mioduszewska, and A. Kacelnik (2018).
[12] Christian Rutz, Barbara Klump, Lisa Komarczyk, et al. (2016).
[13] Researchers have recently found the first evidence that New Caledonian crows can observe a conspecific's tool, form a mental template of the tool, and make the tool, which means that the practice of tool making potentially could be transmitted socially. See S. A. Jelbert, R. J. Hosking, A. H. Taylor, and R. D. Gray (2018).

Much more so than birds, nonhuman primates are flexible users of associative tools, which are composed of two or more distinct objects.[14] Both capuchin monkeys and chimpanzees crack open nuts in the wild using hammer and anvil stones. Because the process involves two spatial relations employed in sequence, biologists consider hammer and anvil nut cracking to be the most complex tool use observed in nonhumans.[15] Nonhuman primates also make and use tools in a variety of different contexts and socially transmit skills from generation to generation. In addition to acquiring food, chimpanzees use tools to play and communicate with others and to clean and defend themselves.[16] Once thought to be the putative hallmark of humanity, great apes and capuchins have also been observed using a tool to make and use a tool. For example, an orangutan and a bonobo have on occasion used a hammer stone to detach a sharp flake from another stone and then used the flake for cutting.[17] These and other examples, however, are quite rare in the wild, and in captivity the nonhuman primates require instruction from their benevolent captors.[18]

As taxonomically widespread as tool use is across the animal kingdom, it is still relatively rare.[19] And as impressive and humbling as it may be that our primate relatives can also use a tool to make and use a tool, no other species than ours routinely *makes and uses* a tool to *make and use* a derivative tool, nor does any other species make and use a composite tool of at least two different material elements (like a spear, knife, or scraper).[20] The symbolic capacity of the human brain foresees tool durability as creating persistent value, and persistent value then becomes *future* value. Sometime in the last five to seven million years, between our last common ancestor with the chimpanzee and the first appearance of *Homo sapiens*, our ancestors overcame some major hurdles necessary for complex tool manufacture and use.[21]

Chimpanzees and capuchin monkeys evaluate potential tools by their suitability for the task. They use heavier rocks to crack open nuts with tougher shells, and they regularly transport and reuse tools.[22] Chimpanzees also

---

[14] See Tables 7-2 and 7-3 on p. 216 in Robert Shumaker, Kristina Walkup, and Benjamin Beck (2011).
[15] Elisabetta Visalberghi and Dorothy Fragaszy (2013).
[16] Christophe Boesch (2013).
[17] Robert Shumaker, Kristina Walkup, and Benjamin Beck (2011).
[18] Ibid.
[19] Gavin Hunt, Russell Gray, and Alex Taylor (2013).
[20] Donald Brown (1991) and Stanley Ambrose (2001, 2010).
[21] Christopher Boehm (2012).
[22] Susana Carvalho, Tetsuro Matsuzawa, and William McGrew (2013).

undergo long-term learning from masters to become proficient at choosing suitable stones for different types of nuts.[23] But how chimpanzees learn to use tools indicates the limits of their use. Chimpanzees learn by copying the result of a demonstration.[24] They attend to the physical properties of the tools and the outcome of the demonstration, not to the purposes of the mentor.[25] In contrast, human children learn by copying the action and not the result of the action.[26] They attend to the demonstration and the mentor's purpose of the tool.[27] The difference is subtle, but important.

Human learners understand the mentor to be doing something *for* them, and by sharing that purpose, children discover the meaning of the mentor's process. Process and purpose are meaningful abstractions of the raw physical signs in the demonstration. This is an important step on the road to property, because property is more than just the physical information of the item of interest. There is meaning in the custom regarding the thing. Pinning down when this occurred in the hominin line is difficult, if not impossible, given what we can and cannot know about our *Homo* ancestors from the archeological record. But doing so is not necessary for my purposes. My claim is that property is unique to humans and that it stems from our customary practices of using tools.

To speak of meaning with human tool use is to get a little ahead of myself, for something else is necessary. Great apes, and possibly capuchin monkeys, comprehend the actions of others as entailing a goal, and they will work with others to help them achieve their ends. [28] But no other primate works *with* others to achieve a joint goal.[29] To do that requires what the comparative psychologist Michael Tomasello calls joint attention, or the simultaneous direction of two minds to the same idea. All great apes cognize two individuals in an interaction as a "you" and an "I," but only two humans can jointly attend to the same end so as to form a "we," a "we" with the mutual knowledge that we both know that each other's end is the joint end. But, you may ask, don't chimpanzees hunt monkeys in groups, to say nothing of lions and wolves? Yes, but as Tomasello explains, there is a difference between hunting with others for the joint end of meat and simply "co-acting" in their own

[23] Tetsuro Matsuzawa, Dora Biro, Tatyana Humle, et al. (2001).
[24] Josep Call, Malinda Carpenter, and Michael Tomasello (2005).
[25] April Ruiz and Laurie Santos (2013).
[26] Josep Call, Malinda Carpenter, and Michael Tomasello (2005).
[27] April Ruiz and Laurie Santos (2013).
[28] Felix Warneken and Michael Tomasello (2009) and Sarah Brosnan and Frans de Waal (2002).
[29] Michael Tomasello (2014).

parallel interests to get, and hopefully keep, whatever meat you can sink your teeth into. The philosopher Raimo Tuomela calls each individual pursuing his own individual goal "group behavior in I-mode."[30] In contrast, *Homo heidelbergensis* appears to have acted in "We-mode."

With a demonstration of tools, children jointly attend to the same goal of the teacher. Children make inferences about what the teacher is thinking about their thinking, that this demonstration is ostensively "for me" to do this. Great apes do not interpret such a demonstration as "for me."[31] They know that a conspecific is dropping a stone onto a nut placed on another stone and that the result is a cracked-open nut with edible goodness inside. But they do not interpret the teacher as hammering a nut "for me" so that "I" may be able to hammer nuts "for myself." The demonstration is not personal to the great ape; it is physically factual. Great apes do not point demonstratively; they point as a request, but not to, so to speak, start a conversation with someone. Human infants do.

Tomasello hypothesizes that joint intentionality emerged with our *Homo heidelbergensis* ancestors some 400 thousand years ago (kya). *Homo heidelbergensis* is the first hominin to hunt live prey as a joint end.[32] To hunt large fleeing prey, the million-year-old technology of hand axes would not do. *Homo heidelbergensis* made and used composite spears.[33] This is significant, for it means that *Homo heidelbergensis* could prune a wooden shaft, set it down, knap a stone into a sharp point, set it down, and then at some later time haft the pieces together with some binding material, which also needed to be prepared in advance. But more than that, *Homo heidelbergensis* was conjointly apprehending these particular pieces as a useful tool. By themselves, the particular pieces were not useful for hunting. Conjointly constituted, the spear had meaning as a tool. How the mind conjointly constitutes the point, the shaft, and the haft into a meaningful whole is more than the sum of the physical facts of the individual pieces. The meaning of such a whole, displaced from the here and now, needs some explanation. What makes it possible for *Homo heidelbergensis* to hold in their minds the following thoughts about the future: a future shaft, a future point, and a future haft, conjointly

---

[30] Raimo Tuomela (2010).
[31] The little word *for* highlights the intentions of the doer behind the doing. Humans jointly attend to those nonphysical ideas behind the doing of something "for me." See chapter 5 for the meaningfulness of *for* as a preposition.
[32] Michael Tomasello (2014).
[33] Harmut Thieme (1997) and Jayne Wilkins, Benjamin Schoville, Kyle Brown, and Michael Chazan (2012).

constituted as a future thing that literally does not exist in the present and that would be useful in a not-so-immediate future activity?[34]

Symbolic Thought Makes Meaning Possible

More than joint attention was changing in the hominin mind. The spear-wielding folk needed to coordinate among themselves when and where to pursue prey that was not immediately perceivable in the present. It is a non-trivial problem to convey information displaced from the here and now. Besides humans, only two other animals (that we know of) have solved the problem of communicating to conspecifics the location of food not present in the here and now. Ants lay pheromone trails and bees perform waggle dances to guide their nest/hive-mates to distant sources of food.[35] But humans voice words. The categorical difference between humans and hymenopterans in solving the problem of displacement is that our communication system is symbolic and theirs are not. Their communication systems are bound to the here and now, while ours is not. In fact, no other animal communication system is symbolic.[36]

Approximately two million years ago our ancestors began carving out a new ecological niche as scavengers.[37] Prior to two million years ago the archeological evidence indicates that large fanged-and-clawed predators ravaged dead carcasses, and then the proto-humans came by to break open the picked-over bones with their hand axes. But then it switches. Somehow the proto-humans armed only with their little hand "axes" were cutting through the tough hides and getting to the meat and bones before several genera of big dagger-toothed cats. How is that possible? The proto-humans would

---

[34] *If property is as old as you claim it is, one might think that there must be a gene-culture co-evolution story.* Dual inheritance theory is predominantly a theory of comparatively recent human behavior (e.g., processing food and lactose tolerance). Given the obvious difficulties, prehuman work is a pretty small part of the literature, the most notable exception being Richard Wrangham's (2009) work on cooking (but even that is hotly debated). I merely aim to show how property is made possible when fully symbolic *Homo sapiens* appears and that *Homo heidelbergensis* is the likely candidate for its proto-appearance in spears. For my purposes we don't need to understand how genes changed in response to hominin behaviors, as they no doubt did when *Homo sapiens* branches from *Homo heidelbergensis*. It's also a whole different project to explain the emergence of symbolic thought in *Homo sapiens* with gene-culture coevolution. My simpler purpose is to use symbolic thought in early humans to explain how we cognize the custom of property.

[35] Derek Bickerton (2009).

[36] Ibid. and Terrence Deacon (1998).

[37] Derek Bickerton (2009).

have to coordinate both their defense of the carcass there and their later consumption of the spoils elsewhere.[38] They would also have to persuade other
members of their band to scavenge a carcass beyond the hill, that is, communicate about objects and events displaced from the here and now. The evolutionary linguist Derek Bickerton hypothesizes that the selection pressure to
solve this recruitment problem could have been strong enough to produce
the first proto-words and to set in motion the very slow and gradual development of symbolic thought.[39]

The archeological evidence indicates various milestones on the road to the
modern mind and its capabilities for symbolic thought. At least as far back
as 100 kya, humans were processing red ochre, perhaps for decoration, and
as far back as 70 kya, humans were deliberately engraving bone tools with
abstract representations.[40] The widespread expression of symbolic thought
in archeological artifacts, however, does not occur until 50 to 40 kya when,
as the paleoanthropologist Richard Klein explains, "structural 'ruins'; formal
bone artifacts; complex graves implying ritual or ceremony; the routine
hunting of dangerous species in proportion to their live abundance; active
fishing; population densities like those of historic hunter-gatherers (im-
plied by a significant reduction in tortoise and shellfish size); and art [appear
as] . . . the MSA [Middle Stone Age] and the Middle Paleolithic were replaced
by the Later Stone Age (LSA) and Upper Paleolithic, respectively."[41]

Symbolic thought, which this artifactual variation from 50 to 40 kya
evidences, is the ability not only to recall concepts at will but also to manipulate those concepts so as to imagine new ways of doing things.[42] It is the
ability not only to think *about* but also to think *with* thoughts free from the
here and now. All other animals think only in the here and now and without
the ability to manipulate their thoughts. When an event external to the animal initiates thinking, the event uncontrollably culminates in an instruction
to the body to act (or not act). Note that I am not saying that other animals do
not store physiological impulses as physiological memory. Nor am I saying
that other animals do not ponder alternatives with their mental maps. I am
saying that only humans can self-trigger thinking without an outside event,

---

[38] Manuel Domínguez-Rodrigo and Travis Pickering (2003).
[39] Derek Bickerton (2009).
[40] Christopher Henshilwood et al. (2011) and Francesco d'Errico, Christopher Henshilwood, and Peter Nilssen (2001).
[41] Richard Klein (2000). For a critical take on this interpretation, see Francesco d'Errico and Marian Vanhaeren (2016).
[42] Derek Bickerton (2009).

about something not before our very eyes, and without any instruction to the body to act.

The key to understanding symbolic thought in humans, the neuro-anthropologist Terrence Deacon argues, is to understand the more general problem of reference in animal communication systems. Many animal communication systems involve both reference, something in the organism's environment, and sense, something in the head of the organism.[43] The difference between human language and other animal communication systems, according to Deacon's careful observations in *The Symbolic Species*, is not that reference is unique to human language, but that human language works with a different kind of reference. Other animal communication systems are not simple versions of human language. Human language is an entirely new species of communication.

When an animal of sufficient size, say a wolf, wildcat, or human, happens upon a black bear sow and her two cubs, she will curl her lips, wrinkle her nose, bare her teeth, and growl. As a sign, the posture and growl refer to her cubs nearby (for without such cubs she may just continue on her way). The approaching animal interprets such a sign as one similar to a display that a conspecific might also make when prepared to fight. In other words, the sow's display points to a class of past experiences in the world involving aggressive, if not mortal, conflict. The sign refers to something in the animal's immediate environment.

Consider vervet monkey alarm calls. Vervet monkeys have a different call to alert the troop to each of three different threats: a leopard leaping from below, an eagle diving from above, and a snake slithering about.[44] When a monkey screams a from-below call, it indicates the presence of a leopard. Such threat-specific calls directly refer to a predator in the neighborhood. But does a vervet monkey's particular vocalization when spotting a leopard mean something to other monkeys like the vocalization 'lɛpərd means something to other Anglophones? No. A vervet monkey's call refers to something about its environment, right here, right now. We humans almost never say "leopard" in the presence of an actual leopard. At the zoo the word *leopard* may indeed point to an actual leopard in the surrounding environment.

[43] Gottlieb Frege (1879).
[44] Robert Seyfarth, Dorothy Cheney, and Peter Marler (1980).

More generally, however, the word *leopard* stands outside the here and now pointing to the other words in the sentence. A vervet monkey's call points in only one physical direction, to the approaching predator. Its calls do not point to other calls, and, more important, its calls do not point to each other and then refer to objects in the physical world.

Words, however, do point to other words, and then we use the sense of the individual words and the whole sentence to pick out the reference in the world. While listening to a live theatrical presentation of *Alice in Wonderland*, we use the other words in the sentence to pick out whether the vocalization *teɪl* (*tāl*) refers to a thin appendage on the mouse's torso or the long and sad story the mouse is narrating. No other animal uses the same signifier to refer to two distinctly different things in the world. The other words in *Alice in Wonderland* point to each other, and those connections then refer to either an appendage or a story in the physical world. Symbolic reference makes such a feat possible because the reference is not tied to the here and now.

If our symbolic communication system isn't tied to the here and now, what holds it together? Other communication systems are supported by the strength of the association between the sign and the external world. When a monkey screams a from-above call, it indicates the presence of an eagle. The fit response is to run down the tree as fast and as far as one vervetly can. If the monkeys used the same call for an eagle as for a leopard, then the strength of the from-above call as an indicator of a diving eagle would be considerably weaker and hence unfit for one of the monkey's hostile forces of nature. Vervet monkey calls are only as strong as the direct associations that support them. It also means that if for some reason all the eagles died out and the monkeys never again used the from-above call, the other calls would independently remain in force.

The link or glue that holds a symbolic system of communication together cannot rely solely on the repeated correlations in the associations that are observed, for a symbol conveys meaning m only in a context in which not(m) could occur but did not.[45] For example, why would we frown to ourselves if a student wrote in a paper, "Pleistocene people gathered mammoths and hunted tubers"? Because a rule of the word *hunt* is that the direct object it takes must *not* be a stationary plant.[46] While the word *hunt* directly conveys

---

[45] Terrence Deacon (1998).
[46] For this example I am using *hunt* as a transitive verb, the Oxford English Dictionary's (OED) first definition of which is to pursue (wild animals or game) for food or sport. As Sarah Skwire pointed out to me, we also hunt for Easter eggs, truffles, and treasure, which typically don't flee from their hunters. But note that we don't simply hunt these stationary things, we hunt *for* them. This is OED definition #2: to make a diligent or energetic search, look *about* (original italics). When we use definition #2,

the meaning of chasing an organism that could flee from its pursuer, it simultaneously does *not* convey the meaning of harvesting something growing firmly in the ground. Every symbol for an organism in the plant and animal kingdoms supports the meaning of *hunt*. If we were to introduce to our class a newly discovered Pleistocene organism called a *boojum*, the students would know from the context of the discussion (except for the one noted previously) whether Pleistocene people "hunted it" or "gathered it" based on the subsidiary knowledge of whether it was a plant or an animal.

There is no such subsidiary link or glue in other animal communication systems. Their call or display is what it is, here and now, and nothing more. It does not signify and carry meaning beyond here and now like a human word does, and it does not simultaneously mean what it is *not*.

Symbolic reference in ordinary human conversations is surprisingly and amazingly deep. To see how words have meaning in a way that animal calls cannot, please bear with me as I explain Deacon's model in more detail, for my explanation of property rests on the marvelous symbolic capabilities of our species. Symbolic reference in humans relies on two other widespread forms of reference in the animal kingdom, iconic and indexical.

When a stimulus or sensory cue s is interpreted as being similar to an object o, s is said to be an icon of o. The iconic reference of s to o is the result of *not* making a distinction or discarding the differences between o and s. For example, when we recognize the image of Bob Hope on an episode of the *Simpsons* cartoon by the similarities of the profiles, the cartoon image is an icon of Bob Hope. At some instant, we discard the yellow-painted skin, the four-digit hands, and the overly large white eyes of the cartoon character to see the commonalities of the image with Bob Hope, a long forehead and a crooked, wise-cracking grin. As Deacon describes it, in iconic reference o is *re*-presented to the mind as s. Consider the growling mama bear. There is a moment when we identify a new animal in view as a mortal threat; it's when we fail to distinguish a mortal threat from the very bear before us (when we might have been able to make such a distinction under different circumstances).

---

hunt is importantly an intransitive verb. In chapter 5, note 36, I discuss how the little word *for* changes the meaning of *hunt* from definition #1 to #2. Hint for the meantime: see note 31 earlier.

The possibility that we might have been able to make that distinction is crucial. Lousy cartoon images of Bob Hope may not be icons of Bob Hope. What makes the guest appearance of Bob Hope on the *Simpsons* work and hence humorous to the viewer is that it is *not* a poorly drawn cartoon character. The object of Bob Hope, the "image" of which is already in our mind, is presented to our mind again as the drawing before us. We see Bob Hope and not mere scratchings on the television screen because the drawing iconically refers to Bob Hope. Such iconic reference is ubiquitous in the animal kingdom, for to survive, animals must be able to distinguish threatening sounds as distinct from nonthreatening sounds. Such mere similarity, though, is only good in the moment it is re-presented to the mind. (I stress the *re-* in *represent* so as to remind the reader each time that a representation means that something is being presented to the mind *again*.)

Unlike iconic reference, indexical reference stretches across space or time to point to something in the external world. An indexical association physically or temporally connects *s* to *o*. Such a connection is built upon three iconic interpretations of similarity.

Let's consider two examples. First, the stimulus of a siren indicates an approaching emergency vehicle. The first iconic relationship is that an approaching emergency vehicle is re-presented to the mind as the sound of a siren. There is nothing that distinguishes this sound from an approaching emergency vehicle, for the loud sound coming from a vehicle could have been something else, say, an obnoxious car alarm. Second, this episode of a siren and an approaching emergency vehicle brings to mind other times and locations when a siren was re-presented to the mind as an approaching emergency vehicle, for example, the last time we were driving on Main Street and heard a siren and saw an emergency vehicle. Lastly, there are correlated features of each of these remembered episodes of sirens and the approaching emergency vehicle so that the siren indicates an approaching emergency vehicle. For example, episodes of a siren and an approaching emergency vehicle are correlated with other vehicles pulling over to the side of the road.

Vervet monkey calls for predators have the same three associations so that the stimulus of a from-below call indicates a leopard at a specific location and time. The first iconic relationship is that this leopard is re-presented to the mind of the vervet monkey as the sound of a from-below call. There is nothing that distinguishes the sound of the from-below call from this leopard, or else no indexical association could exist, but there is also nothing more from this iconic reference to causally link the call to this leopard. The next two iconic relationships are necessary for that.

The second iconic relationship is that this occurrence of a from-below call and this leopard brings to mind one or both of the following: (1) a stimulus of a from-below call at a different time, that is, a temporal proximity, and (2) a stimulus of a from-below call at a different location, that is, a spatial proximity. This second iconic relationship is more than the re-presentation of the leopard to the mind of the monkey as a from-below call in that this re-presentation brings to mind other re-presentations that are temporally and spatially proximal to this occurrence.

The third iconic relationship is that each remembered occurrence of a from-below call and the leopard is correlated; that is, these occurrences are icons of each other such that the mind forms the causal link that the stimulus of a from-below call indicates this leopard from the repeated incidence of these connections. With this hierarchical third iconic relationship, the stimulus of a from-below call causally refers to the leopard.

The first takeaway is that the indexical relation arises because it *does* something, makes a correlation, and so the indexical relationship is only as strong as the repeated correlations that are observed. For example, if passenger cars had sirens and used them regularly, people would stop drawing the conclusion that an emergency vehicle is approaching. Indexical relationships rely solely on what is observed and hence work as a conditioned response. The predictive power lasts only as long as the observed correlation is maintained. The second takeaway is that the indexical relation only does something in the present moment. The siren or leopard call doesn't point to ambulances or leopards of the past or future. The sound points to the ambulance or leopard headed straight for you, right here, right now. So run!

Symbolic reference likewise stretches across time and space, but it also means something beyond the very present. Symbolic reference further means both what is the case, but also, unlike indexical reference, what is *not* the case but could have been had circumstances been different. To see the difference between symbolic and indexical reference, let's compare vervet monkey calls to human words. Each of the three vervet monkey calls *independently* refer to a predator. A leopard call does not refer to any other predator. A leopard call also does not refer to an eagle call or a snake call. The call for a leopard stands alone, and the relationship between the leopard call and its object stands alone from the other calls and other predators. Reference in the vervet communicative system is only between a call and the *directly* associated predator in the present.

Symbolic reference of human words, however, is a closed system in which the symbols refer to *each other* and only *indirectly* refer to an object. Consider the word *cow* (voiced as *kaʊ*). As a from-below call is connected to the animal 🐆, *cow* (*kaʊ*) is connected to the animal 🐄. But unlike a from-below call, *cow* (*kaʊ*) is also connected to the concept COW, which stands outside the here and now. (To distinguish a concept from the word itself, I use small capitals to indicate the concept and italics to indicate the word.) The concept COW is associated with events and experiences with cows ranging from sight, sound, touch, smell, and taste, even if one has never seen, touched, or heard an actual physical 🐄 in person. Moreover, unlike a from-below call but as part of the symbolic system of language, *cow* indirectly refers to the object 🐄 through ideas conveyed in a sentence. For example, in the sentence "Dad was in the barn milking cows," together the words *Dad, barn, milking, was, in*, and *the* indirectly refer to physical cows outside the here and now, so much so that if the sentence was somehow cut off and you didn't hear the last word, you would still have a pretty good idea of what you missed. (Hint for city folk not born on a farm: Farmers don't milk pigs.) What is *not* the case but could have been, had circumstances for the sentence been different, is as important as what is indeed the case when our minds complete the whole that is the meaning of the sentence.

Symbolic reference is hierarchically composed of two types of indexical associations. Words can independently indicate objects (*tuber* can indicate a 🥔), and words can independently indicate other words (*mammoth* can indicate *Pleistocene*). But as a system, each symbol relies on the other symbols through a commonly understood link. The symbols mediated by this link only indirectly refer back to objects (no one has seen a human hunt a mammoth for at least five millennia). Moreover, the link between these symbols rests on all of the impossible relationships among the symbols. The word *hunt* directly conveys the meaning of chasing a fleeing mammoth, and it simultaneously does *not* convey the meaning of harvesting a tuber firmly in the ground. Establishing a symbolic system involves understanding *what is not the case* or what has been discarded as not possible. We either hunt fleeing boojums or gather them. The symbol *boojum* conveys the meaning of a fleeing animal only in a context in which a stationary plant could occur but did not.

At this point I think you'll agree that "symbols aren't simple," as Deacon so warns us in a chapter title. Meaning isn't either, I would add, but we need it to understand property. Property relies on symbolic reference. Property means both what is the case and what is not the case but could have been had circumstances been different. Property operates with the abstract thoughts of a symbolic species.

Meaning Makes Composite Tools Possible

The purpose of this exceedingly short natural history of tools and digression on symbolic reference is to lay the foundation for my claim that tools are the original objects of property in humans and humans only. To do it I must establish that the gulf that separates human and nonhuman tool use is indeed untraversable. I will explain that hammer and anvil tool use by chimpanzees and capuchins, the most complex, socially taught tool behavior in nonhumans, can be achieved by associations alone, that hafted spear use cannot be achieved by associations alone, and that abstract thought is the chasm that separates the two kinds of tools.

The first association in the chimpanzee practice of cracking open a nut is the choice of the object that is a nut. A limited number of physical features indicate whether a hard-walled object is edible. This is not particularly novel—all animals must discriminate between the physical features of an object that qualify it as food and those that do not—except that in this case the reward is not the whole nut itself, but the seed encased in the hard shell. What's impressive for a nonhuman is the number of other simple associations that separate the chimpanzee from its goal.

The next association is the selection of an anvil stone. Again, the physical features that indicate its suitableness are observably few: flat, hard, and in a position not prone to move. The big leap for a nonhuman is to place the nut on the anvil for processing, which is the first of two spatial relations in this practice. The next step is to find a suitable hammer stone. Too light and the nut will never crack; too heavy and the seed inside will be pulverized. What is required of the apprentice is to associate the physical characteristics of the nut with the weight of the stone used. Again, the strength of the association is what matters. The final remarkable step is to cognize the second spatial relationship between the hammer and the nut and apply it sequentially with the release of the stone. In other words, the nut on the anvil indicates dropping the hammer stone onto it.

While impressive when we break it down, the practice requires the concatenation of associations. If the raw computing power of the brain is large enough to hold all of the associations in sequence, emulating the recipe step by step from start to finish is sufficient to obtain the reward. Nowhere along the way must a chimpanzee engage in abstract thought. The chimpanzee need only focus on the physical facts of what *is* the case. Great ape see, great ape do. There is no other glue that holds the demonstration together, no subsidiary knowledge of *what is not* the case regarding the items and the process. No theory of nut breaking.

The key to hafting spears 70 kya is literally the glue. Hafting a point onto a shaft is a major watershed in the natural history of making and using tools. The experimental archeologist Lyn Wadley and her colleagues Tamaryn Hodgkiss and Michael Grant duplicated the trace compound adhesives found on stone tools in Sibudu Cave, South Africa.[47] They find that not all powdered red ochres are the same when combined with plant gum, even if the color is the same. Without knowing anything about chemistry, something unobservable must *not* have been the case for a glue maker 70 kya to use this red ochre and not that one. Wadley et al. also find that not all fires are the same; some woods burn hotter and make longer-lasting coals. Again, something unobservable about the flame must not have been the case for someone to use a specific type of wood with its moisture content and not another type of wood. Wadley et al.'s conclusion from their archeological experiments is that "no set recipe or routine can guarantee a satisfactory adhesive product."[48] The raw observable facts about the inputs are not enough to successfully replicate the process. The glue maker 70 kya must have manipulated concepts abstracted from the here and now. In their words, "qualities of gum, such as wet, sticky, and viscous, were mentally abstracted, and these meanings counterposed against ochre properties, such as dry, loose, and dehydrating."[49] We may not know what word our ancestors used to refer to haft, but Wadley's experiment appears to show that the abstract concepts WET and DRY, STICKY and LOOSE, VISCOUS and DEHYDRATING composed a concept HAFT.

Why does no other animal construct composite tools? Because no other species has acquired the ability to communicate symbolically; no other species has acquired the ability to think with abstract concepts outside the here and now.[50] To construct a composite tool, an organism must be able to

---

[47] Lyn Wadley, Tamaryn Hodgkiss, and Michael Grant (2009).
[48] Ibid. (p. 9593).
[49] Ibid.
[50] Terrence Deacon (1998, p. 22).

manipulate concepts unconstrained by the here and now. It means distinguishing two physically identical red powders in such a way that this one, but not that one, will make good haft. But it also means combining two or more abstract concepts (POINT, SHAFT, and HAFT) in such a way as to create a new abstract concept for the new physical whole. When Alice says to the Mouse, "It is a long *teıl*, certainly, . . . but why do you call it sad?," symbolic thought makes it possible to perceive the vocalizations of the sentence as something more than a concatenation of individual words: our minds create a double pun.[51] In the case of a composite tool, symbolic thought makes it possible to perceive a new physical whole, a spear, as something different than the mere associations of physical parts in such and such physical space at this moment in time. We perceive the created object as a spear, something that did not previously exist in the great commons of nature.

Part of the act of creating a new physical object is to see it—as only a symbolic species can—as something more than the sum of its physical parts. Skeptics find such a claim hard to swallow. *How do you know that a chimpanzee doesn't see a pruned twig as something new, as something different than an unpruned twig?* Yes, the twig is not the same physical thing, but the pruned buds and leaves on the ground attest to a prior physical association. Prior to their removal, the twig would not physically fit into the termite hole. Associating the leaves and buds with the physical problem, the chimpanzee removed them. We are so used to thinking with the symbolic thought we have acquired that it is difficult to perceive the world through associations alone. Associations are all that are necessary for an unsymbolic species to think through a problem of subtraction. When symbolic humans, however, compose a composite tool, we bring, through our thoughts, a new object into existence. *Well, an eagle brings a nest into existence too.* Declared and re-presented to your mind as only a symbolic animal can. Eagles don't communicate symbolically, and there's no reason iconic and indexical relations would not be sufficient to find sticks to interweave, grass and corn stalks to line, and moss and feathers to soften into a nest.

A spear is more than the sum of its parts. A point, shaft, and haft, conjointly constituted as a spear, are things that do not appear in the great commons of nature lying free for any taker. We perceive more than physical features of the object. The created object means something. Spears must be

---

[51] Lewis Carroll then proceeds to double the double pun by typesetting a tail rhyme of the tale in the shape of a tail.

created, and to create a spear one needs to know how to look for this red powder and not that red powder, make this kind of fire and not that kind of fire. *The mouse's tale not the mouse's tail, Alice.* Creating a spear requires a mentor who demonstrates "for me" how to find the right red powder. A composite tool is the joint goal of a mentor and mentee, the simultaneous direction of two minds to the same idea. Moreover, when coming across a spear lying on the ground, the spear is re-presented to the mind of the viewer as the product of a joint goal, something that its creator and the viewer both know does not naturally appear in the common state of nature. The re-presentation to the viewer's mind also includes another person, the creator, not physically present, with whom the viewer jointly attends to the following same end: the person created the spear "for himself" and "not for me." With symbolic thought the viewer interprets what is not the case regarding the spear and the process that created it. In short, the spear physicalizes meaning, both of what is and of what is not the case.

———————➤

If we're impressed with capuchin nut cracking, and we should be, how much more amazing is early *Homo sapiens sapiens*, self-named with pride the wisest of the wise. By the time the human career takes off 50 kya, this symbolic-thinking, joint-goal-attending, composite-tool-making, meaning-forming, precocious little primate is doing things quite unlike any other species in the history of the planet. The modern reflex is to fearfully resist any claim of the uniqueness of our species, to minimize the gulf between humans and our animal relatives. I understand where such a fear comes from. Pride is quick to take hold in our species and with it comes a host of sins. I too would be more partial to human exceptionalism, as the economist Kyle Hampton put it to me, if it were espoused by someone other than humans. But only a human can. Only a human can think with thoughts regarding things not before our very eyes. Only a human can be humane and say, "That thing is yours." So I stand by the claim—more articulately espoused and extensively defended by Terrence Deacon, Derek Bickerton, Matt Ridley, Denis Dutton, Michael Tomasello, John Searle, and many others—that humans routinely do many things that categorically distinguish us from the rest of the animal kingdom. "If the gap between humans and other animals is as small as we've been told," Bickerton asks, "what in the world could possibly be this miniscule difference that makes all other animals do so little and us do so much?

So far as I'm aware, none of those who argue for continuity between humans and other species have ever realized, let alone admitted, that *each time the gap is minimized, the manifold, manifest abilities of humans become more mysterious than ever.*[52] The connection humans make between a person and a tool may not be simple, but it doesn't have to be mysterious either. The connection originates in the symbolic thought of a symbolic species.

---

[52] Derek Bickerton (2009, p. 8, original italics).

3

Primates Socially Transmit Tool Practices, but Humans Share Meaning-Laden Customs

Neither the chimpanzee nor the human is born with the skill for nut cracking or spear hafting; nor are these skills discovered anew each generation. Juveniles of both species acquire the pattern of actions by observing their mentors at work and must practice to become proficient. You learn to hang a door by watching a video on YouTube. Chimpanzees also seek out expert tool users to learn how to better crack nuts.[1] There is a distinct determination of purpose in the individual that seeks to learn from a conspecific. For the chimpanzee, the purpose is eating the seed inside the nut. For the human, the purpose is not so immediate, nor so directly associated with an impulse to eat.

The proximate purpose of hafting a point to a shaft is to construct a new external object that did not previously exist in the world. A spear is a created object. After cracking open a nut, the chimpanzee's anvil and hammer remain stones, to be used perhaps on another occasion when the impulse arises, but they are nonetheless still stones. Nothing new has been created. A stone point when hafted to a wooden shaft is more than a point, a shaft, and some haft. The composite object has been transformed into a tool by virtue of its usefulness for hunting. If a juvenile overhydrates the adhesive or boils it so that air bubbles form, the haft either lacks cohesiveness or is weak. Ruining the usefulness of the object as a tool dissolves the meaning of the object as a tool. The object is not a spear unless all of the elements, skillfully combined, conjointly constitute something that can be used to hunt prey. That conjoint constitution, that meaning, occurs in the mind of the artisan.

The meaning from the shared practice also exists, due to joint attention to purpose, in the mind of the next generation of experts who learn from their

[1] Dora Biro, Noriko Inoue-Nakamura, Rikako Tonooka, et al. (2003).

The Property Species. Bart J. Wilson. Oxford University Press (2020) © Oxford University Press.
DOI: 10.1093/oso/9780190936785.001.0001

master. Many other animals share practices with other members of their social group, practices that are socially, not genetically, transmitted. Primates,
however, are the only order of animals to use tools routinely and flexibly as
a shared practice. But even among the most sophisticated nonhuman tool
users in the wild (capuchins, chimpanzees, and orangutans), no more information than direct associations is passed on from teacher to the taught. What
a nonhuman primate sees is what it acquires as a practice.

As a symbolic species, humans acquire abstract meaning in our practice
of making tools. To share the practice with at least one other member of the
group is to share the meaning of the practice. The meaning-giving process
in making tools is the same as the one at work in language. When someone
speaks, our attention is not on the specific features of the sound waves that
reach our ears. As a meaningful word—jointly attended to by the speaker
and the listener—sound waves lose their external character in the physical
world. We hear through the sound and focus our attention on the meaning
of the sound as a word. We perceive the sound waves as words imbued with
meaning. In the language of the chemist and philosopher of science Michael
Polanyi, we subsidiarily attend to the vocalized sound when we focally attend
to what we hear as a word with meaning.[2]

Meaning works the same way in the human practice of making tools.
A mentor can describe a spear in only physical terms as a particular as-
semblage of a point, a shaft, and a haft. The description would specify the
materials, their arrangement, and the means for combining them. But such
a physical description could only give an account of one particular specimen composed of a point hafted to a shaft. It could not exemplify a whole
class of spears of the same kind, an abstract concept that would include other
specimens of different sizes or materials. What characterizes the class are
the principles of its use as a spear, its purpose. As with language, we subsidiarily attend to the point, shaft, and haft when we focally attend to an assem-
bled specimen as a spear, a long stabbing weapon for thrusting into a fleeing
animal. When our minds integrate a particular specimen into an abstract
thought that bears on its principles of use, we endow the physical object with
a meaning that points, beyond the here and now, to its purpose.

More than a pattern of actions is shared in the human practice of making
tools. While biologists use the term *tradition*, I have used *shared practice* to connote the social transmission of habitual patterns of actions in

---

[2] Michael Polanyi (1958).

nonhumans.[3] I prefer to reserve the terms *tradition* and *custom* for human shared practices because *tradition* and *custom* additionally connote meaning as part of an individual's pattern of actions. The word *custom*, in particular, has the meaning of a long-established practice that carries with it the moral force of what is right. Adding abstract thoughts of what is good and right to patterns of actions is a key element for the human custom of property to emerge out of the shared practices of making tools. The next step is to show how patterns of actions in property arise from making tools. To do this we must first take the intermediate step to connect know-how in making tools to know-how in using tools.

Tool Use Is Embodied Knowledge

Knowing the meaning of a composite tool is an example of what Polanyi calls "tacit knowing," *knowing how* to do something without the ability to articulate how you know it.[4] We know how to convey the meaning of a spear, through words and gestures, but we do not have the ability to articulate how our mind takes the physical facts of stone, adhesive, and wood to give meaning to the composite object as a long stabbing weapon for hunting. The rules of the mind that give meanings to perceptions are supra-conscious and thus inarticulable.[5]

Using tools also involves tacit knowing, but it is more basic than giving meaning to a composite tool and hence not unique to humans. An animal uses a tool to extend its own body to do something that it could not otherwise do with the body alone.[6] For a chimpanzee to locate an underground termite colony or a stingless bee honey chamber, it must probe below the surface with a wooden stick.[7] Termites and bees don't make this easy. The visible signs above ground only give a general indication as to where the chamber may be. The chimpanzee must find its way by feeling the impacts of the stick on its hand as if the impacts occurred where the stick meets lower soil resistance, some 100 cm below the surface.

---

[3] Dorothy Fragaszy and Susan Perry (2008).
[4] Michael Polanyi (1958).
[5] F. A. Hayek (1963). For a proof, see F. A. Hayek (1952).
[6] Benjamin Beck (1980).
[7] Christophe Boesch (2013).

The same is true for humans when we hammer a nail or feel our way around blindfolded by use of a stick or cane. Our focus is on extending our own body to feel what objects may be in front of us. When our stick hits the leg of a table, we feel the table in our body because we are only subsidiarily attending to the actual feeling of the stick on our palm. Likewise, we feel the hammer hit the nail, not the handle vibrating in our palm. We probe and know what's hidden like a chimpanzee presumably probes and knows what's hidden, but with abstract thought we can also reflect upon our probing and knowing, as Polanyi does:

> Our subsidiary awareness of tools and probes can be regarded now as the act of making them form a part of our own body. The way we use a hammer or a blind man uses his stick, shows in fact that in both cases we shift outwards the points at which we make contact with the things that we observe as objects outside ourselves. While we rely on a tool or a probe, these are not handled as external objects. We may test the tool for its effectiveness or the probe for its suitability, e.g., in discovering the hidden details of a cavity, but the tool and the probe can never lie in the field of these operations; they remain necessarily on our side of it, forming part of ourselves, the operating persons. We pour ourselves out into them and assimilate them as parts of our own existence. We accept them existentially by dwelling in them.[8]

Materialists will wince at Polanyi's language. He isn't merely thinking with metaphors to explain how tacit knowledge with tools works, and he isn't using mellifluous metaphors to make his explanation more appealing to our mind. He is thinking in the very metaphors that we think in when we make contact with the external world through tools, for as the cognitive psycholinguist Steven Pinker says, "all abstract thought is metaphorical."[9] Forming a part of ourselves *is* how we think about the use of a spear. Pouring ourselves out and into a spear *is* how we think about the use of a spear. Assimilating a spear as part of our own existence *is* how we think about the use of a spear. Dwelling in a spear *is* how we think about the use of a spear. Once our concepts were no longer tethered to the here and now some 200 to 150 thousand years ago (kya), our minds could combine and recombine a few basic ideas to grasp even more abstract ones, metaphor most definitely intended.

---

[8] Michael Polanyi (1958, p. 59).
[9] Steven Pinker (2007, p. 242).

Polanyi is doing in metaphor to explain tacit knowledge what I conjecture our symbolic thinking ancestors did in metaphor as part of their everyday use of tools: They put themselves in their tools. They perceived a tool in hand to be a physical part of their body such that they felt the external world through it. This is not a wholly original conjecture. For example, the economist and social philosopher F. A. Hayek speculates:

> The notion of individual property must have appeared very early, and the first hand-crafted tools are perhaps an appropriate example. The attachment of a unique and highly useful tool or weapon to its maker might, however, be so strong that transfer became so psychologically difficult that the instrument must accompany him even into the grave.... Here the fusion of inventor with "rightful owner" appears, ... sometimes accompanied also by legend, as in the later story of Arthur and his sword Excalibur—a story in which the transfer of the sword came about *not* by human law but by a "higher" law of magic or "the powers."[10]

How early is very early is not something that we can really hope to answer with the prehistorical record. Thoughts don't fossilize. Nor for our purposes do we need to know how early the notion of property appears. Our project is to explore how we humans cognize the meaning of property beyond asserting a strong psychological attachment.

The knowledge of how to use tools is in our bodies like it is in any animal's body that uses tools. That knowledge may be (almost surely) only genetically acquired in such species as ants and digger wasps, or it may be both genetically and socially transmitted in primates, both nonhuman and human. But the common feature to all animals is that we physically relate to our tools through our perception of them. When interacting with the external world, including our tools, "perception is primary," the animal ethologist W. H. Thorpe explains, "while sensation is the result of secondary analyses."[11] Hayek puts it this way, first correcting a common misconception: "we do not first have sensations which are then preserved by memory, but it is as a result of physiological memory that the physiological impulses are converted into sensations."[12] What Thorpe and Hayek mean is that an animal's

---

[10] F. A. Hayek (1988, p. 30).
[11] W. H. Thorpe (1963, p. 146).
[12] F. A. Hayek (1952, p. 53). The eminent neuroscientist Joaquín Fuster (2003) notes that "Hayek (1952) was the first to propose the representation of percepts and memories in large-scale cortical networks of the kind proposed" in Fuster's book and adds later that "[p]robably nobody has described the processes of categorization better than Hayek (1952)" (pp. 7, 60).

mind, whether operating in an adult human brain with approximately 86 billion neurons or in an ant brain with 250,000 neurons, first identifies and categorizes the neurophysical inputs it receives from the body interfacing with the external world. The mind mediates the physical world and our sensing of it. What we feel with our bodies and then thereby know of our surroundings is our interpretation of our surroundings. "Everything factual," as Goethe recognized in the nineteenth century, "is already theory."[13] Our minds do not directly sense the external world from the neurophysical inputs to our bodies; that is, our nervous systems do not first present sensory data to our mind as a sensation. Rather, physiological memory classifies the neurophysical inputs it receives, and then we feel with the tool to know something about the world, which is why and how a chimpanzee feels the open chamber through a probe, and why and how we feel the table through a cane and the lacrosse ball through a stick.

Such a physical event may then trigger thoughts that uncontrollably culminate in the body to act. For the chimpanzee thinking in the here and now, that could mean switching out the initial stout woody probe for a slender plant stem.[14] For the human thinking with concepts free from the here and now, that could mean thinking to oneself, "I feel the table" or "I feel the ball in the pocket." Even though the person's body does not physically touch the table or the ball, our minds assimilate the tool as part of the very body we feel with. A person with a symbolic system of reference thinks of the tool as part of the abstraction that is ME in the same way that an arm is part of ME.

Property Embodies the Claim "This Is Mine!"

If a spear is a bodily extension of my person, then if someone were to challenge my grasp by grabbing the spear in my hand, I would physically respond in the same instinctive way that I would respond if someone were to forcefully grab my arm, with resentment or fear at the affront. It would be an

---

[13] Johann von Goethe (1981, Volume 12, p. 432): Das Höchste wäre: zu begreifen, daß alles Faktische schon Theorie ist. It is not a large leap to theory as it might first appear when one realizes that Goethe, like Adam Smith in *The Theory of Moral Sentiments*, is using the word *Theorie* with the original sense of the Greek word *theoria*, meaning "to view or behold." Goethe's theory entails both sensing and classifying in the body.

[14] Crickette Sanz, Caspar Schöning, and David Morgan (2010). The brilliance of switching tools is that the ants and termites cannot swarm the slender dipping stick and attack the chimpanzee with painful and dangerous bites.

attack on my person that could trigger a primeval fight-or-flight response. The novel situation is what happens when I lay my spear down and look for a spot to lie down. The spear is no longer a physical extension of my body, *so am I still in it?* For any other animal, the answer can only be no, because there can be no abstract idea of putting myself in the spear in the first place. Nor in any other animal can there be any joint attention to the same end that I had previously put myself in the spear.

But with humans, it would seem as if I am still in the spear. If someone else were to pick up the spear when I lie down, my immediate response would be to shout, "Hey, that spear is mine!" My assumption would be that whoever is picking up the spear would jointly attend to both the object as the spear in question and my purpose in shouting at him. The shout might be accompanied by a physical display as aggressive as Klugh's red squirrels, but I am doing much more than what a squirrel or a scrub jay or a dolphin or a baboon or a chimpanzee does in the defense of a nest, food cache, prey, mate, or territorial domain. The anthropologist and businessman A. Irving Hallowell hits the nail on the head:

> The ambiguity in the use of the term property is no doubt partly responsible for the reputed human analogies found among animals. If one starts with the naive idea that property is some kind of physical object that "belongs" to someone and it is then observed that animals store food or defend their nests or territory against aggressors, it is easy to say that the food, nest, or territory is the animal's "property" and then to generalize further, on the basis of wider observations, and say that animals have "property" as well as human beings.[15]

"Such a use of the word [*property*]," laments the nineteenth-century economist Henry Dunning Macleod, "is quite a modern corruption, and we cannot say when it began," though he is certain that "neither [Francis] Bacon, nor far as we are aware, any writer of his period calls material good property."[16] Focusing our attention on the thing in question is understandable; a thing is the point of contention among conspecifics, both human and nonhuman, and the point of interest among those who study the conspecifics, both human and nonhuman. Nevertheless, by focusing our attention on the thing

---

[15] A. Irving Hallowell (1943, p. 136).
[16] Henry Dunning Macleod (1881, p. 143).

itself, which is but a subsidiary part of the dwelling and scheduling patterns of any species, we are apt to confuse ourselves about how property works, like the pianist who confuses herself when she shifts her attention from the piece she is playing to her fingers touching the keys. So to be clear, never do I use *property* to mean a thing (except perhaps in a quotation where the confusion and corruption are unavoidable). Property is a custom.

What am I doing if I'm doing so much more when I snarl, "Hey, this spear is mine!"? For you to know what the fuss is about, I have to predicate. A mammalian growl delivered with a curled lip and a wrinkled nose doesn't predicate. It is a common characteristic of any mammal's readiness to fight, whether or not you even know that my spear is nearby. All that matters for a mammal to growl is that it sees that you are near the spear. Iconic message sent and received, but that's not property.[17] Even if the interloper drops the spear at the sound of my deep and intimidatingly gruff voice, that's not property either, even though the effect is the same when a wolf takes off at the growl of the sow. Property is priorly predicated upon symbolic thought and the joint attention to the spear and my end regarding it.

The operative word in "Hey, this spear is mine!" is *mine*. *Mine* is predicated on a subject to tell the listener which of the many possible things I mean when I say "mine." In this case the subject is this spear, and because I am predicating, my vocalization is more than a warning sound. My vocalization is a speech act, my utterance a claim. Property consists in a claim imbued with meaning, particularly in the case of disagreement or good faith misunderstanding. The custom entails doing something with words. We speak with the aim of doing work in the physical world. We speak with the aim of changing how people perceive the physical world.

To make the case that property is a human universal, I need to provide some evidence that the custom is universally recognizable between any two human beings on the planet. *How can you prove that two people as different as a Cree and a Finn, a Ewe and a Kinh, a Melanesian and an American think with the same abstract thoughts?* I can't directly, of course. Thoughts, like quarks, aren't something we can see. But like quarks we can infer such elementary particles of thought by observing other effects in the

[17] Carol Rose (2013).

physical universe. Any two human beings can communicate across any two languages, which means, for example, that an Anglophone can bring to a Longgu-phone's mind what is in the Anglophone's mind. For that to be possible there must be some simple expressions universal to all human languages. The linguists who collect and test for such primitive concepts across many disparate languages call their approach to meaning analysis the Natural Semantic Metalanguage (NSM) approach to the study of meaning.[18] NSM linguists search for semantic primes, atomic concepts that are found in every human language and thus presumed to be universally innate. Universal semantic primes make communication across languages possible.

In terms of Deacon's closed system of symbolic reference from the previous chapter, we can think of semantic primes as the conceptual singularities to which semantically more complex words can be decomposed, which is the other major contribution of NSM linguists. Subtle differences between words in the same or different languages become clear when decomposed into simpler concepts. For example, compare Anna Wierzbicka's two decompositions of the speech act verbs *assert* and *claim*:

(a) I say: X
(b) I imagine some people would say that this is not true
(c) I can say that this is true
(d) I assume that people will have to think that it is true
(e) I say this because I want to say what I know is true

versus

(a′) I say: X
(b′) I imagine some people will say that this is not true
(c′) I think that I have good reasons to say this
(d′) I think that I can cause people to have to say that this is right
(e′) I say this because I want to cause other people to think that it is right.[19]

The two verbs are close relatives in that they both are about saying something controversial. But asserting is (c) merely saying that the controversial view is

---

[18] Cliff Goddard (2011, 2012) and Cliff Goddard and Anna Wierzbicka (2014).
[19] Anna Wierzbicka (1987, pp. 321, 324).

Table 3.1. Subset of Semantic Primes (as English Exponents) for Property

substantives	I, YOU, SOMEONE, SOMETHING/THING, PEOPLE
determiners	THIS, OTHER/ELSE
evaluators	GOOD, BAD
mental predicates	KNOW, THINK, WANT, DON'T WANT, FEEL, SEE, HEAR
speech	SAY, WORDS, TRUE
actions, events, movement	DO, HAPPEN, MOVE
"logical" concepts	NOT, MAYBE, CAN, BECAUSE, IF
similarity	LIKE/AS
intensifier, augmenter	VERY, MORE
"possession"	(IS) MINE

Source: Cliff Goddard and Anna Wierzbicka (2014, 2016).

true and (d) assuming that such a statement will mean people also think it is true. Claiming is much more. Claiming is thinking (c′) you can back up your words and thinking (d′) you can cause people to say it is not just true, but right. Claiming is also more forceful than asserting in that it aims to change what other people think. Asserting is saying something because you want to say what you know to be true.[20]

One contribution of such semantic decompositions is that they help us understand how our minds have recombined such conceptual singularities into new words with new meanings and how word meanings have evolved over time because the conceptual building blocks have changed. Since Anna Wierzbicka initiated this research program in 1972, NSM scholars have compiled sixty-five universal semantic primes.[21] Table 3.1 reports the thirty-one most relevant semantic primes for our project.

Consider two of these primes: WANT and DO.[22] One clue that a concept may be a semantic prime is the circularity with which traditional dictionaries define a set of terms. As an example, Wierzbicka reports the

[20] Such decompositions may make translations of words across language possible, but that, of course, need not mean that the network of entailments for such translations are the same across communities. Communities may differ in what constitutes asserting or claiming in practice, and the conditions under which someone can assert or claim may differ by community.

[21] Anna Wierzbicka (1972).

[22] The interested reader is directed to Anna Wierzbicka (1996) and Cliff Goddard and Anna Wierzbicka (2002) for a thorough discussion of these and other semantic primes.

definitions of *want, desire,* and *wish* from *Longman's Dictionary of the English Language*:

> *to want*: to have a desire;
> *to desire*: to wish for, want;
> *to wish*: to have as a desire.[23]

Circular definitions, however, are not sufficient to classify a concept as a semantic prime. NSM linguists also rely on a combination of research on cross-linguistic comparisons and language acquisition in children to designate such primitive concepts as THINK, WANT, DON'T WANT, KNOW, and FEEL as innate components of how the human mind works.[24] The semantic prime DO captures the significant role that the concept of "action" plays in regularized human activity and our ordinary discourse. Human activity is about DOing. One piece of evidence that DO is a semantic prime is that it appears very early in children's speech.[25]

Such atomic concepts are useful for drawing distinctions between two similar expressions. The concepts of THIS, MINE, I, and WANT are as simple as they get in any language, and in every language people know what each individual word for such a concept means. So if I say, "This is mine," I am saying something distinctly different than when I say, "I want this." Chimpanzees—independent of their human captors—may not have tokens (words) connected to their concepts, but they still may share thoughts with humans, even though their thoughts are bound to the here and now and ours are not. Three such concepts would be I, WANT, and THIS.[26] Chimpanzees recognize an "I" in a mirror, and when I visited Georgia State University's Language Research Center, they appeared, like humans, to want things like Wonder Bread and grapes. And while they may not have a word for THIS, chimpanzees point at and request objects like any human who wants something sweet. From our anthropocentric observations, primatologists have good reason to believe that chimpanzees think things like "I want this." It also would not be a stretch to grant that a squirrel, a dolphin, or even a scrub jay may think—in the moment and only in the moment—"I want this"

---

[23] Anna Wierzbicka (1996, p. 48).
[24] Cliff Goddard and Anna Wierzbicka (1994).
[25] Eve Clark (1983).
[26] Anna Wierzbicka (2014, p. 163).

about some food.[27] But "I want this" is not the cornerstone of property. Nor is "I want this" why humans have property. The danger of looking for the origins and meaning of property in like effects in the animal kingdom is that it conflates the very simple thought of "I want this" with the distinct simple thought of "this is mine."

Economists typically use the Hawk-Dove game, first developed by the biologist John Maynard Smith and the geneticist George Price, to model property in humans.[28] In the two-conspecific game, each contestant can either fight or yield to the other for a thing that each organism simultaneously wants.[29] While both organisms benefit from solely using the thing if the other yields, the other organism's best course of action depends on what the other contestant does. If the other contestant yields like a dove, it should fight like a hawk for the thing, but if the other contestant fights like a hawk, it should yield the thing. Such a game-theoretic formulation conflates physical control stemming from I WANT THIS THING with the custom of property built upon THIS THING (IS) MINE.[30]

When I say, "This spear is mine," I am doing something more than merely asserting that I want the spear. I am making a claim, apparently a controversial one to the person picking up the spear, and I am aiming to do something with my words. The content of my claim, from earlier, is that (1) I imagine that the listener will say that this is not true. Why else would he be reaching for the spear when I lie down for a nap? I furthermore make my claim public because (2) I think that I have good reasons to say that this spear is mine. I use it as an extension of myself and to take it is to harm me. (3) I also think that I can cause the listener to have to say that it is right that this spear is mine. I take for granted that my fellow human will jointly attend to these good reasons and upon thinking about it some more concede that it is indeed right that this spear is mine. Finally, (4) I say that this spear is mine because I want to cause other people within earshot to think that it is right that this spear is mine.

Note the following key concepts at work when I claim that this spear is mine: I, SAY, THIS, NOT, TRUE, THINK, GOOD, MINE, WANT, OTHER, PEOPLE, and RIGHT. All but one of these (RIGHT) are indefinable except of themselves.

---

[27] But at some point in the animal kingdom the word *want* becomes too simple for us symbolic thinkers to felicitously describe, for example, an amoeba as "wanting" some algae.

[28] John Maynard Smith and George Price (1973).

[29] See, for example, Robert Sugden (1986, ch. 4) and Herbert Gintis (2007).

[30] See also Carol Rose (2013).

The reason for my speech act is that from my first-person perspective of the world, it appears that the person picking up the spear does not perceive the physical world as I perceive it. Property first involves saying things, not just communicating iconic sounds of aggression.[31] I say something about the action of someone who attempts to pick up my spear, and as part of my claim, I imagine that the listener would say something to the contrary. The concept SAY is one of sixty-five universal semantic primes that NSM linguists have collected and tested across many disparate languages.[32] All human groups say things with symbolic language, and all human groups have a word for saying things.[33] When I say, "Hey, this spear is mine!," I am attempting to introduce agreement on how two conspecifics perceive the spear. The goal is not merely to scare off the interloper, for he may return at some other time beyond the here and now. The goal is to change how the interloper perceives the spear so that I can rely on him not to take it in the future. Property is not in the effect of an interloper leaving the spear on the ground at this moment in time, but in the mutual perception that the spear is indeed mine beyond this moment in time. For humans to do what we do with property we must be able to say things with words. While the dating and character of the emergence of language is controversial, Goddard and Wierzbicka conjecture, based on work by the paleoanthropologist Ian Tattersall, that the atomic concept WORDS emerged when our species emerged 150 kya.[34]

The second key concept in the claim is the predicate that I imagine applies to what I am saying: that the person picking up the spear would say that it is not true. Goddard, Wierzbicka, and Horacio Fabréga conjecture that TRUE originated with cognitively modern humans some 70 kya as one of the last two semantic primes to emerge in human thought.[35] They argue that TRUE would have to follow WORDS because it would be unlikely to evaluate something as TRUE or NOT TRUE "until it became possible to think of 'pinning down' what someone said, which, it seems to us, essentially involves focusing on their words."[36] Property involves other people pinning down oral claims

---

[31] See also Carol Rose (1985, p. 88), who argues that the origin of property rests on "the articulation of a specific vocabulary within a structure of symbols approved and understood by . . . people. It is this commonly understood and shared set of symbols that gives significance and form to what might seem the quintessentially individualistic act."

[32] Cliff Goddard and Anna Wierzbicka (2014).

[33] Donald Brown (1991) and Anna Wierzbicka (1996).

[34] Ian Tattersall (2012) and Cliff Goddard, Anna Wierzbicka, and Horacio Fabréga Jr. (2014).

[35] Cliff Goddard, Anna Wierzbicka, and Horacio Fabréga Jr. (2014).

[36] Ibid. (p. 74).

of "This thing is mine" as true or not true. No other animal superimposes vocalizations with the abstract qualities TRUE or NOT TRUE.

As I mentioned in chapter 1, the concept NOT is essential to how meaning works in symbolic thought, and it is a universal semantic prime. The concept also serves as the glue that holds property together. Property is about counterfactual claims of what could have been the case but are indeed factually not the case.

The third key concept in the claim, RIGHT (the adjective, not the noun), is clearly not semantically atomic.[37] What is right involves more than what is (atomically) good. What is right involves judgments of what is proper, suitable, and fit in informal situations and what is just in formal situations. The molecular concept of RIGHT succinctly captures something that must be true of all cognitively modern human groups, that we have expectations about the regularity of everyone's conduct; that is, there are moral standards that are to be acted. In this case, a standard of this community is that I can claim this spear as mine. Another is that my interloper cannot claim, "This spear is mine." We also have expectations about the appropriate responses to external events, like me and other people orally and physically backing up my claim. In the next chapter I elaborate more on RIGHT and property.

The critical atomic concept in the claim is the predicate of the claim itself. Humans in every language can say, "This (thing) is mine," and in every language it means the same thing.[38] People using such diverse languages as English, Ewe, East Cree, Longgu, Arabic, Finnish, Koromu, Mandarin Chinese, and Vietnamese can all utter the claim "This is mine."[39] Moreover, there is no other way to express the claim in terms of any other atomic concepts. *Mine* means what mine means, just like *do* means what do means, *say* means what say means, and *good* means what good means. Attempting to define these words in terms of simpler concepts fails because these words symbolize atomic conceptual units. And yet in every language every human being knows what *mine, do, say,* and *good* mean.

The claim "This is mine" stands all by itself, in part because it is a normative statement, not only a factual one. If someone else runs off with my spear, I can still say that it is mine, and I'm not simply stating a physical fact. I'm saying that to act as if the spear is not mine is to harm me; that it is not right to

---

[37] See Anna Wierzbicka (2006).
[38] Cliff Goddard and Anna Wierzbicka (2016).
[39] Ibid.

take my spear; and that by the standards of the community the spear ought to be returned to me. Part of the difficulty in working out what property means is that a conceptual singularity, MINE, is at the core of the custom, and it is a normative concept at that.

Along with TRUE, it seems that MINE would be the other of the last two universal atomic concepts to emerge on the Pleistocene plain.[40] The conceptual pronouns *I* and *mine* both may be first-personal, but both I and MINE defy defining the one in terms of the other.[41] Part of the further evidence that MINE is atomic is that it can be readily combined with other semantic primes to capture the meaning of *yours* and its archaic rhyming ancestor *thine*. "This is yours" can be paraphrased as "You can say about it: 'this is mine'" and "This is not yours" as "You cannot say about it: 'This is mine.'"[42] Property is someone saying something beyond the here and now, not merely growling in the present moment. In every language you can also say, "This thing is someone else's."[43] In other words, if there are things about which I can say, "This is mine," then there are other things about which other people can say the same thing. I use the abstract concepts YOU and I to imagine myself switching places with you to say the same things I say. Property is not just about me feeling, thinking, and saying, "This is mine."[44] *Property is jointly reciprocal.*[45] We jointly attend to mine and yours, mine and thine, *meum* and *tuum*. There is no abstract concept of YOURS in Klugh's squirrels or any other animal because there is no abstract concept of MINE in any other animal.

If I can switch places with you and think, "This other thing is yours," then I can do another simple switch with my thoughts. Instead of saying, "This spear is mine," I can say, "This spear is not mine; it is yours." In doing so, something in the social world has changed. The visual perception of the physical world remains unchanged for both of us, yet I have *done* something with these words to alter how both you and I think about the object.[46] We cognize the spear differently: You are now in the spear, and I am not. From this point on, you and only you can say, "This spear is mine." With a few simple words

---

[40] Cliff Goddard, Anna Wierzbicka, and Horacio Fabréga Jr. (2014, p. 74).

[41] Cliff Goddard and Anna Wierzbicka (2016).

[42] Ibid.

[43] Ibid.

[44] See Jon Pierce, Tatiana Kostova, and Kurt Dirks (2003) for a psychological model of the first-personal feelings of "This is mine."

[45] Ronald Coase's (1960) famous examples of cattle raisers and crop growers illustrate this beautifully.

[46] J. L. Austin (1975).

symbolizing a few simple concepts, what we personally know about the external world has changed, even though the physical matter has not.[47] What we know of our surroundings has changed because our interpretation of our surroundings has changed. No other animal can self-trigger thoughts that will change their own perception, as well as a conspecific's perception, of a physical object. What a marvel of the animal kingdom.

Humans Socially Transmit Property with Moral Force

Property is more than one individual claiming, "This is mine," for one claim does not make a custom. Within a band of humans there are many individuals who can claim, "This is mine." Conflict can ensue when a single item is the simultaneous subject in two distinct claims. Whether it is a scrub jay or a human, an animal's scheduling pattern regularizes the nature and timing of its engagements with the external world, including conspecifics. A scheduling pattern is the resulting order from the animal's point of view that "constitutes a set of *expectations* about its actions, their ordering, their probable results, and appropriate responses to outside stimuli."[48] Genetics is one scheduling mechanism; the other is shared practices. In humans, property is a socially shared practice that forms a local order by aligning expectations so as to settle or prevent competing claims of "This is mine."

A defining characteristic of the *Primate* order is that we take pleasure in regularly being in physical proximity and bodily contact with members of our group.[49] Our impulse for sociality is ancient, at least thirty-five million years ancient when extant New World monkeys split from the family tree. Like Adam Smith and his forgotten early twentieth-century heir, the philosopher Samuel Alexander, I take our sociality as an external given and a necessary starting point. For property that means how we deal with each other regarding

---

[47] I have now briefly and unwittingly introduced the first two of David Hume's (1740, p. 337) "fundamental laws of nature, that of the stability of possession [and] of its transference by consent." Paul Sagar pointed out to me that my argument is more Humean than merely that. Hume (1740, p. 202) defines property as a "relation betwixt a person and an object as permits him." As Christopher Berry (1982) explains, by relation Hume means an association in the mind, more specifically "a species of cause and effect" (Hume 1740, p. 324). Property is "not anything real in the objects but the offspring of the sentiments" and "belongs entirely to the soul, which considers the union of two or more objects" (Hume 1740, pp. 326, 112). I see the contours of a resemblance, but given the density of Hume's arguments, a Hume expert, which I am not, would need an entire chapter to flesh out the correspondence between his ideas and mine.

[48] C. F. Hockett (1973, p. 46, original italics).

[49] C. F. Hockett (1973).

things must fit with the general scheduling pattern of our sociality. So far nothing is different than for any other primate. But with symbolic thought, we can—as an end in itself—think about the actions of others and how they fit, or fail to fit, with the scheduling pattern of our group. We can also contemplate our own actions for no other purpose than to think about what we have done in the past or will do in the future. And when we think about our actions, or others', we can evaluate them to be good or bad. The concepts GOOD and BAD are human universals.[50] Humans can universally say that someone has done something good for them or something bad to them, and universally they can feel good or bad when people do such things to them.

When we deem a deed to be good or bad, we are contemplating more than a thing done, an act. We are contemplating our conduct, our character, a whole—just like a spear—that means more than the individual pieces of the thing done. Good conduct includes actions that others can attune their sociable impulses to. Bad conduct includes actions that disrupt the or-derly relations of the group. The other members of our group disapprove of someone taking my spear because they empathize with me in the harm that I feel.[51] They also wish to avoid the conflict that may ensue as my resentment prompts me to beat off this injury and restore my condition. But more than that, others do not empathize with the taker because they themselves do not want to take the spear from me, and they do not want to take the spear from me because we humans judge our acts "for their own sakes, for their bearing on our character."[52] Sociability hafts the point of actions to the shaft of moral valuations to form the whole of our character.

As a social species, we have expectations regarding the regularity of each other's conduct. This regularity, this harmony of conduct, forms the back-ground of a human band and the basis of what is right in the sense of what is pleasingly coincident or fitting with the entire scheduling pattern or order of the band.[53] A single act is thus not good unless it is also right with the whole of human intercourse. Out of the habits of responding to claims of "This is mine" emerged a fitting custom found presumably in every human society: Do not steal. This general rule is stated in the negative be-cause not following the custom leads to harm, discord, and violence. It is

---

[50] Cliff Goddard and Anna Wierzbicka (2002).
[51] Vernon Smith and Bart Wilson (2019).
[52] Samuel Alexander (1933, p. 237).
[53] The word *right* and its cognates in Old Saxon, Old Frisian, Old Norse, Gothic, Dutch, German, and Latin mean straight; not bent, curved, or crooked; direct, going straight towards its destination; directed straight forwards (*OED*).

furthermore stated in the abstract, making it applicable to future unforesee-able circumstances. Finally, because it is not genetically transmitted, we must be taught how to follow the rule and submit to its authority. We are taught by our mentors not to steal for the sake of not stealing. Children may acquire the concept MINE by age two, but it is by teaching, imitation, and practice that they learn how to meaningfully apply the custom of property here and now, which includes learning when to say, "That is yours."[54]

---

[54] Celia Brownell, Stephanie Iesue, Sara Nichols, and Margarita Svetlova (2013).

4

What Is Right Is Not Taken Out of the Rule, but Let the Rule Arise Out of What Is Right

Following the seminal work of Armen Alchian and Harold Demsetz—the most prominent representatives of the neoclassical school of new institutional economics—no economist is unclear as to the meaning of the term *property rights*.[1] The distinction between property and property rights, however, is less clear. The early twentieth-century economist and statistician Irving Fisher defines a property right as "the right to the chance of obtaining some or all of the future services of one or more articles of wealth" and property as "the abstract right of ownership."[2] He then plainly differentiates these two definitions from the quotidian notion of a thing itself as "property": "a loaf of bread is concrete wealth, not a property right; the right to eat it is the property."[3] Alchian is more succinct on the meaning of property rights: "the rights of individuals to the use of resources."[4] So are Elizabeth Hoffman, Kevin McCabe, Keith Shachat, and Vernon Smith when they design an experimental treatment condition around the idea: "A property right is a guarantee allowing actions to occur within the guidelines defined by the right."[5]

While economists broadly accept property rights as indispensable for understanding economics, we define the nominal phrase circularly in terms of "the right to do *X*."[6] To channel the eighteenth-century jurist and judge

---

[1] Armen Alchian (1965), Harold Demsetz (1967), and Armen Alchian and Harold Demsetz (1973).

[2] Irving Fisher (1906, p. 22).

[3] Ibid. (p. 23).

[4] Armen Alchian (1965, p. 53).

[5] Elizabeth Hoffman, Kevin McCabe, Keith Shachat, and Vernon Smith (1994, p. 350).

[6] Terry Anderson and Laura Huggins (2003, p. 2) are a rare exception: "Property rights are the rules of the game that determine who gets to do what and who must compensate whom if damages occur." I too will use the concept of rules and rule following as the core of property emerging as a moral custom.

The Property Species. Bart J. Wilson. Oxford University Press (2020) © Oxford University Press.
DOI: 10.1093/oso/9780190936785.001.0001

Sir William Blackstone, we seem to be afraid to put the question mark further down and ask what the right to do X means, as if fearful of opening a Pandora's box of morality; or at best, we rest satisfied treating the noun *right* as a universal semantic prime, self-evident and incapable of being further decomposed, indefinable except of itself.[7]

But being fearful is a mistake and by resting satisfied we are mistaken. Yoram Barzel avoids the morality of rights by defining so-called economic property rights as "the individual's ability, in expected terms, to consume the good (or the services of an asset) directly or to consume it indirectly through exchange."[8] The thug would agree as he whacks me on the head and takes the messenger bag from my shoulder. Exactly how is an "ability to consume" a right, or property, or a property right? In the grand tradition of weasel words, the modifier *economic* empties the content of *property right* but leaves the visible shell of the term untouched. With the moral premises sucked out, economists need not fear the moral connotations inherent in right, property, and property right that might eventually hatch and challenge their positivist analysis.

Economists go out of their way to quarantine their positive economic analysis from moral and legal considerations. In a widely cited article, Douglas Allen, for example, justifies the "essential . . . distinction between legal and economic rights" with an appeal to Blackstone.[9] Allen interprets Blackstone as "defin[ing] property rights" when Blackstone says, "The third absolute right; inherent in every Englishman, is that of property: which consists in the free use, enjoyment, and disposal of all his acquisitions, without any control or diminution, *save only by the laws of the land*."[10] When Blackstone qualifies the absolute right of property (n.b.: *ius proprietatis*, never "property right" or "property rights"), he is not drawing a distinction between so-called

---

[7] From Blackstone's *Commentaries on the Laws of England* (1803, book II, pp. 1–2):

> There is nothing which so generally strikes the imagination and engages the affections of mankind, as the right of property; or that sole and despotic dominion which one man claims and exercises over the external things of the world, in total exclusion of the right of any other individual in the universe. And yet there are very few, that will give themselves the trouble to consider the original and foundation of this right. Pleased as we are with the possession, we seem afraid to look back to the means by which it was acquired, as if fearful of some defect in our title; or at best, we rest satisfied with the decision of the laws in our favour, without examining the reason or authority upon which those laws have been built.

[8] Yoram Barzel (1997, p. 3).
[9] Douglas Allen (1991, p. 15, note 5).
[10] Sir William Blackstone (1803, p. 138, Allen's italics).

economic and legal rights, because qualifying a statement is not the same thing as making a distinction in kind. When Blackstone defines and qualifies liberty, the second absolute right inherent in every Englishman, as "the power of locomotion, of changing situation, or moving one's person to whatsoever place one's own inclination may direct, without imprisonment or restraint, unless by due course of law," he is not drawing a distinction between two kinds of liberty, between a power-of-locomotion liberty right and a legal liberty right.[11] He is describing the circumstances under which the customary rule of liberty can be abridged by the customary force of law, that is, when legal and moral boundaries have been crossed. The same is true of the right of property. Blackstone spends 518 pages of book II specifically qualifying what abridges the customary rule that people are free to use, enjoy, and dispose of their things. Under English law, limitations on the right of property include the legal and morally accepted power of taking an individual's things for public use through forfeiture, eminent domain, and taxation. The distinction of economic and legal property rights is a purely late twentieth-century analytical one, not a 250-year-old distinction found in a major treatise of the common law.[12]

To be clear, my criticism of work by economists—like Armen Alchian, Steven Cheung, Douglas Allen, and Yoram Barzel—is not with the content of positive economic analysis.[13] Barzel's work is particularly important in highlighting the costs associated with using things that we want to use. My criticism is with the jargony abuse of common words in the service of positive economic analysis. Rights, by any stretch of the word, are not plain abilities. Abilities to enjoy things or consume them need not be moral. Rights, properly considered, on the other hand, are moral, *all the way down to their micro- and meso-core*. Why refer to rights when abilities will do fine? For example, why say, as Barzel does and any economist would, "when transaction costs are positive, rights to assets will not be perfectly delineated," when the following would do just fine: "when transaction costs are positive, the abilities to use assets will not be perfectly delineated"?[14] Such a restatement befits the positivist, consequentialist, avowedly nonmoral purposes of an economist. Where things would change would be in statements like "the ability to

---

[11] Ibid. (p. 134).
[12] See also Daniel Cole and Peter Grossman (2002) and Geoffrey Hodgson (2015), who criticize economists for separating "economics rights" from "legal rights."
[13] Armen Alchian (1965), Steven Cheung (1969), Douglas Allen (1991), and Yoram Barzel (1997).
[14] Yoram Barzel (1997, p. 4).

receive the income flow generated by an asset constitutes part of the property rights over it."[15] The alternative sentence—"The ability to receive the income flow generated by an asset constitutes part of the abilities to use it"—doesn't have the same ring to it, however, which is to say it lacks the moral dominion of having "rights over" an asset. Phrases like "The Abilities to Use Things Model" and "The Abilities to Use Things Approach" would also seem to lack some luster when substituting "abilities to use things" for "property rights," but neither replacement should matter if that is what we economists truly mean. Barzel's book is an economic analysis of contractual exchange, not property rights.

The fear in broaching property as a moral concept is that when we look into the box of morality, we are privy only to our own moral values, so we must settle for plumping for what feels right to us. Moral reasoning, however, is neither wholly objective nor wholly subjective. When we find ourselves in a new situation with strangers, we can search our personal databank of experiences for common principles that might bring agreement. The twelve jurors who unanimously convict my thief can agree in and on principle because morality is not purely subjective. Our moral reasoning is intersubjective.

On the mistaken second point, a right to do X is not a simple irreducible concept in English, nor is its cognates in French (*droit*), German (*Recht*), or Italian (*diritto*). Meaning 9d in the *Oxford English Dictionary*—the legal, equitable, or moral entitlement to do something—reveals two conceptual units of a right to do X, the first of which is morality. Presuming that the legal connotation historically follows and is derivative of the moral connotation, it would be tempting and convenient in the modern era of legislature-instituted rights to subsume the moral sense within the legal sense.[16] But as positively uncomfortable as it may be to economists, morality is a critical component of understanding the emergence of property.[17]

The other key concept is entitlement, the grounds for laying a claim, not any claim, but a moral claim to do X. This brings to the foreground the assertion of and an appeal to facts as part of a justification for doing something. Anna Wierzbicka argues that the word *right* as an adjective has three senses (moral, intellectual, and conversational), which are all unique to English.

[15] Ibid. (p. 7).
[16] John Salmond (1907).
[17] Thomas Merrill and Henry Smith (2007) argue that for property to work it must be recognized as moral, but they do not explain how property emerges with its moral charge.

One common thread to each sense is that "human conduct can be seen and assessed 'objectively,' 'rationally,' and in accordance with 'evidence.' There are 'rules,' there are 'procedures,' and there are objective criteria that people can refer to."[18] As an entitlement to do something, a subsidiary sense of empiricism similarly permeates the noun *right* with appeals to rules and evidence to support a moral claim to do something.

While appeals to empirics almost always have a positive connotation in English, *empirique* in French is rarely neutral and mostly negative.[19] So we should not be surprised that *droit*, the French word of import for the abstract noun *right*, does not evoke evidentiary appeal and is conceptually decomposed in French differently. The online *Dictionnaire de l'Académie française* defines *droit*, in the sense demanded, as *ce qui est juste; ce qui est conforme à une règle implicite ou édictée*, that is, that which is right (*juste*), that which is consistent with an implicit or enacted rule. Again, *droit* carries both a moral and a legal sense, but for our purposes the important semantic work to note is in the explicit evocation of following a rule, an implicit rule, a moral rule. What is translated into English as the adjectival *right* is the French word *juste*, which, when one realizes that Latin in classical Roman times had no letter *j* and instead used the letter *i*, indicates that we have made a full turn to the chapter title, a maxim by the third-century jurist Julius Paulus, and its keystone of *ius*.

One of the three classical Roman uses of *ius* is "a right, moral or legal," as in the familiar Justinian phrase *ius suum cuique tribuere,* to grant a right to each one his own.[20] Translating *ius* as "a right," however, sounds too much like a physical thing for the modern ear. The Roman *ius* is not something that can be felt by the senses, like the grain of a wooden chair. *Ius* is incorporeal, of the mind. A better translation for the intangibility of *ius* would be "to grant what is right to each one his own." That is the meaning I employ in the chapter title, which is a near-literal translation of a Julius Paulus maxim: *Non ex regula ius sumatur, sed ex iure quod est regula fiat.*[21] I say "near literal translation" because the chapter title omits a weighty relative clause, "which is" (*quod est*).

---

[18] Anna Wierzbicka (2006, p. 79).

[19] One example of the latter, of several, that Anna Wierzbicka (2010) gives is "*l'astrologie est un rapport naïf et empirique au cosmos* (astrology is a naïve and empirical relationship with the cosmos)" (p. 11). In contrast, in English an empirical relationship is desirable and sound: "Efforts are being made to research it scientifically on the basis of empirical evidence instead of philosophical logic and reasoning" (p. 12).

[20] John Salmond (1907, p. 467): The two other uses of *ius* are (1) justice, from which *iustitia* and *iustum* are derived, and (2) law, in the juridical sense.

[21] Friedrich Hayek (1973, p. 72).

Friedrich Hayek artfully translates the maxim as "What is right is not de-rived from the rule, but the rule arises from our knowledge of what is right."[22] "Knowledge" is not literally in the maxim, but it captures the emphatic in-corporeality of the literal "let the rule arise out of what is right, which is," full stop. Julius Paulus is saying that what is right is firmly established. It just *is*. And we know what it is—right. The emphasis in the full clause also comes from the hortatory subjunctive of "Let the rule arise," as in the familiar phrase from Genesis, "Let there be light." I use Julius Paulus's maxim to ex-plicate a theory of the emergence of property as a bottom-up custom. Let the rule of property arise out of what is right for the situation at hand. To help us understand what that means, I show how the third-century maxim manifests itself in twenty-first-century laboratory experiments on property.

One element of my approach is Demsetzian. If "the emergence of prop-erty rights can be understood best by their association with the emergence of new or different beneficial and harmful effects," such as a case study of the Native American trade of beaver pelts on the Labrador peninsula, then the novel circumstances of laboratory economies likewise present an opportu-nity to further that theory by observing property in its nascence, with the additional benefit that these virtual economic terraria are replicated several times over.[23]

Given the unexamined use of the term *property rights* in economics, the tendency in economics is to think out the question of what property is in terms of how property is known, namely, the externally surmisable benefits and costs of using a resource. What Demsetz did not have access to were the moral debates concerning such benefits and costs that the Labrador Native Americans engaged in to establish new rules of property. In the chapter, I focus on the actual deliberations of strangers interfacing in an unfamiliar context, out of which emerge, or fail to emerge, a mutual delineation of mine and thine, *meum* and *tuum*.

More broadly, my approach follows in the tradition of Adam Smith and clas-sical political economy. The framework is further founded in rule-guided ac-tion and rule-guided perception, which, in turn, rely on morality. Following Hayek, a *rule* "means simply a propensity or disposition to act or not act in a certain manner, which will manifest itself in what we call a *practice* or custom," with the practice or custom in question being what I call *property*.[24]

---

[22] Ibid. (p. 162).
[23] Harold Demsetz (1967, p. 350).
[24] Friedrich Hayek (1973, p. 75, original italics).

Articulating the relationship between the rules of property and the manifest practice of them is a crucial step that the chapter takes, and one that is impossible for neoclassical economics to take. What a theory of the emergence of property needs is an approach that begins by treating property as a sphere of actions, perceptions, and things that appears regularly in human intercourse.

What Is Right Is Not Derived from the Rule

Our sense of what is right is an abstract whole, operating with symbolic thought. When people talk with us, we tend to act or not act in a certain manner. We don't interrupt the speaker, and we take our turn. We also tailor the conversation to the listener, which entails discarding that which is not suitable for the current circumstances. We call such a propensity, for short, following the rules of polite conversation.

Like sound and sight, our sense of what is right is a feeling in our body by which we thereby know something about our environment external to our body.[25] Our sense of what is right consists in the capacity to follow rules that we appear to "know," not "know" in the sense that we can declare them axiomatically and exhaustively, but "know" in the sense of being able to describe roughly what actions are suitable for the situation.[26] If this is not self-evident, try listing all the rules of polite conversation. Have you included what "Do not bore" or "Do not show off" means? They may not be on your list of general rules of conversation, yet when we are challenged with someone who imperviously breaks one out of the uncountable number of rules, we can call forth *ex tempore* the specific rule relevant for this encounter. We have a kind of background sense, which, although quite inarticulable, allows us to formulate in the foreground a reason as to why this person has diminished the genial atmosphere. As Ludwig Wittgenstein put it, "there is a picture in the foreground, but the sense lies far in the background; that is, the application of the picture is not easy to survey."[27]

The first implication of not being able to explicitly know or specifically state the rules that govern how we act is that only *in their totality* does a whole system of rules, the custom, form the sense of how to conduct ourselves

---

[25] Vernon Smith and Bart Wilson (2019, pp. 29–31).

[26] F. A. Hayek (1963).

[27] Ludwig Wittgenstein (1953, §422).

rightly.[28] To embed our understanding of property in practices is to consider it as implicit in our rule-guided actions, and hence we are going well beyond the brute economistic weighing of benefits and costs. In short, our actions are governed by abstract rules, not concrete algorithms of benefit-cost analysis. As sensitive as our actions are to the external benefits and costs of our circumstances, much of our intelligent action arises from knowledge that is largely inarticulate. Moreover, the assessments of benefits and costs that we make are only intelligible against the background provided by this inarticulate understanding. The practice provides the context within which the assessment of benefits and costs makes the sense that it does. Benefits and costs are islands in the sea of property. Strategically important islands they may be, but islands nonetheless.

The second implication is that the rules that govern our actions also govern our perceptions of actions, and it is rule-guided perception that poses the fundamental problem for the emergence of property as a moral custom.[29] While different individuals will recognize a specific set of circumstances as one of the same kind involving property, we are unable to present the precise stimulus condition that will replicably produce the same perception in different people and hence the same action in different people. Rule-guided perceptions carry the understanding in patterns of appropriate action, which conform to a sense of what is right for this circumstance. But while agents can perceive when they or others have or have not done what is right, that others share that perception is not a given. The perception of an action as one of a kind that fits a pattern of what is right depends critically on the agency being shared.

Actions constituted as a custom are shared among those who practice the custom because the common perception of the action has integrated the individual agents into a shared regularized whole, a "we." Shared perceptions serve as the foundation for actions within a practice, actions that are what the Russian philosopher and literary critic M. M. Bakhtin calls dialogic, in continual active dialogue and multilaterally extending to and from an agent.[30] A rule doesn't apply itself. It must be followed in real time, under ever-fluxional circumstances, and against the unarticulated background of the entire custom. The interpretation of what a rule means is done on the fly and in dialogic concert with those around the agent.

---

[28] F. A. Hayek (1952). See also Francis Heylighen (1999).
[29] F. A. Hayek (1963).
[30] M. M. Bakhtin (1982).

In contrast, framing property rights as the internalization of the benefits and costs of an individual's right to use a resource, *in response to others*, is monologic. Specifying a property right as "*W* has the right to do *X* with *Y*" doesn't allow for the difference between the formulation and its application in particular circumstances of time and place. It also doesn't take account of the bidirectional relationship between a rule and the entire custom of property. The custom is what keeps the rule *active*, and the application of the rule reaffirms the custom. But *the current application of the rule also modifies the custom by amalgamating into the background all of the inarticulable nuances of its application here and now*. Stating that what is owned are rights to use resources is like Macbeth numbly concluding that life "is a tale/Told by an idiot, full of sound and fury,/Signifying nothing." Macbeth is engaging no one, and no one him. He is simply responding to the news of Lady Macbeth's death in a moment of epiphany. *Enter a Messenger.*

But the Rule Arises from Our Knowledge of What Is Right

The nineteenth-century German jurist Ferdinand Mackeldey explains one meaning of *ius* as *ius est norma agendi*, which he translates as *ius* "is a rule of conduct." Literally translated, *ius* is the standard which is to be acted.[31] (Curiously, *agendi*, translated as the future passive participle of the verb *to act* [*agere*], is considered to be the marking of the *jus*sive mood.) From everyday human intercourse, we have expectations of the regularity of each other's conduct. The moral *ius* is the background practice of what is right, out of (*ex*) which arises the rule (*regula*). When does a rule arise? When one needs to be formulated. When does a rule need to be formulated? When someone does something contrary to what is right, that is, when a disagreement in the perceptions of what is right leads to an act contrary to the *ius*, an *iniuria*. Such an act challenges the existing multilateral dialogue of actions. It interrupts the regularity of everyone's conduct. Rules of property arise as remonstrance to injuries, hurts, and losses willfully inflicted on others. Returning to the example of conversation, the rule "Do not bore" is called to the foreground when we are confronted with a veritable bore in the room, and what it means

---

[31] Importantly, Ferdinand Mackeldey (1883) is talking about the external relations of free Roman men. Another meaning of *ius* is *ius est facultas agendi*, the license to act, or, literally, the opportunity which is to be acted.

to bore us to tears (say, with the semantics of Latin phrases) relies on all the inarticulable rules of polite conversation.

Finally, we consider the negative portion of Julius Paulus's maxim: *Non ex regula ius sumatur*. The reason the *ius* is not taken out of the rule is that the inarticulable background cannot be taken out of an articulated foreground. The everyday practice of what is right is not derived from a rule, not only because the custom is inarticulable *in toto*, but also because a rule not summoned from custom cannot anticipate the unknowable local circumstances under which it might conflict with another rule subsumed within the larger community practice of what is right.

We are now in the position to apply rather straightforwardly Julius Paulus's maxim to the case of property: *A rule of property regarding things arises from our background knowledge of what is right regarding people and things.* To explicate the proposition, I draw from the spontaneous conversations of participants in several laboratory experiments.[32]

Two Different Experiments Illustrate the Proposition

Erik Kimbrough, Vernon Smith, and I designed an economic experiment to explore what happens when the experimenters do not enforce property in a virtual world.[33] The basis for the heuristic experiment was a platform designed to investigate how a market might emerge endogenously when participants have to discover (1) that trade is possible and that once discovered, (2) specialization is possible to exploit the wealth-creating benefits of trade.[34] Sean Crockett, Vernon Smith, and I took the institution of property for granted and built the platform accordingly: What one could produce and what one could consume, no one could interrupt. The simple change that Kimbrough, Smith, and I made to the platform was to relax that assumption built into the original software.

Figure 4.1 displays a screenshot of the experiment interface. Every session consists of eight participants who each control the production of two types of fictitious goods, red and blue. In Figure 4.1, Person 2 controls the

---

[32] Erik Kimbrough, Vernon Smith, and Bart Wilson (2010); Erik Kimbrough (2011), Bart Wilson, Taylor Jaworski, Karl Schurter, and Andrew Smyth (2012); and Taylor Jaworski and Bart Wilson (2013).

[33] Erik Kimbrough, Vernon Smith, and Bart Wilson (2010). See also Erik Kimbrough, Vernon Smith, and Bart Wilson (2008).

[34] Sean Crockett, Vernon Smith, and Bart Wilson (2009).

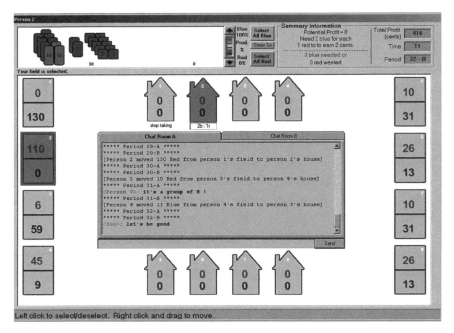

Figure 4.1. Screenshot of the homestead experiment platform.

production displayed in the rectangle numbered 2 (and in green only on Person 2's screen), which is called a field. All participants are informed in the instructions, deliberately in the passive voice, that

> when the clock expires [at the end of the period], you earn cash based upon the number of red and blue items that have been moved to your house. To select items to be moved, *left* click on an item or click on the red or blue buttons at the top of the screen. The yellow highlighted items can be moved by dragging with the *right* mouse button.

Person 2's house is in green (on Person 2's screen). What the participants are not told is that they can move items to other people's houses and fields (as was only the case in the original design) and that they can move items from other people's houses and fields. The participants must discover that such movements of items are possible.

The participants are also not informed, but can discover, that the odd-numbered persons (even-numbered persons) are capable of increasing returns for producing red (blue):

For the first 10 seconds of each period, you will produce items in your green field. Using the scroll bar in the upper middle portion of your screen, you can change the proportion of each second allocated to producing red and blue. Each person's production is displayed on their field.

An odd (even) can earn 30 (26) cents in autarky (the economist's word for "isolation"), but with specialization and exchange at the competitive price, an odd-even pair can earn 90 and 80 cents, respectively. Anytime an item is moved to another person, the movement is recorded in a chat room in the middle of the screen, and anytime an item is moved from another person, the movement is recorded in red. At any time during the session, the participants are free to chat with the other participants in one of the two publicly accessible chat rooms. The instructions for the chat room give the participants wide latitude within an explicit constraint of civility:

> Everyone in this experiment can send text messages. Everyone can read all posted messages. In the center of the screen, you can type a message in the line in either of two chat rooms and click on the Send button.

> Under your house you can also post a one-line message that will be visible at all times to the other players.

> You are free to discuss all aspects of the experiment, with the following exceptions: you may not reveal your name, discuss side payments [outside of the laboratory], make threats, or engage in inappropriate language (including such shorthand as "WTF"). If you do, you will be excused and you will forfeit your earnings.[35]

Unlike the well-circumscribed action spaces in traditional economic experiments, this one is as wide open as the Wild West. Participants interact in real time from the moment the experiment begins until it concludes sixty-seven minutes later. The software imposes no order of moves, except that red and blue are produced during the first ten seconds of a period and that

---

[35] Many people find it curious that the instructions refer to "your house." *Wouldn't that bias the groups in favor of establishing property?* Perhaps, that's testable. We originally wrote the instructions for an experiment in which the software enforced property because we first wanted to see what happened when nothing but the software enforcement changed. The interested reader will notice that the results in the second experimental platform are similarly unsuccessful when there is no such thing as "your house" in the open sea.

consumption occurs at the moment the period concludes ninety seconds later. In the experiment and a follow-up study with Taylor Jaworski in which people are free to migrate from the original group, the participants start in pairs, and without hint or notice, two pairs appear as one group of four on the screen, and finally the two groups of four become one group of eight, but in Erik Kimbrough's extension, all eight people are together for the entire session (which makes things much more unsettling).[36] The participants inhabit a hurly-burly uncertain world. The experience is fast paced, you might even say suspenseful, to such an extent that after a pilot session, we made every seventh period a day of rest in which nothing is produced but during which the participants can still converse with each other.

At this point the naysayer interjects to make the highly original observation that the participants live in a physical world with secure property and that we gave the participants their own house and field in the virtual world. *How can a contrived task with college sophomores help us understand the emergence of property as a moral custom?* Obviously, my coauthors and I are not claiming to have recreated the Big Bang of property. That would be cool but a little dangerous. Instead, we are observing how real people making decisions of salient monetary consequence interface with each other on a frontier with no externally enforced custom of property. Some groups will succeed and prosper, and some will fail, spectacularly so. The question is, can we identify why from a complete historical record of what happened, including their heat-of-the-moment conversations? New experiments can also be designed to test any *ex post* synthesis.[37] If a nagging intuition questions whether endowing the participants with their exclusive control over a field and house is important to these observations from the laboratory, then let's bring that to the foreground in another experiment.

The second experiment platform is inspired by the property law scholar Robert Ellickson, who studied how North Atlantic whalers in the eighteenth and nineteenth centuries solved the problem of property for things that lie free for any taker (which is how the seventeenth-century German jurist Samuel Pufendorf described the problem in his discussion of natural law and

---

[36] Taylor Jaworski and Bart Wilson (2013) and Erik Kimbrough (2011).
[37] Erik Kimbrough, Vernon Smith, and Bart Wilson (2010) do just that in three successive treatments.

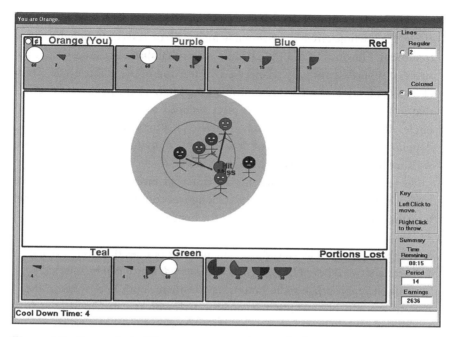

Figure 4.2. Screenshot of the open sea experiment platform.

property, *res in medio quibusvis exposita*).[38] I and three bright undergraduates at the time, now professors of economics themselves, tested Ellickson's admittedly *ex post* explanation with an *ex ante* experimental design.[39] Figure 4.2 displays the software interface for the experiment.

Each participant, first in pairs and then later without notice as a sextet, controls a stick figure that can move around the white open area in the middle of the screen. The range of vision for a stick figure is limited to the gray area displayed in Figure 4.2 for Orange. White circles move randomly around the wide Sargasso Sea until a stick figure right clicks on one within its range. Five seconds later the computer determines according to an unannounced probability whether the stick figure is successful in hauling in the circle. Within that five seconds, however, any other stick figure within range

---

[38] Robert Ellickson (1989).

[39] Bart Wilson, Taylor Jaworski, Karl Schurter, and Andrew Smyth (2012). The resources in Peter DeScioli and Bart Wilson (2011) also lie free for any taker, but the participants are unable to discuss the situation. Their avatars can only inflict damage, benignly smile, or extricate themselves from a showdown in which two participants wish to consume the same resource.

or capable of reaching the circle can also "throw a line" and attach itself to the circle. Each whole circle is redeemable for $v = 60$ or 100 cents, depending on treatment. However, if multiple people are probabilistically successful, each successful participant only receives a $1/n^2$ portion of the whole circle. Thus, $(1-1/n)v$ of value is wasted if multiple people lay claim to the same circle that lies free for any taker. After ninety seconds for "gathering"/"catching" circles, the stick figures figuratively return to port for sixty or ninety seconds, depending on treatment, and are free to discuss anything in the experiment within the same guidelines reported previously.

To test Ellickson's proposition that different circumstantial conditions lead to different rules of capture, the stick figures could use two different lines to gather circles, or as it is explained in the instructions:

> On the top right side, you will see the number of lines that you have left. There are two types of lines, *regular* and *colored,* which can be selected by using the appropriate radio button next to them. Both lines work in the same way with one exception. If you hit a circle with a *colored* line, the circle will turn your color whether or not the computer determines you are successful in catching it.

Later, the instructions state:

> You may also purchase additional lines by clicking on the BUY button next to the type of line you would like to purchase. The cost of the lines is taken out of your earnings. You will be given an initial allotment of lines. After that you will be able to purchase *colored* lines for 12¢ [or 20¢ depending on treatment] and *regular* lines for 6¢ [10¢].

With regular lines, the participants can implement the whaling rule, which was called fast-fish-loose-fish. If a ship's harpoon was in the whale and held fast to the boat, no one else would attempt to catch that whale. However, if the harpoon was not attached to the boat, that is, the fish was loose, then the whale was fair game for any other ship to harpoon. Ellickson notes that whalers in the North Atlantic used this rule for preying upon right whales, slow-moving baleen whales that don't dive when harpooned and aren't particularly feisty.

When whaling moved off the coast of the United States, American whalers preyed upon sperm whales, which have teeth, will use them on a boat, and will dive, pulling the boat down with them. With this change in conditions, Ellickson reports that American whalers switched from a fast-fish-loose-fish rule to what was called an iron-holds-the-whale rule. If a ship's harpoon is attached to a whale and identifiably so, then no other ship would attempt to catch the whale. The colored lines allow the participants to identify the first striker. The colored lines are more expensive in the experiment so the participants can reveal their preference for a colored line to a regular line. The participants will only choose to use the more expensive colored line if there is a valuable reason to do so. Otherwise, the cheaper regular line will do just fine. Participants were randomly assigned to one of two treatments. In the first the circles move slowly and are easy to catch on the first strike with $p = 0.75$. In the second, the whales move 50 percent faster and are three times more difficult to catch on the first strike ($q = 0.25$). In a subsequent third treatment, the participants first experienced right-like whales for the first two-thirds of the session and then unannounced the same-looking circle began behaving like a sperm whale.

Beginning with What Is Meant by "What Is Right"

Despite the functional differences in the platforms, common themes run through the discussions of both experiments, and the emergence of property follows the same process in both platforms. The students, all undergraduates, participate in only one session within a platform and only a small number of the 480 participants would have been recruited to participate in both platforms. As the excerpts of the instructions listed previously hint, the instructions are deliberately sparse. We beam the strangers onto an unfamiliar virtual world, like Jean-Luc Picard and the metaphor-phonic Dathon, and ask them to make sense of whatever comes next. The question is whether and how they make it work.[40]

Not surprisingly, at the beginning of the session or when additional stick figures or houses and fields suddenly appear around them, the participants use the chat room to get their bearings. The screen is a picture in the foreground, but what is the sense that lies in the background? What subsidiary perception fits the application of the representation in focus? The chat transcripts provide a glimpse into the sense they are attempting

---

[40] "Darmok and Jalad—at Tanagra."

to make.[41] Here are some examples of the first steps of that process (the dashed lines demarcate distinct sessions):

D: should we be trying to help each other?
D: or is selfishness the way to go?
H: that's a super good plan . . .
H: if everyone just agrees to not steal other peoples then we will get more
A: that is very true
D: I think so too
G: true
D: I'm down
H: so just do that

G: so r we working together or against each other
H: i think we are supposed to work together
G: ok sounds fine

B: its a way to collaborate and help each other or steal from each other

Notice first that while the instructions on actions are amoral, and in the first platform presented in the passive voice, the participants readily imbue the observed actions with morality, calling certain movements of pixelated chits and certain clicks on a circle "stealing." This isn't a rare occurrence. According to the 450-million-word Corpus of Contemporary American English (COCA), the frequency of the word *steal* is 20,296 (#1,798 on the list and right below *politician*).[42] The four experiments discussed in the chapter include a total of 480 participants in sixty sessions who typed 175,143 words (space delimited units of text). The words *steal, stealing, steals, stole*, and *stolen* appear correctly spelled 397 times. That is 50.3 times the frequency in

---

[41] Because the participants are identified as Person *i* in the first platform and by a color name in the second, to standardize the presentation of the conversations, I use letters to denote the different participants within a session. Sometimes the context incidentally reveals which platform the session comes from, and other times not. The latter case is intentional. Each panel is from a distinct session. Several but not all of the conversations are presented in the original papers, which also include many more details on the context of the specific session.

[42] http://www.wordfrequency.info/.

the COCA.[43] *But of course they call this "stealing." They come from a physical universe with formally and informally enforced property.* The question to ask, if you are not peering into the mists of time, is: Why is it that the perceptions of these participants lead them to apply that word with its full moral force to these particular circumstances?

Note also how *B, D,* and *G* parse the context into one of two big bins. Either we help each other, work together, and collaborate *or* we selfishly work against and steal from each other. *D* and *G* are in part seeking clarification on what is right in this virtual world, but why pose the question? They are re-cognizing the background and have a subsidiary interest in the first perceptual bin, which is the first alternative in each of the three cases. Not once is the question in the transcripts posed in the reverse: "Should we be trying to be selfish, or is helping each other the way to go?" *D* and *G* are also raising the question as the foundation for seeking agreement on the former of the two possible answers. The problem then becomes one of integration into a "we":

E: do you want to do this the right way?
F: wht is the right way
E: the right way is I produce red you make blue then we split it nobody gets 100 percent profit but we both win
F: tht wat i been doing then u started stealing

F: [*E*] do u wanna start talkin about maximizing our production or keep fighting over it?

Integrating into a regularized whole involves changing the moral view of those who do not share the same background perception of what is right. Observed contradictions are one hurdle. *F* claims that *E*'s harmonizing plan is inconsistent with *E*'s prior actions. Another hurdle is virtual vertigo. The declaration of "im confused" is not uncommon in this type of experiment following digitization into the e-world. In the homestead platform, the

---

[43] In stark contrast, Joy Buchanan and Bart Wilson (2014) find only one instance of anyone objecting to the "re-selling" of a nonrivalrous good produced by another person, and the words *steal, stealing, steals, stole,* and *stolen* were never once used in 5,183 words of a treatment with no enforcement of property.

transition is achieved by clarifying, as E does, how to specialize and trade.[44] But there is also moral confusion:

D: So it would benefit us all if no one was a thief. [A]!
A: the point . . . is to make a big profit?
D: yes but to make a long term profit teamwork helps a lot

Participants volunteer for these experiments for the opportunity to earn cold hard cash. Profit is the common goal. To achieve that goal as an integrated group, D reasons with A by liberating from moral disregard a principle that A cannot contest. Once the concept of teamwork is shared, the transition to a whole can follow quickly:

F: lets agree to not hit once someone is on it alot of money is lost
D: hahah
A: true
F: my partner and i did and it worked well
E: yup
F: agreed??
A: agreed
F: [D]??
F: [C]??
A: lol
E: haha
A: guess not
C: yea that sounds like a plan

However, with the intransigent, integration is not inevitable:

D: look, if we all stop stealing, we can all help each other maximize
: . . .
A: yea [B] push it
D: but . . . we can help you
B: no
D: what do you need?
D: how many blue for red?
D: we can give you what you need, without you hurting us

---

[44] Sean Crockett, Vernon Smith, and Bart Wilson (2009) observe that roughly half of the pairs never discover exchange (and hence specialization). Groups of four always discover exchange and early on.

C: [B] everyone else hit it were trying to help each other
A: no one can get screwed if we don't steal
C: you aren't making ANY money now
: . . .
D: and we have all been helping each other the whole time
B: Chill out . . it is just a game
: . . .
D: so we are reputalbe
C: uh
C: for MONEYYYYYYYYYYYYYYYYYYYYYYY
C: real money
C: why are you even here
D: we can help you earn more
C: [B] is BALLIN
D: if you let us
D: and then, you would stop hurting us
: . . .
C: we are working together
C: but [B] doesnt want to help
: . . .
C: [B] why would you steal my red fopr someone else[45]
B: just because
: . . .
B: Stop whining
D: gaah! when will it end!
C: your taking MY MONEY
C: real money

This is one of the rare cases of an obdurate "baller" chatting with, or better, antagonizing, everyone else. Individuals who have not attuned themselves to the group are generally quiet to the point of ignoring pleas to engage in conversation. (They also tend to avert their eyes when they are privately paid their earnings at the conclusion of the session.) A, C, and D have integrated into a regularized "we" who are "working together" and "helping each other" (these are common phrases across sessions), but B clearly has not. B is interrupting the dialogue of A, C, and D and challenging the integration of the We, which the We remonstrates as "hurting us."[46]

---

[45] Moving the items to an unsuspecting location is a commonly employed strategy when possession is particularly unstable.
[46] See Erik Kimbrough and Bart Wilson (2013) for an experiment that uses geography as a treatment condition to induce the solidaristic tribal instinct of "us versus them." We subject the world to an unforeseeable productivity shock to ask whether the rules of property can adapt to outsiders.

Until this point, I have described the situation somewhat disinterestedly as one of disagreement in the perceptions of what is right, out of which a rule of property arises. Can either *B*'s propensity to act in a certain manner or the We's disposition not to act manifest itself in a custom? The reflexive answer is, well no, both are not possible if the telos of a rule is to regularize activity and create an order, as the participants are well aware:[47]

G: teamwork evryone wins
H: right right right
: . . .
G: in this exp. the access to other peoples stuff really just causes problems
: . . .
H: lets make some money
G: muah ha ha ha. order fights chaos i love it!!!!
E: hahahaha
G: no taking. ask and you shall recieve
: . . .
G: the only chaos is if the other half doesn't play nicely

E: seriously people your going to mess it up for everyone because this will
      turn into everyone messing eachothers up
E: and noone winning

But why will this mess it up for everyone is a good question, and relevant to answering the bigger question of how moral sentiments undergird the rule of property that emerges.

Resentment Prompts People to Act

Consider baller *B* and the We of *A*, *C*, and *D*. The We perceive certain clicks of *B*'s mouse as stealing that screws them over and hurts them. If they leave the experimental session with zero earnings, they still receive $7 for showing up on time, which is more than they walked into the laboratory with. So what

Adam Smith, David Skarbek, and Bart Wilson (2012) also find that such tribal sentiments feed wasteful investment in capabilities to plunder and to defend against predation.

[47] The Latin word *regula* is the common root for both *rule* and *regular*.

makes *B*'s clicks hurtful to the We? *A*, *C*, and *D* perceive themselves to be falling from a superior to an inferior position. The superior position is that each person is the only person who controls how much red and blue are produced in one specific field. For each person there is also only one house that will convert red and blue items at the end of the period into cash earnings, provided that items have been moved to it. The inferior position obviously is no red and blue items in either a field or house following *B*'s clicks and hence no cash earnings. Adam Smith summarizes the situation to a T when placed in the context of this session:

> To disturb [the We's] happiness merely because it stands in the way of [*B*'s] own, to take from [*A*, *C*, and *D*] what is of real use to [*A*, *C*, and *D*] merely because it may be equal or of more use to [*B*], or to indulge, in this manner, at the expence of other people, the natural preference which every man has for his own happiness above that of other people, is what no impartial spectator can go along with. . . .
>
> Though it may be true, therefore, that every individual, in his own breast, naturally prefers himself to all mankind, yet he dares not look mankind in the face, and avow that he acts according to this principle, and that how natural soever it may be to him, it must always appear excessive and extravagant to them. . . .
>
> [*B*] is to them, in every respect, as good as [*A*, *C*, and *D*]: they do not enter into that self-love by which [*B*] prefers himself so much to [the We], and cannot go along with the motive from which he hurt[s] [*A*, *C*, and *D*].[48]

Part of the background of what is right, as Smith details, is that "there can be no proper motive for hurting our neighbour," an emergent principle alive and well in the experiments.[49] Notice that part of the *ius* is that every person in every respect is as good as another in the experiment. The closer we look, the more rules we see come out of the background to support the ones we are focally attending to.

B's clicking on the red and blue items in the fields and houses not under his control is an act contrary to the *ius*, an *iniuria*, not just in the secondary sense of harm in the modern use of the word *injury*, but also in the primary moral sense of an act contrary to what is right. With the hope of bringing him into the group, the We are calling out *B* as callous and morally perverse so

---

[48] Adam Smith (1759, pp. 82–83).
[49] Ibid. (p. 82).

that a rule of property may emerge. In the homestead platform, the form of the rule seems rather straightforward. In one lone case, someone spells it out precisely as a rule:

E: but let's start with the rule of: don't take stuff from other people's houses
   or fields

While this rule may appear obvious, it is not the only possible rule of property for the homestead platform. When followed in real time and under fluctuating circumstances, a different rule may arise out of a minor change in the background. Recall that the design in Erik Kimbrough's follow-up study differs slightly from the others in that all eight participants are together from the beginning of the session. Because the harmony of possession is more difficult to achieve from the outset in octets than in duets, every single one of his sessions discusses a different rule never proposed elsewhere in the homestead platform:

E: the fields are fairgame, lets decide on that from now on, nobody takes
   ANYTHING from a house, if you have stuff to share you can put it in
   your field

For the last ten periods, Kimbrough's virtual world is literally identical to our original experiment, with participants drawn from the same population, and yet his participants always propose a slightly different rule. While part of property is in our bodies, in our genes, namely that people universally resent injury, the other part of property—the solution to the problem of injuries—is external to our bodies. The rules of property reside in our environment, in our sociality, and hence can vary from group to group, place to place, thing to thing, time to time.

   The same process is at work in the open sea platform. When a stick figure is the first to click on a freely roaming white circle, the first striker suffers harm (probabilistically) when anyone else subsequently clicks on the same circle. As "things," these pixels on a computer screen are within the virtual grasp of the whalers and homesteaders before a baller *B* snatches them away. This perception of harm is the common thread across these two different platforms and why double clicking a circle is considered just as much to be stealing as moving red and blue items out of a creator-endowed field or house. In both platforms, the different participants perceive the actions of the baller *B* types as one of the same bad kind. Just as the We resent *B*, so integrated groups of stick figures in the open sea platform also resent the *iniuria* of double clicking on circles, which can prompt them to retaliate:

B: [D] you took mine! haha
F: what ever happen to our deal??
D: hhahah im the best
D: im the master
C: i know right
A: [D] u suck\
D: i leraned the best from [C]
F: ok everybody only steal from [D]
C: LOL
A: k
B: haha
D: hahah hey no fair
E: deal
F: deal
C: deal
E: haha
F: blue??
F: dude come on
A: sorry . .
E: hahahaha
F: or dudet u in??
F: steal from [D] no one else
F: ??
A: i will
E: me 2
F: sweet

Regardless of the form of the rule that arises out of the background to fit the local circumstances, there is a compelling emotion, which Adam Smith astutely identifies, that buttresses the sentiments regarding a rule of property as moral: "Resentment seems to have been given us by nature for defence, and for defence only. . . . It prompts us to beat off mischief which is attempted to be done to us, and to retaliate that which is already done."[50] No one learns from their mentors how to feel resentment when someone harms them. By nature we feel bad when someone injures us, and we want to think bad things about the person who made us feel that way.[51] What we discovered is that Adam Smith's model of thinking about hurt and resentment is at the core of what the participants express in solving the problem of property—what is mine. Do people mix their labor with things? Yes, but so what? Who cares? Property is defined negatively by what people will *not* tolerate: injury.

In a two-page-long footnote, Smith anticipates and refutes a reluctance to accept resentment as part of a sense of moral demerit:

> Resentment is commonly regarded as so odious a passion, that they will be apt to think it is impossible that so laudable a principle, as the sense of the ill desert of vice, should in any respect be founded upon it. They will be more willing, perhaps, to admit that our sense of the merit of good actions is founded upon a sympathy with the gratitude of the persons who receive the benefit of them; because gratitude . . . is regarded as an amiable principle, which can take nothing from the worth of whatever is founded upon it. Gratitude and resentment, however, are in every respect, it is evident, counterparts to one another; and if our sense of merit arises from a sympathy with the one, our sense of demerit can scarce miss to proceed from a fellow-feeling with the other.[52]

Within the integrated community, everyone empathizes with everyone else in their resentment of the harm inflicted by people like *D*, the self-proclaimed master. Such empathy is a necessary component for supporting a rule of property, and what makes such empathy palpable is that the individuals have harmonized into a "we." Resentment is the sentiment, the predisposition, that makes the rule of property a moral goal.[53] The rule of property

---

[50] Ibid. (p. 79).

[51] Vernon Smith and Bart Wilson (2019, p. 29).

[52] Adam Smith (1759, p. 76).

Samuel Johnson's dictionary (http://johnsonsdictionaryonline.com/) from 1755 defines *sympathy* as fellow-feeling; mutual sensibility; and the quality of being affected by the affection of another. Our word *empathy*, which wasn't available to Smith, fits better than *sympathy* for the modern reader not familiar with eighteenth-century diction.

[53] Stephen Pack and Eric Schliesser (2006) argue that Smith out-Humes Hume by showing that resentment is not just relevant for the origins of justice, but the sentiment that gives lift to justice in the first place. Resentment and property are so intertwined that Lionel Shriver's brilliant 2018 collection of stories could have easily been entitled *Resentment: Stories between Two Novellas*.

is moral, not merely because the community is in fact committed to the rule, *but because the community feels compelled through (morally justified) resentment to commit to the rule.* When *E* says that "seriously people your going to mess it up for everyone because this will turn into everyone messing eachothers up," *E* is concerned that the commitment to the rule might erode. That it often doesn't in the presence of an incorrigible is a testament to the work that morality does. *F*'s plan to "steal" only from the master of mischief *D* and no one else actually worked. Why? Because everyone else held to their moral convictions. Resentment of harm, the mutual empathy of desiring to avoid harm, and the compelling moral commitment to a rule to avoid harm are what give meaning to property as a practice.

Property Emerges to Protect Us from Real and Positive Hurt

As the natural law theorist Samuel von Pufendorf noted so eloquently, humankind is capable of "kindness by the furtherance of mutual good," but humans are also "often malicious, insolent, and easily provoked, and as powerful in effecting mischief, as [they are] ready in designing it."[54] It's not hard to find evidence to confirm the latter with participants' comments in these experiments:

- you're all a bunch of crooks
- o! damn the heathen
- we[']re turning into vultures
- It's a madhouse! A madhouse!
- this is madness
- I'm gonna have nightmares about this tonight
- This is like lord of the flies, they leave us to fend for ourselves, lol

Every virtual economy opens with vicious chaos, and roughly only one out of every six groups ever overcomes the havoc by the time the experiment ends. Those few who do appeal first to one another's own interests and their repeated experiences with the mutual harm of war. Once the injustice of real and positive hurt becomes common to everyone, that is, once the practice

---

[54] Samuel Pufendorf (1672, p. 136).

of justice becomes a common virtue, they then establish regular and orderly conduct by instituting specific rules for the stability of possession. These experiments demonstrate what Pufendorf expounded upon nearly 450 years ago: "we may hence too discover the falsity of that vulgar saying, Mine and Thine are the cause of all the wars and quarrels in the world. For on the contrary the distinction of Mine and Thine was rather introduced to prevent all contention."[55] Property is the moral scheduling pattern that emerges to eliminate injustice, real and positive hurt.

As a system of rules, property is more than a first-person moral claim, "This is mine." The custom includes second-person conditions that other people recognize the harm and participate in my resentment when someone acts on "I want this" when by custom they cannot say, "This is mine." Property includes reciprocal humane claims of "That is yours." A distinguishing feature of such a step toward a theory of the emergence of property is its negative character. Nominalizing the problem of property as a right to do X with Y diverts our attention from the rule-guided actions and perceptions of people involving things. As Ludwig Wittgenstein recognized, "a substantive makes us look for a thing that corresponds to it."[56] Rather than focusing on what people do, say, know, think, and feel for property to emerge as a custom, we look for the distinguishing features that define a macro-level noun, but a right does not have well-defined boundaries like a chair does. So to aid us with the conceptualization, British lawyers in the late nineteenth century began employing a metaphor, property as a bundle of rights, which still persists, though not without its vocal critics.[57] Treating rights bundle-able like sticks only more deeply reinforces the notion that rights are things, but because rights aren't things, equally amorphous substantives, such as duties, privileges, powers, and immunities, are called upon to explicate the intricacies of property.[58] With such a focus on things, the purpose of property becomes the use of the things.[59]

As difficult as it may be to read without falling out of your chair, the purpose of property, the custom, does not lie in thoughts of "I want this" or the use of things. The end of a rule of property is to secure from *iniuria*. That

---

[55] Ibid. (p. 368).

[56] Ludwig Wittgenstein (1958, p. 1).

[57] Stuart Banner (2011) traces its first uses to George Sweet in 1873, with respect to proprietorship, and to Robert Campbell in 1881, with respect to property. See Symposium (2011) for a debate on the merits of the metaphor.

[58] See Wesley Hohfeld (1919).

[59] J. E. Penner (1997).

is the sense in which property is negative. The use of things is the ultimate purpose of having things and satisfies thoughts of wanting things, but a rule of property such that someone can say, "This thing is mine," does not arise from the use of things.[60] If things were not scarce and people not mischievous, selfish, and limited in generosity, we would not need a rule of property regarding things.[61] Rather, a rule of property arises out of our background knowledge of what is right, which includes protecting us from real and positive hurt. A rule of property "acquires force by a slow progression, and by our repeated experience of the inconveniences of transgressing it."[62] We have rules of property, not because we have an ultimate interest in using things within our grasp, but because, proximately, someone with an equal or stronger hand may challenge our grasp. And we will not tolerate such injury to ourselves or to others.

---

[60] Henry Smith (2012, p. 1704) similarly concludes that "rights to exclude are a means to an end, and the ends in property relate to people's interest in using things." Eric Claeys (2012, p. 143, original italics) credits Henry Smith for that conclusion but critiques his theory for failing to explain "*how, why,* or *to what extent* exclusion and governance each institute or embody the moral norms internal to property in practice." This chapter takes the step of incorporating the morality of harm into the emergence of property regarding things.

[61] David Hume (1740).

[62] Ibid. (p. 315).

5

The Custom of Property Is
Physically Contained

The modern bourgeois world has largely forgotten that property confers peace to its conspecifics. As Samuel von Pufendorf clearly understood, such a peace evolves differently depending on "the temper or condition of men, the nature of the things themselves, and the difference of place required; and as was judged most convenient for the cutting off all manner of quarrel or dissension."[1] Having made the case that property and the concept of mine is a human universal, in this chapter I trace with broad strokes one such trajectory of the custom, the Anglophonic, by its linguistic remains, not as a moral exemplar, but as an informative example.

Etymology Evidences Both Custom and Containment

Few documents on private law remain to record the custom of property prior to the Roman Empire. The Code of Hammurabi merely registers the fine for robbery in general (death) and for theft of temple items in particular (also death), so we know precious little about how the custom worked in practice except that we have taken it seriously for at least 4,000 years. A small piece of etymological evidence remains in the Latin word *mancipium*, which came into use sometime after the founding of Rome but before the Republic. This word is derived from *manceps*, which can be glossed as "hand (*manus*) + taker (*-ceps*)."[2] As the nineteenth-century French jurist Joseph Ortolan explains it, the distance was not that great from the Pleistocene plain to Rome in the seventh to fifth centuries BCE:

---

[1] Samuel von Pufendorf (1672/2005, IV.IV.XIII).
[2] The Latin word for "to belong (to)," *pertinere*, also originally connoted a sense of grasping, meaning literally, "to hold (*tenere*) through/constantly (*per*)." The connotation of constancy seems to imply that one must persevere to maintain that which belongs to one's self.

The Property Species. Bart J. Wilson. Oxford University Press (2020) © Oxford University Press.
DOI: 10.1093/oso/9780190936785.001.0001

The hand (*manus*) was the symbol of power in the widest sense. Chattels, slaves, children, wife, and freedmen, all were subject to the chief—*in manu*—an expression which, at a later period, lost its wide and acquired a more special signification. But the means by which the warrior acquired power and was enabled to get his property within his grasp (*manu capere*), was by the lance, the wielders or possessors of which were the Quirites—a symbol that long remained in use after the actual prototype had disappeared. . . . That which we now call property bore a name very expressive of the then state of civilization—*mancipium*.[3]

There are, however, subtle differences to note. First, the singular for Quirites, the name for an ancient Roman citizen, is *quiris*, or spear.[4] Sometime in the last 70,000 years the meaning of *spear* began to point to more than the purpose of the tool; it began to point to a social class of people who wielded them. We also extended the use of the abstract notion of "this is mine." An ancient Roman citizen could say, "*Hoc est meum*," about the spear in hand *and* the multitude of things that he acquired from using the spear. Symbolic thoughts were further recombining with the customary scheduling pattern for acquiring things.

By the classical period, we have records on vestigial private acts for transferring corporeal things. Two of these procedures explicitly incorporated physicalness and orality, as hypothesized in chapter 3, into the conveyance. The first, *mancipatio* (from *mancipium*), took the form of a fictitious sale, and the second, *in iure cessio* (surrendering in court), the form of a fictitious lawsuit.[5] In both choreographed acts, the transferee would grasp the thing, say, a slave, and pronounce a precise statement in the presence of the transferor, who would remain silent. The specific formula for the *in iure cessio* was: *Hunc ego hominem ex iure Quiritium meum esse aio*, or literally, "I assert (or <u>say</u>) from the law of the Quirites this man to be mine." The transferee didn't simply stand in the vicinity of the thing being transferred even though everyone present would know why they were there, nor did the presiding praetor or provincial governor say the magic words. No, the Romans, notorious sticklers for procedures, were precisely and symbolically marking—with physical contact

<hr />

[3] Joseph Ortolan (1896, p. 64).

[4] In one of Plutarch's answers in *Questiones Romanae* (no. 87), he says that "for a spear is decreed sacred to Juno, and most of her statues are supported by a spear, and she is surnamed Quiritis, and a spear of old was called *quiris,* wherefore they surname Mars Quirinus?" See Plutarch (1874).

[5] Fritz Schulz (1951).

and oral work—a cognitive transfer. One person's abstract notion of MINE in a thing was disappearing and being replaced by another person's notion of MINE in the same thing. With practice, a marvel of the animal kingdom becomes a custom.

These two procedures indicate that there is much more at work in the custom than transferring the grounds for someone to say, "This is mine." The *in iure cessio* was a formal proceeding before a magistrate, and the *mancipatio*, while private, required the presence of six Roman citizens.[6] Such public display is a key component of the custom, for when the transferee asserts his first-person claim in the future, other people will know what he says to be true. The basis of a custom is more than a subjective claim. It is simultaneously objective in the sense that the resulting order constitutes a set of expectations for the transferee grounded in what other members of the community know, namely that they know that it is true that the transferee can say, "This is mine." The visibility of the custom also implicitly contrasts its meaning, for the transferee and everyone else, for other people cannot say, "This thing is mine." They must say, "That thing is yours." If these features feel familiar and belabored, they are, because for the past 500 years Anglophones have had a pithy little verb, which the Romans did not, to succinctly summarize the situation:[7] The transferee now *owns* the thing.[8]

As the scheduling pattern of the Romans changed with the overthrow of the monarchy c. 509 BCE, a new word supplanted *mancipium*. Roman society, ordered around the family/household (*domus*), recognized the oldest male citizen (*dominus*) as the head of the house. Within the *domus*, other members could use things in the household, but the expectations were that only the *dominus* could decide to transfer household things to and from

---

[6] Barry Nicholas (1962).

[7] Cliff Goddard and Anna Wierzbicka (2016) define the verb *own* with only semantic primitives. Since every language contains these primitives, any human being could comprehend this deconstructed concept in the semantic primes of their own language even if they do not have a corresponding verb for *own* in their own language. Whether every human society would use the concept in the same way is an entirely different question, the likely answer to which is no, except for some tools, utensils, or ornaments.

[8] Herein lies a difficulty with applying human concepts of property and ownership to nonhumans like baboons and long-tailed macaques. Nonhuman primates are incapable of thinking with such concepts as SAY, TRUE, MINE, and KNOW, which are integral to the meaning of *own* and *ownership* for humans. Property in humans is more than the physical acts in the present that demonstrate the recognition of another conspecific's mate and a refrain from treating it as part of its harem. Recognizing this awkwardness, Hans Kummer, W. Götz, and W. Angst (1974) put the word *owned* in quotation marks the first time they apply it to baboons. More recent articles are less sensitive to the differences between human and nonhuman primate concepts regarding things. See, for example, Hans Sigg and Jost Falett (1985) and Hans Kummer and Marina Cords (1991).

other families. What was right was that he alone generally held the *patria potestas* (power of a father) to alienate things and to exclude others from using them. This abstract concept came to be called *dominium*.[9] Unlike *mancipium, dominium* never referred to a thing; a thing itself was *materia*.[10] The concept evolved from a thing taken and within one's grasp to an abstract notion representative of people of a particular stature. Like "ownership," *dominium* connotes a *-ship*-ness, the abstract condition or status of being the *dominus*, that is, what is solely and despotically right for the *dominus* to do. (Despotic is not a stretch. Capital punishment was not beyond the power of the *dominus*.) In Old English/Middle Age terms *dominium* is lordship.

By the time of the early emperors, expectations had evolved further so that other members of the household, for example, non-firstborn sons in the imperial army, could act like *domini* with regard to the booty they acquired in war.[11] Eventually a second term came into use consistent with the new expectations that some things were exclusively, particularly, peculiarly, and properly distinct from the reach of *dominium*. The ancient adverb ripe for nominalizing this distinct abstract concept was *proprie,* from which came the noun *proprietas*. Notice, then, that *dominium* and *proprietas* were originally not perfect synonyms even though both have been translated simply as "ownership." Both are about what is right for someone to do with things when by custom he can say, "*Hoc est meum*." The word *dominium*, however, draws upon grander, absolutist connotations from rule and dominion that *proprietas* does not. The idea of property is further undergoing a shift from a narrow class of privileged individuals to the broader notion of general propriety. This evolutionary etymology illustrates the important sense that property is a custom. More is involved than the mere thing about which by custom someone can say, "This is mine." An individual's actions regarding such things must fit with the larger scheduling pattern of society. What is right is not derived from the rule, but let the rule arise from our knowledge of what is right.

After 1,200-some years, the distinction between *dominium* and *proprietas* begins to blur. The Spiritual Franciscans, extreme proponents of poverty, argued that Christ and the Apostles had renounced *dominium* over all things, even the food they ate.[12] In their withering attacks on this position, the secular

---

[9] Charton Lewis and Charles Short (1879).
[10] Henry Dunning Macleod (1881).
[11] Ibid.
[12] Jonathan Robinson (2013).

theologians William of Saint-Amour and Gerard of Abbeville seem to treat *dominium* and *proprietas* as synonyms for ownership.[13] For Bonaventure, a defender of the Franciscans, *proprietas* is a special case of *dominium* and most aptly translated as "ownership."[14] His defense of the Franciscans, by the way, rests on distinguishing *dominium* from the simple use (*simplex usus*) of things like clothes, shoes, food, books, and other utensils. Bonagratia of Bergamo, however, a well-trained lawyer who defended the Spiritual Franciscans at the papal curia, maintains the distinction between *dominium* as lordship and *proprietas* as ownership, a distinction that had remained in civil law.[15]

A Linguistic Convention Emerges with the Tiny Word "In"

In this debate I find the earliest use of a noun phrase that would later become a broad linguistic convention in English jurisprudence. As part of his argument, Henry of Ghent, another scholastic critic of the mendicants, describes a usufructor this way: *Non habet dominium aut proprietatem in re.*[16] To translate the Latin into modern English, the theologian Virpi Mäkinen renders the sentence as "He does not have ownership (*dominium* or *proprietas*) of the thing."[17] A literal translation would be "He does not have *dominium* or *proprietas* in the thing." Note the original preposition *in*. For Mäkinen and the modern ear for whom she is translating, *ownership of the thing* has the right ring for *proprietatem in re*. For our purposes, though, the literal prepositional phrase *in the thing* is revealing because *in* can take two cases in Latin, and Henry of Ghent chose the ablative case, not the accusative. One of the uses of the ablative case in Latin is for location. When a preposition like *in* takes both the ablative and accusative case in Latin, the ablative indicates no motion, and the accusative motion toward something. With the ablative case, something is not moving with respect to the prepositional complement *re*, the thing.[18] Henry says that the bearer of a usufruct does not have *proprietas* in the thing. Such a construction reflects and reveals how the mind is cognizing the custom as an abstract concept. By the Middle Ages,

---

[13] Virpi Mäkinen (2001).
[14] Ibid. The other special cases of *dominium* that Bonaventure notes are possession and usufruct.
[15] Virpi Mäkinen (2001).
[16] Quoted in Ibid. (p. 108, fn. 13).
[17] Ibid. (p. 108).
[18] Henry of Ghent also didn't choose the genitive case for *of* without a preposition.

we are no longer simply putting ourselves inside things when we assimilate them as a part of our body; we are putting abstract concepts of *dominium* and *proprietas* inside things, and because they are contained as such, they are not moving with respect to the thing.[19]

Godfrey of Fontaines, another critic of the Franciscans, similarly uses the *in*-with-ablative construction when he argues that the pope as the vicar of Christ "does not have right (*ius*) and *dominium* in them [ecclesiastical goods]."[20] The pairing of *ius* with *dominium* is interesting for it substantiates Mäkinen's thesis that a new language of rights came out of the Franciscan poverty debates, which, she argues, eventually led to the idea and expectations of individual natural rights. For us, Henry and Godfrey are examples of people putting more than themselves inside things; they were cognizing the custom as part of the very thing itself. The *Institutes of Gaius* and the *Corpus Iuris Civilis* contain a few uses of *habet proprietatem,* but never *habet proprietatem in* with the ablative (or the accusative, for that matter). Ideas are continuing to mate in marvelous ways.

Proprietas makes its way to English through the Old French word *propriété* and then by the Anglo-Norman word *propreté.*[21] In the *Confessio Amantis,* the Middle English poet John Gower provides us with the oldest instance in English that I have found—c. 1393—of an *in* prepositional phrase modifying *propreté* or *property*:

> Bot yit it is a wonder thing,
> Whan that a riche worthi king,
> Or other lord, what so he be,
> Wol axe and cleyme propreté
> In thing to which he hath no riht,
> Bot onliche of his grete miht.
> For this mai every man wel wite,
> That bothe kinde and lawe write
> Expressly stonden theragein.[22]

---

[19] David Seipp (1994) reports that English lawyers in the Year Books from 1290 to 1490 would regularly say, "I have property in *X*" in Latin or "The property of *X* is to me" in Law French.

[20] Quoted in Virpi Mäkinen (2001, p. 134, fn. 98).

[21] Sherman Kuhn and Hans Kurath (1952, pp. 1405–1406).

[22] John Gower (c.1393, book 3, l. 2323–2331). Note also that Gower uses *propreté* as part of an explicit claim. Here is my novice literal translation with some much-needed help from Sarah Skwire:

> But yet it is a wonder thing,
> When that a rich and worthy king,

Other contemporaries of Gower, like the theologian and biblical translator John Wycliffe, use the preposition *of*: "for they wil haue propretie of Ghostly goods where noe propertie may be, and leauen propretie of worldlie goods where christian men maie haue propretie."[23] One difference between the two is that Gower may have been a lawyer and thus familiar with the Law French term *propreté* and its usage. If Gower wasn't a lawyer, there is evidence that he was a litigant and that he regularly used technical legal terms in his work.[24] Gower's use of "property in thing" is interesting because a century and a half earlier the English judge Henry of Bracton never once uses *proprietatem in* in his celebrated legal treatise, *On the Laws and Customs of England*.[25] While *habet* (or *habuit*) *proprietatem* appear in a few places, Bracton never employs the *in* prepositional phrase of his contemporary Henry of Ghent. Gower is perhaps supplying for us the earliest trace in English for how we think about the conception of property.

In the early 1500s another power dispute erupted with the papacy. As part of his engagement with the church, a young professor of theology, Jacques Almain, revisited the thirteenth-century arguments of another Spiritual Franciscan, William of Ockham.[26] Whereas the first uses of "have *proprietas* in the thing" are stated in the negative (a pope or usufructor does not have *dominium* or *proprietas* in the thing), Almain provides the earliest instances in Latin (that I have found) for a statement in the affirmative, that the Pope "*habet proprietatem in aliquibus rebus* [these things]," which he further elaborates upon to mean "*in talibus habet proprietatem proprie propriam.*"[27] By the third successive *propri-* I think the point is firmly made: the pope has *proprietas* in such things properly his own (i.e., those things properly his own before he became pope, like his favorite pair of shoes). All told Almain uses the construction *habet proprietatem in* seven times in the page-long

Or other lord, what so he be,
Would ask and claim property
In thing to which he hath no right,
But only of his great might.
For this may every man well know,
That both natural and written law
Expressly stand there against.

[23] John Wycliffe (d. 1384, p. 33).
[24] Conrad van Dijk (2013).
[25] See Bracton Online, available at http://bracton.law.harvard.edu/. Last accessed April 2, 2016.
[26] This is the same prominent Spiritual Franciscan more famously known for the razor principle that bears his name.
[27] Jacques Almain (1706, p. 1079).

second chapter, including the chapter title. He also uses the phrase frequently throughout the rest of the piece and in his other works. Almain's teacher, the Scot John Mair, likewise uses the phrase, but just once in his 1518 commentary on the power of the pope.[28] In every instance, the preposition takes the ablative case.

Until the early part of the sixteenth century, English lawyers use three words interchangeably in ownership disputes involving chattels: *proprietas, propreté,* and *property.*[29] By the end of the sixteenth century, the usage of *have property in Y* is firmly established in English jurisprudence. Sir Edward Coke's report on *The Case of the Swans* (1592) is a landmark decision and nicely illustrates the usage.[30] As solicitor general, Coke represented Queen Elizabeth against Lady Joan Young and Thomas Saunger. At issue was whether the Keeper of the Queen's Swans could seize 400 unmarked swans in a public river from where the swans would travel to the plaintiffs' adjoined, privately owned estuaries. Coke's report includes eight instances of the phrase *have property in*, three of which are in the negative:

- That the subject might have property in white swans not marked, as some may have swans not marked in his private waters, the property of which belongs to him, and not to the King.
- That everyone who hath swans within his manor, that is to say, within his private waters, hath a property in them, for the writ of trespass was of wrongful taking his swans.
- A man hath not absolute property in any thing which is *ferae naturae,* but in those which are *domitae naturae.*
- But in those which are *ferae naturae,* and by industry are made tame, a man hath but a qualified property in them, *scil.* so long as they remain tame, for if they do attain to their natural liberty, and have not *animum revertendi,* the property is lost, *ratione impotentiae et loci:* As if a man has young shovelers or goshawks, or the like, which are *ferae naturae,* and they build in my land, I have possessory property in them, for if one takes them when they cannot fly, the owner of the soil shall have an action of trespass.

---

[28] John Mair (1706, p. 1151).
[29] G. E. Aylmer (1980).
[30] Sir Edward Coke (1600, Trinity Term, 34 Elizabeth I).

- But when a man hath savage beasts *ratione privilegii,* as by reason of a park, warren, &c. he hath not any property in the deer, or conies, or pheasants, or partridges, and therefore in an action.
- He shall not say *(suos)* for he hath no property in them, but they do belong to him *ratione privil'* for his game and pleasure, so long as they remain in the privileged place.
- But a man may have property in some things which are of so base nature, that no felony can be committed of them; and no man shall lose life or member for them, as of a blood-hound or mastiff, *molessus.*[31]

These excerpts summarize several of the important findings of the case, for which judgment was given in favor of the Crown. When a swan is marked on the beak or foot, the person who marked the swan has property in that swan, even if it strays into someone else's waters. If an unmarked swan flies into private waters, the owner of the water has property in the swan while the swan is in her waters. But the moment an unmarked swan leaves private waters for a public waterway, the property in the swan vanishes and the Crown now has property in the swan. Depending simply on where a swan swims, one person's abstract notion of MINE in a swan can disappear and be replaced by the queen's. And the marvel is that if that same swan were to swim back into private waters the next minute, the queen's notion of MINE would disappear in the swan and someone else's would instantaneously replace it. Physical touch and uttered words are no longer necessary. The mind is doing all the work.

The custom is different, however, for animals that are tame by nature. A person has property in a cow when the cow is on private land, when it strays onto someone else's private land, and when it wanders onto public land. No matter where the cow may saunter, as cows are wont to do from time to time, the property in the cow never changes. That is the sense in which Coke says the property in the thing is absolute; the property in a naturally tame animal is independent of time and place. Property in a naturally wild animal is not absolute; it's relative, dependent upon the circumstances of time and place. The scheduling patterns of animals are interconnected. The human scheduling pattern regarding animals in the external world depends on the generally different scheduling patterns of wild and domesticated animals.

---

[31] Sir Edward Coke (1600).

The Semantics of "In a Thing" Physically Contain Property

The preposition *in* isn't the only one Coke uses in his report on *The Case of the Swans*. On two occasions he also modifies *property* with an *of* prepositional phrase:

- For one white swan, without such pursuit as aforesaid, cannot be known from another, and when the property of a swan cannot be known, the same being of its nature a fowl royal, doth belong to the King.
- That if any swan cometh on the land of any man, and there builds, and hath cignets on the same land, that then he who hath the property of the swan shall have 2 of the cignets, and he who hath the land shall have the third cignet, which shall be of less value than the other 2.[32]

In the first instance, the phrasing is not about having a property, but in the second instance it is precisely about having the property. So why choose *of* here but *in* for the other eight cases? For the eight uses of *have property in*, the context of the sentence involves questions of who has, and under what circumstances does someone have, property in a swan. Those eight instances explicate the specifics of the custom by which someone can say, "This swan is mine." In the sole case of having the property *of* the swan, there is no question about who has property in the swan. It is assumed that someone does and that a swan has wandered onto someone's private lands to build a nest and raise some cygnets. The question is about the cygnets, not the swan itself.

In both instances a little two-letter word does the heavy work of orientating the noun being modified, *the property*, to the prepositional complement, *the swan*. The preposition *of* connotes an intrinsic, part-whole relationship between the property and the swan.[33] As another example, consider *the front of the swan*. The swan is a whole, and an intrinsic feature of a whole swan is that it has a front, a back, and two sides. The swan also has feathers, a beak, and two webbed feet, but what is contextually important in referencing *the front of the swan* is the part of it that is the front. By choosing *of* to say he who has the property of the swan, Coke is highlighting to the reader that it is an

---

[32] Ibid.
[33] Andrea Tyler and Vyvyan Evans (2003).

intrinsic feature of the very swan itself, that someone has the property in it when it builds the nest on private land.[34]

The linguists Andrea Tyler and Vyvyan Evans develop a cognitive model of English prepositions that is composed of two entities, a spatial relationship between the two entities and a functional element that reflects the interactive relationship between the two entities.[35] The model explains how a change in a preposition subtly changes the meaning of a sentence. Different contexts call for choosing one preposition over another. Consider Tyler and Evan's example of *He ran to the hills* versus *He ran for the hills*. In both cases the person has a goal of reaching the hills, and the relationship between the person and the hills is that the person is in motion toward the hills. But the functional element concerning the interactive relationship is quite different in the two sentences. The preposition *to* places emphasis on the prepositional complement as the primary goal. If the context is that a city jogger wants to exercise somewhere peaceful and free of smog, then *to* would fit the bill as it highlights the goal of getting to the hills and subordinates the current location in the city. But if getting to the hills is secondary or oblique to the context of, say, getting the hell out of Dodge because there are guns ablaze in the streets, then a bank robber would run *for* the hills. The preposition *for* puts the hills in the background and emphasizes the intentions behind the running.[36]

Now let's consider our preposition of interest. As far as English prepositions go, the polysemy (multiple meanings) of *in* is rather extensive and complex. Tyler and Evans identify twenty-seven distinct senses of *in* and organize them into six different clusters. The canonical sense of *in* involves one thing spatially located within a second three-dimensional entity that has

---

[34] Coke's rival, Francis Bacon, similarly uses both prepositions. He writes both that there are "several ways whereby a man may get property in goods or chattels" and that one may "dispose the property of their goods and chattels" (1838, pp. vii, 586). These two uses are consistent with two different contexts in which Coke uses *property in Y* and *property of Y*.

[35] Andrea Tyler and Vyvyan Evans (2003).

[36] Recall the two meanings of *hunt* in chapter 2, note 46. As a transitive verb, *hunt* emphasizes the direct object and the action it receives. The mammoth is why men go a-hunting. Append *for* to *hunt*, as in hunting for Easter eggs, and the emphasis of the sentence shifts to the diligence and energetic search of kids dressed in their Easter Sunday best. When we use *hunt for*, there is no direct object to receive the verb's action; Easter eggs, truffles, and treasure are prepositional complements. We could say, "The kids gather Easter eggs," but only if the parents were more interested in the cheap plastic eggs than the activity of their adorable kids. *But I can say both "I am hunting for rabbits" and "I am hunting rabbits."* I do not claim that one use precludes the other. I claim that the two sentences convey slightly different meanings. When Elmer Fudd whispers to the audience, "Be vewy vewy quiet. I'm hunting wabbits!," the focus of the sentence, and episode, is on the direct object, Bugs Bunny, as Elmer Fudd's punchy accent on *wabbits* further testifies. Saying "I'm hunting for wabbits!" simultaneously emphasizes Elmer Fudd and his intentions and de-emphasizes Bugs Bunny.

a boundary, an interior, and an exterior—for example, *the tea in the cup*. The interactive relationship between the two entities is that the cup contains the tea. Move the cup and the tea moves with it. The tea is not in motion and will not move by itself because the tea is in the cup.

Every one of the twenty-seven senses of *in* that Tyler and Evans identify, even the noncanonical ones, involves a bounded entity and the functional relationship of containment, whether, for example, *The cow is in the pasture* or *The cow is in heat*. Even though the cow is not literally located within a three-dimensional entity but instead standing on a planar pasture, our minds flexibly conceptualize the spatial and functional relationships of *in* as applying to the cow and the pasture. Because the pasture is bounded and because the cow is located within the interior of the pasture, we say, "The cow is in the pasture" like we say, "The tea is in the cup." Our minds likewise process the cow and its estrous cycle as fitting the requisite spatial and functional components of *in*. I learned on the farm that the estrous cycle of a cow lasts about fifteen hours and recurs every twenty-one days or so. Because the biological process is temporally bounded, and because the cow cannot free itself from an estrous state, we say, "The cow is in heat" like we say, "The tea is in the cup."

British Anglophones, however, would not say, "The cow is in heat." They say, "The cow is on heat." As Tyler and Evans explain, the choice of the preposition can be conventional when there are multiple functional elements of the situation on which to coordinate.[37] The preposition *on* connotes a functional element of a relatively short state, as in "The family is on vacation" or "Aaron Rodgers is on fire." Family vacations end, and Aaron Rodgers, unfortunately, isn't always on fire. So both *on* and *in* fit the case of a cow's estrous cycle. The semantics of *in* and *on* reflect and reveal the supra-conscious principles by which our minds cognize the external world.

What, then, does *in* reveal about the relationship between property and the thing when someone has property in the thing? The abstract notion of property is located within a three-dimensional thing, say, a spear, which has a boundary, an interior, and an exterior. The interactive relationship between property and the spear is that the spear contains the property. Just like where the cup moves so moves the tea, so where the spear moves so moves the property. The property does not move by itself when the property is in the spear. The same is true of domesticated animals, which, unlike spears, have

---

[37] Andrew Tyler and Vyvyan Evans (2003, p. 188).

a tendency to wander about on their own accord. The cow contains the property no matter where it strays. Property is but another characteristic of the very thing itself. The custom is contained in the thing.

The case of property in swans marks an interesting and illuminating example. The same property that is in a cow can be located in a horse and a sheep and a goose, but it cannot be located in a swan or a deer or a fox. Our powers of conceptualization are flexible such that different kinds of custom can be located in different kinds of things. That is the ancient difference between *domitae naturae* and *ferae naturae*. Presumably we could try to put the same property that is in a cow into a swan, but the property in a cow is likely to conflict with the scheduling pattern of swans more generally, which is to say that the property in a cow is likely to conflict with how we think about swans, which is further to say that the property in a cow is likely to conflict with the scheduling pattern of humans regarding swans. The rules for when someone can say, "This animal is mine" differ based on the type of animal in question. Our minds perceive an animal through the customary ways of perceiving an animal to be wild or domesticated. WILD and DOMESTICATED are concepts outside the here and now, and an essential component of how we regularly think about animals. The customary rules by which someone can say, "This animal is mine" are another way we regularly think about animals, and the two customary ways of thinking about animals are mutually dependent.

Eventually the Use of "Property in a Thing" Wanes

The phrase "have property in" is commonplace in seventeenth- and eighteenth-century writing, most frequently in legal contexts.[38] Locke uses it twelve times in chapter V: *Of Property* in the *Second Treatise* (1690). Sir

---

[38] In the *Metaphysics of Morals* (1797), Immanuel Kant also uses an *in* prepositional phrase when he says, "all rights in this thing" (*alle Rechte in dieser Sache*). Consistent with discussion of Latin phrases earlier, the German *in* here takes the dative case meaning *within* or *contained by*, and not the accusative. The full sentence is about *dominium* and external objects:

> Der äussere Gegenstand, welcher der Substanz nach das Seine von Jemandem ist, ist dessen Eigenthum (*dominium*), welchem alle Rechte in dieser Sache (wie Accidenzen der Substanz) inhäriren, über welche also der Eigenthümer (*dominus*) nach Belieben verfügen kann (*jus disponendi de re sua*).

The original German can be found on p. 79: https://archive.org/stream/immanuelkants-me00kircgoog#page/n278/mode/2up. Last accessed June 22, 2016.
   Mary Gregor's translation is (Kant 1797, p. 56):

William Blackstone refers to *property in Y*, where *Y* is a moveable thing, over twenty times in the *Commentaries on the Laws of England in Four Books,* vol. 1 (1765).[39] In his *Lectures on Jurisprudence* (1760s), Adam Smith discusses property in goods, crops, a hare, a watch, flocks, cattle, furniture, moveables, and possessions. David Hume only uses the phrase once in the main text and twice in footnotes in *A Treatise of Human Nature* (1740).[40]

This way of thinking about the relationship between property and things so penetrated Henry Dunning Macleod's thinking in the late nineteenth century that he misremembers Wycliffe and quotes him as saying, "and leave property in worldly goods," when, as quoted earlier, Wycliffe actually says, "and leave property of worldly goods."[41] Macleod also translates Justinian's "*transfert proprietatem mercium*" as "transfers the property in the goods," when the literal translation of *mercium* is in the genitive case, "of the goods."[42] Macleod's mind cognizes *proprietas* to be more than an intrinsic feature of the goods; *proprietas* is in the goods.

The Dutch jurist Hugo Grotius in his magnum opus *De Jure Belli ac Pacis* (*Concerning Law of War and Peace*) says that "*Est . . . filius aut filia capax dominii in res ex jure gentium.*"[43] In 1738 John Morrice translates this sentence as "children in their infancy are, by the Law of Nations, capable of having a property in things."[44] More literally, the gloss is "a son or daughter is capable of *dominium* against things by the Law of Nations." Grotius uses the plural accusative case for things (*res*), not the plural ablative (*rebus*), yet Morrice interprets *in res* as meaning *in things* in the way that Blackstone, Coke, Locke, Macleod, and Smith refer to property in things.[45] *In res* is the plural of *in rem*

An external object which in terms of its substance belongs to someone is his property (*dominium*), in which <u>all rights in this thing</u> inhere (as accidents of a substance) and which the owner (*dominus*) can, accordingly, dispose of as he pleases (*ius disponendi de re sua*).

[39] Sir William Blackstone also uses other physical prepositional complements like a king, dwelling, soil, land, copyholder, and bailor, and other abstract complements like possession, action, and debt. James Madison (1792) likewise talks about property in such abstract things as opinions, the use of faculties, and rights. Locke precedes them in this by writing about "property in his own person." As our thoughts continue to mate and evolve in our flexible symbolic minds, it is beyond the scope of the book to discuss these extended cases.

[40] One footnote is a paraphrase of Locke.

[41] Henry Dunning Macleod (1881, p. 143).

[42] Ibid.

[43] Hugo Grotius (1625/1913, p. 146).

[44] Hugo Grotius (1625/2005, p. 510).

[45] John Morrice elsewhere uses the language of "property in *Y*" when there is no *dominium* or *proprietas* at all in the original. He translates Grotius as saying that "we lose our property in wild beasts, as soon as they recover their natural liberty" (Grotius 1625/2005, p. 636). A more literal rendering would be that "the wild beasts cease to be ours as they recover their natural liberty" Grotius (1625/1913, p. 196).

and connotes action directed against (*in*) things (*res*). Considering that the context of the section is that even children can by custom make legal claims regarding *dominium*, Grotius's sentence perhaps conveys a sense of legality in a way that Morrice's translation fails to.

Over a hundred years later William Whewell's translation of the same sentence begins to sound modern: "a son or daughter is capable of ownership over things *jure gentium*."[46] The choice of *over* for the preposition is a nice touch to convey the lordship in the original *dominium*, particularly when the subject of the sentence is the little lord of a child exercising *dominium*. But it also indicates that the use of "property in things" may be waning by the mid-1800s, for Whewell prefers *ownership* to Morrice's *property* as a translation for *dominium*.

By the early twentieth century, Francis Kelsey renders Grotius's sentence succinctly familiar to the modern ear: "a son or daughter, according to universal customary law, is capable of ownership of property."[47] Because Kelsey naïvely thinks of property as a physical object, Macleod would anachronistically consider Kelsey's translation to be a modern corruption. Recall that the preposition *of* connotes an intrinsic, part-whole relationship between, in this case, ownership and property. For Kelsey, ownership is an intrinsic feature of "property," the thing itself. When Coke talks about the property of a swan, he is referring to one of the many features of the swan, to wit, the property in it. Kelsey is doing something different, using a specific part of a thing, its property, to refer to the whole thing. In other words, "property" is a synecdoche for the thing itself. He then refers to ownership in "ownership of property" as an intrinsic part of *pars-pro-toto* property. To Macleod, "ownership of property" is pleonastic. It's like saying the ashiness of a gray beard. If we are synecdochically referring to an old man by the feature of his facial hair, ashy grayness is redundant.

I conjecture that synecdoche is how *property* came to refer to both the custom and the thing itself.[48] Synecdoche is, I further conjecture, the reason that the use of "property in a thing" begins to wane. Once the part becomes the whole so that our minds cognize "property" as the physical object itself, having property in a thing becomes redundant; the thing *is* "property."

Even though the Oxford English Dictionary defines *property* in terms of *ownership* and *ownership* in terms of *property*, "ownership of property"

---

[46] Hugo Grotius (1625/1853, p. 93).
[47] Hugo Grotius (1625/1925, p. 232).
[48] Only a language maven would fret about the creative uses of language.

doesn't sound redundant to the modern ear. Neither does "If you own something, it is your property." We treat the concepts OWNERSHIP and PROPERTY as complements. Ownership is the state or condition of being able to say at this time, "I own Y" or "Y is my property," which in noncircular atomic concepts means (1) I can say about Y: "It is mine"; (2) people can know that what I say is true; and (3) other people cannot say, "It is mine" about Y.[49] Both *own* and *property* are about states of the world. In some states you own a cow, and in others you don't. In some states a swan is your "property," and in others it is not. The difference between the two words in modernity is that *own* is a static state verb and "*property*" the corresponding noun for the class of things that the verb *own* can take as a direct object.

But "I Have Property in X" Conveys Richer Meaning Than "X Is My Property"

Does it matter that our language has evolved from "She has property in the swan" in the sixteenth century to "The swan is her property" and "She owns the swan" in the twenty-first century? Yes, if different language can bring different ideas to the foreground for how we think about the world. Suppose there is a dispute about a particular swan. The modern statements involve a swan, a woman, and a claim of a relationship between the two. The verbs *own* and *is* convey the claim, namely that the state of the world is such that this woman and only this woman can say, "This swan is mine" and that by custom people can know that what she says is true. The focus is on whether the state is such that the woman can claim this swan to be in the set of things she owns. Is the swan her "property"? Or is it not? To then ask why the swan is her "property" is to ask for a function that maps things into one of two mutually exclusive sets, her "property" or not her "property." The primary question is about the objective criteria for the static mapping and whether this swan meets the criteria to be in the set of things that are her "property." The features of the swan itself, swans in general, and the scheduling pattern of humans regarding swans are all secondary. At best, they shape the function that does the mapping; at worst, some or all of these features are ignored.

The quaint-sounding statement "She has property in the swan" likewise involves a swan, a woman, and a claim of a relationship between the two. But

---

[49] Cliff Goddard and Anna Wierzbicka (2016, p. 102).

it also involves—thanks to the nonthingness of property and to the powerful word *in*—an interactive relationship between property and the swan. The swan contains the property. Moreover, because the swan itself isn't property, the statement contains three distinct substantives, which means there is a third relationship at play between the woman and property. In our modern vernacular, there are only two distinct noun phrases, the first linked to the second (which is what the copula *is* does), and hence only one relationship between two substantives. The quainter vernacular "She has property in the swan" contains three substantives and three relationships between them: the woman and the swan, the woman and property, property and the swan.

If a woman has property in a particular swan, we simultaneously know from the context that something is not true about the statement "The woman does not have property in this swan." "The woman has property in this swan" simultaneously means that in such a situation (1) some other person does not have property in this particular swan and/or (2) there is not a different custom these people practice, say, one for domesticated animals like cows, such that the woman would not have property in this particular swan, and/or (3) there are many other things in the world besides this particular swan in which the woman does not have property. While our modern minds project the question onto the Flatland of just two dimensions, the sixteenth-century language of property operates vividly in three dimensions.

At this point, evolutionary-minded psychologists and linguists will be quick to raise their shields when their sensors detect sci-fi conditions suitable for the slightest possibility that someone may be saying and thinking that language determines thought.[50] Cancel the red alert: A hostile Klingon vessel of the Sapir-Whorf hypothesis is not approaching. First, recall that I posited in chapter 3 that every human being shares a core set of semantic primitives, which means that any human being can think with the same concepts, including combining them to form more complex thoughts and words. Second, I am not saying that language unidirectionally determines thought, that language determines what *can* be said.[51] I am making the rather uncontroversial claim that two different concatenations of words can have two different meanings. Specifically, my point is that custom adds metaphorical depth and time to our perception of property. Where we moderns cognize the problem

---

[50] Or is it thinking and saying that language determines thought?
[51] See Aneta Pavlenko (2011, p. 19) for her discussion on how North American psychologists shifted the conversation on language and thought from "what is said" to testable hypotheses of "what can be said."

as whether or not to put a flat circle around the swan and call it "her property," the Elizabethan jurist locates the woman, the swan, and the property within a three-dimensional sphere of actions. The features of the swan itself, swans in general, and the custom regarding swans are not secondary, but indeed primary to the three-dimensional problem before our mind's eye. Property is an evolving process. It matters how we, with our first- and second-person views of the world, get to the here and now.

PART II
CLAIM AND TITLE: EFFECTS

6

My Claims Tie Together Modern Philosophies of Property Law

The Language of "Possession" and "Rights" Muddies the Meaning of Property

Called the foremost teacher of law in the late nineteenth and early twentieth centuries, the Harvard Law School Dean James Barr Ames submits that "only he in whom the power to enjoy and the unqualified right to enjoy concur can be called an owner in the full and strict sense of the term. . . . A true property may, therefore, be shortly defined as possession coupled with the unlimited right of possession."[1] Legally founding property on possession is not just Anglo-Roman fashion and an Anglo-Roman fetish but also useful, for, as the weighty legal authorities Sir Frederick Pollock and F. W. Maitland attest, "to prove ownership is difficult, to prove possession comparatively easy. . . . Possession then is an outwork of property."[2] The metaphor is apt. Outside the principal fortification of ownership, possession is a minor fortification for maintaining the enjoyment of the thing.

But defining "true property" as the conjunction of possession and the right of possession does more than fortify ownership. It appears to change the ordinary meaning of the term. Ames continues, "If these two elements are vested in different persons there is a divided ownership."[3] It changes the meaning of the word *ownership* to say that my dispossessor has an element of ownership in my spear. Nay, the dispossessor has physical control. It is I and my spear that have been divided. And upon the division I am vested with something more than a right of possession. No matter where the spear goes, the property contained therein goes with it, and no matter where the property contained therein goes, my claim still stands: "That spear is mine."

[1] James Ames (1913, pp. 193–194).
[2] Sir Frederick Pollock and Frederic Maitland (1895, p. 42).
[3] James Ames (1913, p. 194).

The Property Species. Bart J. Wilson. Oxford University Press (2020) © Oxford University Press.
DOI: 10.1093/oso/9780190936785.001.0001

What is separated are possession and ownership, physical control *of* a thing and property *in* a thing.

Ames's definition appears at first blush to confuse the issue until we distinguish a first-person from third-person point of view of the events. When I think about what has happened, I cognize the situation as: I can say about that spear: "It is mine"; people can know that what I say is true; and other people cannot say, "It is mine" about that spear. When I say, "That spear is mine," it is predicated on some good reasons that I can say that spear is mine. Based on those good reasons, I think I can cause people to have to say that it is right that that spear is mine. And so I say out loud for everyone to hear, "That spear is mine," because I want to cause other people by a speech act to think that it is right that that spear is mine.

Well, that's what I'm claiming anyways. Does it matter if I had previously taken the spear from the person now in physical control of it? Or if I had previously taken the spear from someone else who has now disappeared? Or if—and this is not as far-fetched as it may seem in human history—I had taken the spear from someone else who has now disappeared and a fourth person has in the meantime taken the spear from the person who took it from me?

Part I is a first- and second-person account of how we as a species cognize the meaning of property in a thing. It does not address how a traditional legal theorist or judge sifts through conflicting claims of "This is mine" and "That is mine" from a third-person point of view. In a concrete conflict, someone must decide what is indeed true and what is indeed right, which is a problem logically, cognitively, and temporally posterior to the dispute between my dispossessor and me. You, the dispossessor, and I both have first-person and second-person expectations about what each other will or won't do, the state of the affairs concerning the spear, and the appropriate responses to the events regarding the spear. We disagree *ex hypothesi* on how we perceive the spear and what we know about who can say, "This spear is mine." Dean Ames, however, isn't defining property to explain how you and I cognize the meaning of property. He is summarizing a practical definition of property for third parties to settle such disputes between you and me.

Blackstone, I submit, organizes the problem a little more skillfully. Rather than defining property as the unity of possession and a right of possession, he construes the problem in terms of what constitutes an unassailable title. Should there be a dispute, a trinity of possession, a right of possession, and a right of property completely substantiate a claim of "This thing is mine":

For it is an ancient maxim of the law, that no title is completely good, unless the right of possession be joined with the right of property; which right is then denominated a double right, *jus duplicatum*, or *droit droit*. And when to this double right the actual possession is also united, there is, according to the expression of Fleta, *juris et seisinae conjunctio*, then, and then only, is the title completely legal.[4]

Bracton too treats *dominium* as the union of the right of possession (*ius possessionis*) and the right of ownership (*ius proprietatis*). The job of judges and jurists is to explicate that which justifies a claim of "This thing is mine." To do that they separate possession and ownership in parallel with the claim that someone has separated possession from ownership.[5] The legal scholar Richard Epstein explains:

> At this point, lawyers ask the question, what is the basis of the action to recover possession of property or damages for its loss—ownership or possession? To an economist [or an average person too] that question looks largely empty, given that the original owner and possessor were the same person. But for the classical lawyers in both the Roman and the common law tradition, the primary actions to recover the possession of land, animals or chattels were said to rest on the violation of the fact of possession, and not of the ultimate right of ownership. The difference between these two conceptions becomes critical in any situation in which the location of ownership is in dispute.[6]

As part of the tradition of resolving conflicts regarding things, judges and jurists have nominalized two features of that ancient process into the concept of an incorporeal right—the right of possession and the right of ownership. What is right regarding the physical control of a thing and what is right regarding the property in a thing lie dormant until a dispute arises. When a disagreement occurs, judges call upon these concepts to explicate what should have guided expectations of the parties for the situation in question. The ancient rights of possession and ownership are scheduling patterns in conflict resolution, the resulting order of which constitutes a set of expectations about

---

[4] Sir William Blackstone (1765, p. 199). *Seisina* is the Latinization of the Law French term *seisin*, meaning freehold possession of land or chattels.
[5] Richard Epstein (1998, pp. 62–68).
[6] Ibid. (p. 64).

what we ought to do, the state of affairs and probable results of those actions (what is true and what is good, respectively), and the appropriate responses to external events. While it may be easy to forget, such scheduling patterns are not genetic; they are shared moral practices that form an external order by aligning expectations among conspecifics. These expectations fit with and are founded upon the internal order of the mind, how we think about claims of "This thing is mine." Complications arise, however, when moving from first- and second-person perceptions of property to third-party adjudicators when the scheduling patterns of first and second persons regarding things are ignored.

The Conception of Possession Discards Mind and Custom from Property

In 1803 and at the tender age of twenty-four, Friedrich Savigny published *Das Recht des Besitzes* (*The Law of Possession*), a groundbreaking treatise in the history of jurisprudence. Savigny reads Roman law to say that the legal concept of possession is the conjunction of acts that demonstrate (1) physical control of the thing (*corpus possessionis*) and (2) an intention to hold the thing as one's own, as the mind of an owner (*animus domini*). While agreeing with the first element, Oliver Wendell Holmes famously takes issue with the second in *The Common Law*. For Justice Holmes, acting with the mind of a *dominus* is too strong to establish possession. When a *dominus* treats something as his own, the point of the law is "to prevent other men to a greater or lesser extent from interfering with [his] use or abuse."[7] Holmes argues that the limited intention to exclude is all that is needed to establish possession and that this streamlined intention makes a related type of dispute, though legally distinct, easier to handle. Suppose a *domina* leaves something with a shopkeeper to sell on her behalf and then someone else absconds with it while in the shopkeeper's trust. Savigny would deny possession to bailees like the shopkeeper because they cannot, by definition, hold the item with the mind of a *dominus*. And without possession, the bailee does not have access to a standard legal remedy called trover to recover the value of the thing (not the thing itself) from the absconder. Holmes argues that the common law has

---

[7] Oliver Wendell Holmes (1881, p. 220).

found a way to settle more cases of dispossession by limiting the intention in possession to that of mere exclusion.

Judge Richard Posner expertly sifts through the differences between Savigny and Holmes.[8] True to his reputation, Posner compares and contrasts them through a third lens, the economics of the law of possession, to expose an anomaly in Holmes's definition of possession. If Savigny's definition is anomalous with regard to bailees, Holmes inconsistently handles the case of an employee who steals from an employer.[9] By Holmes's definition, an employee has possession of an employer's goods because he has both physical control of them and the requisite intent to exclude all others from using them. But if an employee has possession, how can he be treated as a thief who has taken the goods from his employer's possession? Posner explains that Holmes wriggles his way out of this inconvenient case by saying that employees have been historically treated as slaves. Because slaves could not be legally regarded as possessors, an employee-slave can thus be deemed a thief when he physically takes goods from the employer's possession. Note that Savigny's definition has no problem with this case. The moment the employee carts off the goods for his own use, he is acting as a *dominus* and is, hence, in possession of the goods.

Both definitions run into problems regarding theft. Savigny's definition is inconvenient for bailees because the intent is too strong; for Savigny the *animus domini* must always be present. But by weakening the intent, Holmes's definition creates a *corpus possessionis* problem (we are unable to distinguish two possible motives attached to the same matter of fact), the solution to which is to treat thieving employees as slaves.[10] I find it curious that in the case of swans and cattle, property in a thing depends on the scheduling patterns of the thing itself and the scheduling patterns of the humans regarding the thing. But in the cases of bailors and bailees, and employers and employees, property in the thing does not depend on human scheduling patterns. In an important way, the life of the law of possession has not been experience, despite what Holmes may famously exhort.[11] The legal concept of possession has been about axioms and fictive corollaries.

When a *domina* places an item in the hands of a shopkeeper, she can still say, "That is mine," even though she no longer has physical control of the

---

[8] Richard Posner (2000).
[9] Ibid. (p. 548).
[10] For legal purposes only, of course.
[11] Olive Wendell Holmes (1881, p. 1): "The life of the law has not been logic: it has been experience."

thing. Where the item moves, so moves the property in it. Another feature of the scheduling pattern is that the *domina* places her trust *in* the shop-keeper to treat the item as she treats it, that is, *as her own*, which includes maintaining its condition and defending it against would-be dispossessors.[12] This is to say that the bailor and the bailee jointly attend to the same end, that the bailee will maintain the item's condition and defend it against would-be dispossessors.

For the bailee to treat the item as the *domina* would treat it, he must treat the item as if he can say, "This thing is mine" (1) to himself as he cares for it and (2) to others who would dispossess him of it. When someone becomes a bailee, he divides himself, as it were, into two persons.[13] The first is him-self, someone who is not the *domina* and who cannot say, "This is mine." The second is himself, the bailee, who treats the thing as the *domina* treats the thing, maintaining its value and pursuing dispossessors. To a third person, the bailee acts like the *domina* acts and to the same effect. The first has no property in the thing; the second has something that looks and feels like pro-perty in the thing but only against would-be dispossessors who are not the *domina*. The jurist A. M. Honoré describes the second as having a "lesser interest" in the thing.[14] "Yet, without more," he adds, "we feel no temptation to say that the bailee owns the thing." The didact might claim that it is as im-possible for the first to be, in every respect, the same with the second as it is impossible to identify cause with effect. However, without such abstract thinking beyond the here and now, never would a bailor place goods in trust and joint attention with a bailee. Such is the scheduling pattern of our (and only our) species. Perhaps the common law could recognize it explicitly as it explicitly recognizes the scheduling patterns of wild and tame animals.

Holmes must weaken Savigny's intent to act with the mind of an owner because he is intent on defending the outwork of property, not the bastion of property itself. By doing so, Holmes leaves unguarded the back door to the castle, wherein the concept MINE sits singularly on the throne. Holmes's logic is that "if what the law does is to exclude others from interfering with the ob-ject, it would seem that the intent which the law should require is an intent to exclude others."[15] There exists not a slight temptation to begin with the as-sumption that possession must be the first line in the defense of property and

---

[12] Where the shopkeeper goes, so goes the *domina*'s trust.
[13] In what follows, compare with Adam Smith (1759, p. 113).
[14] A. M. Honoré (1961, p. 125).
[15] Oliver Wendell Holmes (1881, p. 220).

that the intent of import is that which protects possession, namely, the intent to exclude others. This provisional assumption is treated as a necessary practical consideration that can be dropped later without much consequence for philosophical, legal, and economic foundations of property. Yet the concept MINE is the basis for the *animus domini* and central to how we cognize the meaning of property in things. The practical consideration by which the *animus domini* is put aside is typically never explicitly reconsidered, but simply conveniently forgotten. The discussion then proceeds as if the mind of the *dominus* does not matter. The mind of the *dominus* matters.

A. M. Honoré Would Seem to Agree

Despite A. M. Honoré's explicit admonition, twentieth- and twenty-first-century legal scholars and philosophers tend to treat his well-known list of eleven "standard incidents" of ownership (*ownership* is his word) as a blueprint for demarcating various subsets of the incidents as the necessary and sufficient conditions of property.[16] Such a conclusion stems from a preoccupation with a public administration of rights, despite his further objection of thinking about property as a bundle of rights. The twentieth-century American tradition of legal realism maintains that property is not about things, but a bundle of incorporeal rights and legal relations between people.[17] The error of such thinking rests in misunderstanding how humans cognize the custom of property and why the custom arose in the first place. I submit that my claims about property are—à la Hume's self-associated link to Grotius—"in the main, the same with that hinted at and adopted by" Honoré closely read.[18]

The essay opens with a claim he shares with me that "ownership is one of the characteristic institutions of human society."[19] All peoples distinguish *meum* from *tuum*. Honoré aims to present a "clear idea of what ownership is" by "giving an account of the standard incidents of ownership."[20] The technical-sounding "incident," *Black's Law Dictionary* informs us, "denotes anything which is usually connected with another, or connected for some

---

[16] A. M. Honoré (1961, pp. 112–128).
[17] For legal realist theories of property as a thing-free, socially constructed concept, see, for example, Stephen Munzer (2001) and Laura Underkuffler (2003).
[18] David Hume (1751, p. 307, fn. 1).
[19] A. M. Honoré (1961, p. 107).
[20] Ibid.

purposes." Unlike my project, Honoré goes straight to the law to understand what ownership is. Specifically, the standard incidents of ownership are "those legal rights, duties, and other incidents which apply, in the case, to the person who has the greatest interest in a thing admitted by a mature legal system."[21] First, notice that Honoré's definition of ownership includes the prepositional phrase "in a thing." The "most general term" in property, interest, is contained in the thing.[22] Where the thing goes, so goes someone's greatest possible interest.

Second, note that the operative phrase in the definition is "the greatest interest." The superlative indicates that ownership is a matter of degree. Ownership varies from thing to thing and also from people to people. Honoré peppers the essay with examples of how different legal systems and different people treat ownership differently. The customary character of ownership is a presupposition of the essay. That said, Honoré seeks to explain the "substantial similarity in the position of one who 'owns' an umbrella in England, France, Russia, China, and any other modern country one may care to mention."[23] He is compelled to put the word *own* in quotation marks for the obvious reason that the English transitive verb *own* doesn't directly translate one to one into many (if any) languages. His English-to-French example is that "He owns that umbrella" means the same thing as "Ce parapluie est à lui," even though the latter uses a copula, literally, "That umbrella is to him." The equivalent, not simply similar, position that would have been useful for Honoré is that in every language, with mature systems of law or not, people can by custom say, "This is mine," "C'est à moi."

When Honoré gets to the point of listing the incidents that apply to ownership, he explicitly states that they are "not individually necessary, though they may be together sufficient, conditions for the person of inherence to be designated 'owner' of a particular thing in a given system."[24] The passive voice of the designation indicates the legal lens of his analysis. A third party, a court, designates which of the two disputants can say, "This thing is mine." The particulars of the case determine which incidents taken together comprise the designation as to whether you or I can say by custom, "This is mine." When you and I disagree about the perceptions of what is right regarding

---

[21] Ibid.
[22] *Black's Law Dictionary*, 2nd edition, https://thelawdictionary.org. Last accessed September 8, 2018.
[23] A. M. Honoré (1961, p. 108).
[24] Ibid. (p. 113).

some *thing*, a third party takes stock of the situation and pulls out of the background and into the foreground the expectations that ought to have guided your and my expectations. Expressed as a rule, the judge articulates the moral scheduling pattern that you and I ought to have followed under these specific circumstances.

Honoré cautions against reading his list of standard incidents as a way to derive deductively and abstractly what is right regarding ownership: "As we have seen, the use of 'owner' will extend to cases in which not all the listed incidents are present."[25] Rather, Honoré's incidents arise from our cumulative knowledge of what is right regarding ownership. Over the course of the human career, we have discovered that the moral scheduling pattern regarding things includes the following (in Honoré's language of ownership and right):

1) The right to possess: to have exclusive physical control over the thing;
2) The right to use: to personally enjoy the thing;
3) The right to manage: to decide how and by whom the thing shall be used;
4) The right to the income: to enjoy the fruits, rents, and profits arising from the personal use of the thing;
5) The right to the capital: to alienate the thing and to consume, waste, or destroy the thing;
6) The right to security: to remain the owner of the thing indefinitely if he chooses and he remains solvent;
7) The incident of transmissibility: to transfer ownership of the thing to another person;
8) The incident of absence of term: to be entitled to the ownership of the thing for a duration of time;
9) The prohibition on harmful use: to be restrained from using the thing in ways that cause harm to others;
10) Liability to execution: to dissolve or transfer ownership of the thing in case of debt or insolvency; and,
11) Residuary character: to return ownership to vest in the owner of the thing.[26]

---

[25] A. M. Honoré (1961, pp. 112–113).
[26] Ibid. (pp. 113–128).

I second Honoré in saying that "it is of no help towards understanding society to speak as if [ownership] were [a bundle of rights]."[27] Our symbolic minds do not aggregate specific concrete rules regarding things to create the abstract custom of property. Our symbolic minds operate in the abstract and point out the specifics of the world as the circumstances of time and place demand (as further classified by our supra-conscious minds). What is right regarding things is not derived by a finite list of specific rules, by a list of standard incidents, the effects of property. Rather, the rules of property arise from our knowledge of what is right.[28] An adjudicator will ultimately decide the two-dimensional question as to whether the swan is your or my property, but the decision comes out of a process of discovering the expectations that should have guided the three-dimensional problem of whether you or I have property in the swan. A third party settles disputes regarding things by considering the facts of the situation as they relate to you and me, the custom, and the thing. The thing itself is as central as the third-party scheduling patterns—the standard incidents of property—are for settling disputes regarding things.

A new wave of research has reintroduced the thing to the study of property. While this substantial body of new work has re-thingified the study of property over the last twenty years by rediscovering how people long ago thought about property, the step that this legal research has not taken is to treat property as, first and foremost, abstract thought embodied in customary human action.[29]

When we make a composite object like a spear, as only a human can, we create something. That physical object is not the end of the action. One feature of the action itself is that an object now exists that previously did not. We perceive the thing as something different than the sum of its physical parts. A second feature of the action itself is that we have self-directed purposes for which that object is a means.[30] An "I" has plans beyond the here and now for it. A third feature of the action itself is that for anyone

[27] Ibid. (p. 134).
[28] *Quod est*, full stop.
[29] For an excellent survey and the references therein, see James Penner and Henry Smith (2013).
[30] Douglas Rasmussen and Douglas Den Uyl (2005).

else to assert physical control of that object is to interfere with those self-directed purposes. Those purposes carry with them expectations that are the consequence of creating an object. Created goods are something about which by custom someone can say, "This is mine." I thus join Douglases Rasmussen and Den Uyl in concluding that such an object (with a single creator) "must be considered an extension of what one is (assuming no dichotomy between oneself and one's action) and not as items contingently attached to oneself."[31] Property is more than an external dichotomous mapping of things into one of two sets, "my property" and "not my property." Property is a scheduling mechanism of human action that first-personally takes the concept I in my body and places it in an object as the moral concept MINE.

Note the cognitive similarities between the semantically related, but noncompositional, concepts I and MINE. Both are first-personal, but neither can be defined in terms of the other.[32] Just as only I can use I to refer to myself, only I can use MINE to predicate a claim on something that I have property in. A body is a physical container for the concept I. Move the body, and I move with it. Likewise, a thing is the physical container for the concept MINE. Move the thing, and the property moves with it. Mine, however, is not *dominium*. Mine is not absolute, nor is mine the right to exclude. Mine is mine like I is I and you is you. Mine is singular, atomic, reflexive, the core of property. When, at the urging of his parents, the three-year-old Miles gingerly hands over the object of his fixed gaze, his prized Thomas the Train toy, to fellow three-year-old Owen, Miles learns that even though he can say the toy is "Mine!," he does not have *dominium* in the toy, nor an absolute right to exclude. The custom of sharing among young Southern Californian boys circa 2018 applies to such circumstances of time and place. But when Owen, also at his parents' urging, eventually returns the train to Miles ten minutes later, Miles learns that his property in the train never left the train while the train was within Owen's grasp. He can still say, "Thomas the Train is mine" and take it to bed with him that night. Sole and despotic dominion and the right to exclude are consequences that follow from the customs of time and place and thing by which someone can say, "This is mine."

---

[31] Ibid. (p. 100).
[32] Cliff Goddard and Anna Wierzbicka (2016).

The Neo-Lockean Theory Invokes Custom but Doesn't Go Far Enough

Locke's is perhaps the most well-known theory of property. If not the most well known, it's the most intuitive to the average person. The labor theory of property holds that someone can say, "This is mine" if he or she does something productive with the thing. The popularized version of the theory is that we have property in the things with which we mix our labor. Philosophers interpret Locke's theory as a metaphysical argument about mixing substantives, a version of which we will discuss when we examine Robert Nozick's and Jeremy Waldron's critiques of Locke. I follow the legal scholar Eric Claeys, and the philosopher Stephen Buckle before him, who explain that Locke's theory of property, carefully read, is a theory of purposeful activity that creates value.[33] Because Locke is writing in the natural rights tradition, he bases his theory on something that appears to be naturally right. For Locke this entails the unarguable proposition that "every Man has a *Property* in his own *Person*. This no Body has any Right to but himself."[34] From this it follows that "the *Labour* of his Body, and the *Work* of his Hands, we may say, are properly his."[35]

I don't want to push this too hard, but is there not something awkward, some conceptual tension, about saying that someone has property in her own person? In a world in which slavery was commonly accepted, Locke is making more than one statement when he says that everyone has property in their own person. But even though slavery is no longer condoned, there is still another source of conceptual tension in his phrasing. Modern restatements of Locke frequently use the verb *own*, which Locke never does, to say that a person owns herself, owns her body, and owns her actions. Sometimes authors put this use of *own* in quotation marks, and that nonfelicitousness is what I am referring to.[36] What does one say when pointing at oneself: "This is mine" or "This is my body"? We say, "This is my body." Saying "This is mine" while pointing at one's (own) body seems infelicitous. I submit that such conceptual tension—saying, "I own myself" or pointing at one's body and saying, "This is mine"—stems from how MINE cognitively works. While

---

[33] Eric Claeys (2013) and Stephen Buckle (1991).
[34] John Locke (1689, p. 287, original italics).
[35] Ibid. (pp. 287–288, original italics).
[36] John Thrasher (2019) argues that a conception of self-sovereignty avoids problems of applying property notions of "self-ownership" when considering issues of the supreme authority over one's own body.

we can say about our body in all its thingness, "This body is mine," it sounds infelicitous to say, "This self is mine" or "This I is mine." Because MINE is something we felicitously put in physical things external to ourselves, like tools, our minds resist locating an abstract MINE inside in the same physical body which contains an abstract I or SELF.[37] The singular concepts I and MINE are both first-personal but not, I conjecture, colocational. While the location of I is a philosophical puzzle and up for debate (where in space and time is I located?), MINE is in things, generally external things, and not in the abstractions we call ourselves.

Since the abolition of slavery, we similarly resist referring to people as "mine." Even though we say, "This truck is mine" and "This is my truck," we generally don't say, except with love and a shoulder hug, "This sister is mine," even though we regularly introduce her as "This is my sister." Saying "This sister is mine" in a particular moment has the lovingly ironic effect that it does because we, as a general rule, don't think of our sisters as things we have property in. *But parents at their kid's first soccer practice respond to questions like "Which one is yours?" by saying, "That one is mine."* I'm not saying we *can't* use language flexibly and stretch the meaning and use of words for the wry effect of connecting ourselves to our children. We clearly do. I'm saying we generally, regularly, as a rule, *don't* introduce our child to someone new by saying, "This daughter is mine." Why is that? Because the concept MINE is something we generally put in things, not people, which, for a symbolic species, means something.

If I prune a stick whose original tree matter had been "in the common state Nature placed it in," Locke's theory is that by the work of my hands I can say, "This stick is mine." Why? Because I have "mixed [my] labour with it, and joined to it something that is [my] own."[38] The stick has "by this labour something annexed to it that excludes the common right of other men."[39] The philosophers Robert Nozick and Jeremy Waldron mock the mixing metaphor with examples of pouring radioactive tomato juice into the Atlantic Ocean and dropping a ham sandwich in wet cement.[40] So successful are these amusing critiques that even a Lockean scholar like Claeys feels compelled to concede that "true, the mixing image is somewhat hyperbolic."[41] No, the

---

[37] See also the "separability" thesis in J. E. Penner (1997, p. 111).
[38] John Locke (1689, p. 288).
[39] Ibid.
[40] Robert Nozick (1974, pp. 174–175) and Jeremy Waldron (1983, p. 43).
[41] Eric Claeys (2013, p. 23).

metaphor is not hyperbolic, nor easily dismissible as a mere image. Locke is using how we think about property to explain how the custom works. "Something of oneself," the Swedish legal philosopher Karl Olivecrona deftly explains, "is infused into an object."[42] There is a reason Locke's labor theory of property is intuitive and well known; people actually think about property that way. The concept of mine and the property constituted thereby is in the pruned stick. What this means is that other people cannot say, "This stick is mine."

Sometimes, though, someone else may say, "That stick is mine." No custom stands independent of other customs. Only in its totality does a social system composed of customs form the sense of how to conduct ourselves rightly, and Locke's is no different.[43] Claeys identifies in Locke's treatise three of the numerous other customs that qualify when I can say, "This is mine": Do not waste, leave a sufficient amount ("enough and as good") for others to do the same, and charitably give to those whose very life or safety depends on my thing. [44] In the case of my pruned stick, I suppose someone could come up with an entertaining statement that would qualify my claiming of the pruned stick such that I could no longer say, "This stick is mine." But what would be the point? Neither Locke's nor my claim is that property is absolute. (Nor is my claim that we can interpret the custom to be as we wish it to be, including wishing it away.) Property is embedded in a system of good conduct. One of Locke's and his interpreters' major contributions to the study of property is that they embed it in a social system with other customs.

Where modern Lockeans miss the mark is that they don't go far enough and treat property itself as a custom. They stop short with an appeal to an incorporeal substantive, a right: "productive use . . . grounds ownership of property in each person's non-conventional right to acquire and deploy external assets to satisfy some aspect of his self-preservation or -improvement."[45] Property is a scheduling pattern of actions distinct from the patterns of actions associated with using the thing. When I say, "This stick is mine," I am doing something different in the world than when I do something productive with the stick, like prune it, or when I use the stick as a shaft for a spear. Of course, it is because I intend to do something with the stick that I go out, find it, and prune it. And, of course, there are customs that govern when and

---

[42] Karl Olivecrona (1974, p. 225).
[43] F. A. Hayek (1952).
[44] John Locke (1689, pp. 288, 291) and Eric Claeys (2013, pp. 20–21).
[45] Eric Claeys (2013, p. 46).

how I may acquire and deploy an unpruned stick. But none of that makes the physical facts of labor mixing and productive use a theory of property. Recall that physical facts are insufficient in and of themselves to explain how you and I cognize the external world differently when we jointly attend to a spear and I say, "This spear is not mine; it is yours." You have property in an object that you create because humans (and only humans) re-cognize created objects as objects that don't appear in the common state placed by nature. We recognize the purposes of an "I" in a created object, and one meaning of a created object is that by custom I can say, "This thing is mine."

Property, to borrow from Michael Polanyi, "transcends the disjunction between the subjective and objective."[46] Insofar as the custom establishes contact with the external world, such as mixing labor with a thing, it is not subjective; and insofar as I confidently say, "This is mine" based on that contact, it is not objective either. I have property in the thing because other people and I jointly comprehend that (1) I can say about the thing: "It is mine"; (2) people can know that what I say is true; and (3) other people cannot say, "It is mine," about the thing.[47] Physical facts and productive use do not account for the personal presence of the singular I and the singular MINE in cognizing the custom and, thus, cannot explain how property works.

Exclusive Use Cannot Explain Property as a Scheduling Pattern

Like my account, J. E. Penner rejects the claim that property is a culturally relative conception. He posits, contra the modern orthodoxy in law, that an "idea" of property transcends local customs. As a foundational point, it is exactly right and a long overdue reorientation for the study of property. The question is, what is the universal human idea of property? My answer is that all human beings emphysicalize the concept of mine in socially taught customs of when someone can and cannot say about certain things, "This is mine."

Similar to Claeys, Penner conceives of property in terms of a right "grounded by the interest we have in the use of things," though expressly

---

[46] Michael Polanyi (1958, p. 300).
[47] Saying "This is mine" does more than represent the world in words. Language, as Kenneth Burke (1966) argues, is a mode of doing something in the world.

without a labor mixing metaphor.[48] Note the common diction. Both Penner and Claeys "ground" property in the use of things. Penner's ground is "the interest in exclusively determining the use of things."[49] Yet, how does an interest in the use of things ground a right? The common-sense argument is that there must be a reason we exclude others from using things. Unless they're a curmudgeonly Mister Wilson with a menacing neighbor kid, people generally don't go around excluding others for the sake of excluding others. The reason we exclude other people, Penner argues, is that we want to use the things ourselves.

All animals "want" to use things themselves.[50] Consider the feisty American red squirrel. A red squirrel excludes conspecifics from the pine nuts it has gathered by caching them and defending its caches with impressive paroxysms of rage. If a squirrel didn't hide coniferous cones, its primary food source, an unguarded, neat, and convenient pile of them would surely be consumed by a conspecific that happened upon it. The hiding squirrel has an interest, so to speak, in the nuts and the species a scheduling pattern in larder-hoarding them that allows the species to survive. Now consider brown bears. Brown bears also have an interest in eating nuts, and they have the morphology to cache them. But brown bears don't cache nuts. Why does grounding the scheduling pattern in the use of nuts fail to generate larder-hoarding in bears? Because something is missing from consideration. Bears and squirrels fill different ecological niches. Bears are omnivores and sit comfortably on top of the food chain. Compared to squirrels, the benefits are rather low, relative to the costs, for bears to cache nuts. With slow feedback and innovation there is little value for a species-wide pattern of food caching to form in bears. Variations in the costs and benefits of exclusion would likewise fail to universally ground the human custom of property in the simple use of things, particularly food. Exclusive use is a consequence, the secondary effect, not the content, of the meaning of property in things. "I want this" and "This is mine" mean distinctly different things in the human animal. Only in humans does MINE ground property in every community.

---

[48] J. E. Penner (1997, p. 71).

[49] Ibid. (p. 49).

[50] I am again using my human-tinted lenses to comprehend how red squirrels act. The semantic prime WANT is a universal human concept; see Anna Wierzbicka (1996). Primatologists would add that their subjects also think with the concept of want. At some point, say, with ants, we would feel the need to put quotation marks around ants "wanting" things like humans and chimpanzees want things. Pinpointing that line is beyond the scope of my project.

Kantian a A Priorism Cannot Account for the Moral Significance and Transmission of Property

The philosopher and legal scholar Arthur Ripstein identifies a different value missing in the move to ground property in the exclusive use of things. Ripstein rejects the idea that the value of following the custom of property can be characterized "without reference to property-like concepts."[51] Specifically, he argues that the value in excluding others from using a thing cannot be characterized in terms of the use of that thing. Penner's theory mixes the moral valuation of the means with a valuation of the ends that need not be moral.

We do not deem a single act good—like excluding you from my thing— because in general it would be good for me to use the thing. Rather, in general it is good for me to use the thing because it is indeed right, that is, fitting with the entire scheduling pattern or order of society, for me to exclude you from using it. As Ripstein summarizes, "the relevant value is not something separate, which the rules try to achieve or even instantiate . . . because the value exists in the rule," to which he adds for Kantian good measure, "it is the form of interaction that has moral significance."[52]

Ripstein, however, doesn't show what the moral significance of property is. Why does the form of interaction have moral significance? Just prior to the previous quotation he says that "in the case of property, each property owner is master of his or her property, as against all others. That is the justification of the rule in property."[53] But what makes a rule of property moral? Elsewhere in a book-length treatment of Kant's legal philosophy, Ripstein explains the Kantian argument regarding the physical control and use of things external to our bodies. The short answer—without getting into the sticky aprioristic details of Kant's Universal Principle of Right, the Principle of Acquired Rights, and his conception of freedom—is that it would be morally wrong not to have rules of property.[54] While the logical conclusion of a universal proposition and a postulate may well be that it would be "illegitimate" to have "anything less than fully private rights of property," it does not follow that rules regarding the physical control and use of things are *moral* shared

---

[51] Arthur Ripstein (2013, p. 164).
[52] Ibid. (p. 176).
[53] Ibid.
[54] Arthur Ripstein (2009).

practices.[55] After all, such rules could simply be socially transmitted, like the capuchins' use of hammer and anvil stones to crack nuts, or they could even be genetically acquired, like the ants' use of leaves to transport liquid foods.

Ripstein's contribution is to (re-)inject moral evaluations into a study of property that had largely become anormative. The open question is, where does the moral significance of property come from? I would argue that the morality of property is built upon valuations of the basic claim "This thing is mine." The valuation of such a normative speech act is secondary to the comprehension of it. I do something in the physical world when I say, "This is mine," and other people then judge the claim-act to be good or bad (as well as true or not true).[56] We, in the full jointly attending meaning of the word, superimpose the abstract concepts GOOD or BAD on the idea of the act itself.[57] We do not merely apprehend the bare physicality of the vocalized act; we contemplate the claim-act for itself.[58]

What makes us want to contemplate our action for its own sake? We are a symbolic-thinking, motive-ascribing species, which means we abstract the thinking and feeling from which an action proceeds and then deem the action to fit or not fit with the order of the group's scheduling pattern. But that we do so is not in itself the contemplation of actions for their own sakes. Something more is required to elevate actions to the subject of attentive consideration for their own sakes. That something more is the primate impulse for sociality and the connatural pleasure of being in the company of conspecifics. A solitary mammal with symbolic thought—if such an animal could even acquire symbolic thought—would not self-direct its attention to the actions of others so as to become interested in them and consequently in its own actions for their own sakes. Adam Smith sums it up beautifully when he considers the counterfactual condition of *Homo sapiens*:[59]

---

[55] For the details in Kantian terms, see Arthur Ripstein (2009, p. 62, italics added): "First, . . . the only way that a person could have an entitlement to an external object of choice is if that person had the entitlement formally, because having means subject to your choice is prior to using them for any particular purpose. Second, . . . the exercise of acquired rights is consistent with the freedom of others, because it never deprives another person of something that person already has. *So anything less than fully private rights of property . . . would create a restriction on freedom that was illegitimate based on something other than freedom.*"

[56] See also Carol Rose (1985).

[57] See also Vernon Smith and Bart Wilson (2019, ch. 3).

[58] Samuel Alexander (1933).

[59] Adam Smith (1759, p. 110).

Were it possible that a human creature could grow up to manhood in some solitary place, without any communication with his own species, he could no more think of his own character, of the propriety or demerit of his own sentiments and conduct, of the beauty or deformity of his own mind, than of the beauty or deformity of his own face. . . . Bring him into society, and he is immediately provided with the mirror which he wanted before. It is placed in the countenance and behaviour of those he lives with, which always mark when they enter into, and when they disapprove of his sentiments; and it is here that he first views the propriety and impropriety of his own passions, the beauty and deformity of his own mind. . . . He will observe that mankind approve of some of [his passions], and are disgusted by others. He will be elevated in the one case, and cast down in the other; his desires and aversions, his joys and sorrows, . . . will now, therefore, interest him deeply, and often call upon his most attentive consideration.

If we ask, why do people consider stealing to be morally bad, the answer is that they disapprove because, through empathy with the victim, they feel the victim's and others' resentment from upsetting the expectations of the group's order, an order that is the product of generations of humankind. The moral reasoning of property is objective in that it is an external social formation independent of the thinking and feeling of any individual. Though the moral reasoning of property is not subjective, meaning that it doesn't exist only in the thoughts and feelings of the individual, it is not purely objective either. Every individual that submits to this external social formation personally commits an "I" to following the rules of property. Our moral reasoning, in general, and of property, in particular, is intersubjective.

Following the rule for the sake of following the rule is to submit to its authority, and authority is precisely the kind of the property-like concept that Ripstein invokes to explain how property works: "the problem to which exclusion is the solution is one of determining who has authority over what."[60] When a *domina* says, "This is mine" to anyone, including a bailee, she is invoking the concept of authority. Authority of someone over something is only half of the equation.[61] Why would the bailee accept that authority? Because he follows the rule of property for its own sake, but also because

---

[60] Arthur Ripstein (2013, p. 174).
[61] Notice the preposition *over* and compare "the authority of someone over something" with "something under the authority of someone." Aren't prepositions marvelous?

he learned from his mentors to follow the rule for its own sake. He learned from his mentor when he can and cannot say, "This is mine." A crucial step in forming an ethicizing animal is to accept someone as an authority on how to conduct oneself. The *domina* here and now is a composite eidolon of all the teachers the bailee accepted as a moral authority and from whom he subsequently learned the rules of property. Accepting someone as an authority is more than submitting to the dominance of the brawniest bully, which is merely yielding to the basic impulse to avoid pain. Accepting someone as an authority involves the teacher and the taught jointly attending to the same end: following the rule of property for its own sake.

The *In Rem* Theory Operates at the Macro-Level

The legal scholars Thomas Merrill and Henry Smith have spent over fifteen years blazing a new trail in the scholarship of property.[62] The trail is an economic one, marked with instrumental values and transaction costs. In their account, property "is the right to a thing, good against the world" and works the way it does because it "emerges from the process of solving the problem of how to serve use interests in a roughly cost-effective way."[63] If you and I dispute that a particular spear can serve both our interests simultaneously, the local adjudicator must decide whether any action can be taken to remove the spear from your physical control. The question in settling a dispute like this is not whether any action will be taken against you or me personally. Rather, the question is whether any action will be taken against the thing itself to transfer its physical control to me. The former is what the Romans called an *actio in personam* (action against the person) and the latter an *actio in rem* (action against the thing).[64] The cost-minimizing way of dealing with numerous disputes is not to sort through the web of personal social relations in each and every case, but to bring the thing itself to the foreground and decide by the dictates of custom who can and cannot say, "This spear is mine." Once only one of us can say, "This is mine," the other can say nothing upon being excluded from the thing.

---

[62] See, for example, Thomas Merrill and Henry Smith (2000, 2001, 2007).
[63] Thomas Merrill and Henry Smith (2001, p. 358) and Henry Smith (2012, p. 1704).
[64] George Long (1842). Here the Latin preposition *in* means "against" and takes the accusative (motion toward) case and not the ablative case. The action is imposed from the outside on the person or thing.

Smith argues that the reason property is the "law of things" is that it is informationally less costly to decide who can exclude others from using something than it is to specify the social relations between each person regarding the affirmative use of something. Such a conception stands in stark contrast to modern legal thought, which treats property as a bundle of rights, a thicket of social relations in which "things form the mere backdrop . . . and a largely dispensable one at that."[65] Merrill and Smith invert the modern picture of a bundle of rights.

When you come across a spear lying on the ground, you know that you cannot take physical control of it without needing to know anything about any social relations, such as who I am, how I relate to you, what I use it for, what I cannot use it for, who else might have an interest in using it, how they might relate to you, and so on. The complement of the set of things for which you can say by custom, "This is mine" is the set of things for which you cannot say, "This is mine." If you cannot say by custom, "This is mine," you do not have the authority to assert physical control over the spear. And because I can say, "This is mine," I have the authority to exclude you from using my spear. What everyone needs to know is that simple.

Smith lays bare the bundle-of-rights metaphor as an untenable theory of property.[66] He, like the philosopher David Schmidtz, takes the right to exclude as a core principle for how property works, though Smith prefers to think of exclusion as a strategy.[67] Exclusion, for Smith, is "a convenient starting point" for minimizing the information costs of delineating mine and thine, "a rough first cut—and only that—at serving the purposes of property."[68] It reduces the problem of how property works to two dimensions, "by defining the thing in an on/off manner."[69]

Smith places the physical thing front and center in his philosophy of property law, but the thing resides in Edwin Abbott's Flatland as the domain of a simple indicator function. Just as A Square cannot perceive A Sphere while in two dimensions, so an indicator function cannot account for the third dimension of moral abstract thought at work in property. The value judgments that support property are part and parcel of the concepts by which we practice the custom of property. At the very core of property is the moral claim "This

[65] Henry Smith (2012, p. 1691).
[66] See also the references in Henry Smith (2012) for more of his articles on this topic.
[67] David Schmidtz (2012).
[68] Ibid. (p. 1705).
[69] Ibid. (p. 1709).

is mine." To make a myriad of these moral claims compossible, rules and order emerge as embodiments of how, why, and to what extent people have property in things. Property operates in the three-dimensional Spaceland of human action regarding things. *She has property in the swan.* The perceiving person and the moral custom are as important as the thing itself.

While a right to exclude is indeed a core expectation in the practice of property, it is not the right place to look to understand the emergence of property, for it is difficult to see how exclusion becomes moral. What is the emotion, or more precisely, the mind-mastering passion, that compels commitment to exclusion and is distinct from and prior to resentment as a defense against loss?[70] A right to exclude is a secondary scheduling pattern in the practice of property because it is not proximate to the emergence of the primary scheduling pattern of property.[71] When unaligned expectations lead to a conflict, the open question is whether the conflict should be settled with a positive statement of a right to exclude or a negative statement of either (1) what harm did *not* occur or (2) what should *not* have been done to cause the harm.

To exclusion, Smith adds the information costs of governing the thing to complete his modular theory of property. Information costs are certainly a problem that shapes the custom of property, but predominantly at the macro-level of society, particularly when settling disputes between people from different communities. Smith's theory of property is fundamentally about governance, an account of current law and legal institutions in the great society. When courts must settle disputes with jurisdictions spanning many communities, Smith hypothesizes that judges are more likely to adopt a local custom into law the less demanding its information processing is for third parties whose schedules must adapt to the law.[72] Information costs, however, are ultimate problems of an evolving, open society, not the proximate problem from which property emerges at the micro-level of the individual or the meso-level of the community.

---

[70] See Vernon Smith and Bart Wilson (2019, ch. 2).

[71] See chapter 9.

[72] Henry Smith (2009). For case studies on the hypothesis in East Asia and Taiwan, see Yun-chien Chang and Henry Smith (2015).

7

Disputes Explicate How We Cognize Property, Out of Which We Discover a Clear General Rule

The Custom for Created Goods Is First-in-Hand

Among the property cases that every common law student learns is the land-mark English case of the chimney sweeper's boy and the jewel. The official re-cord of *Armory v. Delamirie* (1722) summarizes the dispute in one extended sentence:

> The plaintiff being a chimney sweeper's boy found a jewel and carried it to the defendant's shop (who was a goldsmith) to know what it was, and deliv-ered it into the hands of the apprentice, who under pretence of weighing it, took out the stones, and calling to the master to let him know it came to three halfpence, the master offered the boy the money, who refused to take it, and insisted to have the thing again; whereupon the apprentice delivered him back the socket without the stones.[1]

A gem set in a ring is not something found in the common state of nature. Someone created the composite object for a self-directed purpose and could by custom say, "This ring is mine." Moreover, every person (and only a person) who happens upon a jewel lying around in some soot re-cognizes it as a composite object, one meaning of which is that someone at some time ex-clusively, particularly, peculiarly, and properly had property in it. Sir Edward Coke calls it a "maxim of the Common Law . . . that property of all goods whatsoever must be in some person."[2] But when that someone is unknown or no longer around to say, "That ring is mine," what happens to the property in

---

[1] *Armory v. Delamirie* (1722, p. 664).
[2] Sir Edward Coke (1642, p. 167).

The Property Species. Bart J. Wilson. Oxford University Press (2020) © Oxford University Press.
DOI: 10.1093/oso/9780190936785.001.0001

it? Can someone else have property in the ring? If so, who becomes the next person to have property in the ring, and how does one acquire property in it?

Recall the work that words do on the physical world when I say, "This ring is not mine; it is yours." Vocalizing those eight simple combinations of sounds changes how you and I think about the physical world. If the ring was mine, but I am unknown or no longer around, how would Marc Armory and Paul de Lamerie cognize the ring?[3] I cannot affect how they think about the ring because I'm not around to make such a claim. As far as Armory and de Lamerie are concerned, any property in the ring has been suspended. To paraphrase the English comedian Eddie Izzard: no claim, no property. If you don't make a claim, then you can't have property in the thing.[4] The property could reappear if I reappear to claim, "This ring is mine," but until then, there is no property in the ring.

Until I do in fact return, or if there is no reason to expect that I may return, the prudent course of action is for someone else to enjoy the thing and claim it with MINE. The question is, who? Who can say about the ring, "This is mine," such that other people will think (1) that he has a good reason to say, "This ring is mine" and (2) that no one else can say, "That ring is mine"? Armory or de Lamerie? Because such a situation is not uncommon, humans have a scheduling pattern that constitutes a set of expectations about what people can do regarding such things; namely, the custom is that the first person to find the thing, especially to grasp the thing with his hands, can say, "This is mine." This is nearly how Lord Chief Justice John Pratt rules: "That the finder of a jewel, though he does not by such finding acquire an absolute property or ownership, yet he has such a property as will enable him to keep it against all but the rightful owner, and consequently may maintain trover."[5]

Of the two claimants, Pratt awards the ring to the one who first had it in hand and laid claim to it, though, as the legal anthropologist Simon Roberts notes, the chief justice's statement is somewhat imprecise. Whatever property Armory may have had in the ring, it did not bind "all but the rightful owner," but only all persons without a better claim to say, "This ring is mine."[6] Relative to de Lamerie, Armory first grasped the ring, but someone else relative to Armory could have also turned up later to say, "That ring is mine," and that person need not be the person who "rightfully" had property in the ring

[3] The court reporter misspelled the defendant's name.
[4] "Those are the rules . . . that I just made up!"
[5] *Armory v. Delamirie* (1722, p. 664).
[6] Simon Roberts (1982).

before it was lost.[7] What this means is that *Armory v. Delamirie* may not illustrate so starkly "the fact that a right to possess will accrue from the mere fact of possessing" nor that "the mere taking possession of a thing creates a right to its exclusive possession."[8] As the legal scholar Robin Hickey argues, albeit with a different line of reasoning, "the proposition that possession, without more, generates title" is a late nineteenth-century interpretation of the early eighteenth-century case.[9] *Armory* may simply illustrate the first-in-hand custom by which someone can say, "This is mine."[10]

For future reference, Table 7.1 summarizes the cases in this chapter in the order I present them, which is not chronological.

An episode of the British animated children's show *Bing* illustrates how mentors teach their mentees that created goods lying around are things generally about which someone can say, "This is mine." The eponymous Bing is a preschool bunny who learns how the world works from his guardian-babysitter, Flop. In the episode entitled "Not Yours," Bing and Flop visit Padget's corner shop to purchase groceries and a treat for dinner (carrot muffins, naturally).[11] While Flop pays for the groceries, Bing wanders around the store and discovers a box of lollipops on the far wall. He irresistibly but gingerly picks one up, twists open the wrapper, and with luscious anticipation takes a lick. When Flop calls Bing to leave, he discreetly slips the lolly into his pocket. As they walk down the street, a driver pulls over to ask for directions. Disinterested in the grown-ups' conversation, Bing turns his back and pulls out the lollipop. Flop returns to Bing's side and sees him licking the lollipop. The show delivers the bulk of the lesson in a simple fifty-second conversation:

Flop: Oh, what have you got there, Bing?
Bing: Mmm. A lollipop. It's strawbry.
Flop: Where did you get that from?
Bing: It's mine. I found it in the shop.

---

[7] Ibid. (p. 686).
[8] Peter Birks (2000, ¶ 4.40) and William Swadling (2008, p. 650).
[9] Robin Hickey (2015, p. 143).
[10] When the psychologists Ori Friedman and Karen Neary (2008) tell children a story about two kids who sequentially play with a ball and then ask them, "Whose ball is it?," two-year-olds respond with the first person in the story to play with the ball.
[11] *Bing* (2015).

Table 7.1. Who Has Property in X, Which Is in Y, if Neither Person Had Property in X before X Was Acquired?

Case[*]	X	Y	Did someone have property in Y? If not, who has firstness in X?
Armory v. Delamirie (1722)	jewel	unknown	No, Armory (first in hand)
Haslem v. Lockwood (1871)	manure in piles	public highway	No, Haslem (first in the creation)
Pierson v. Post (1805)	fox	public beach	No, Pierson (first in hand)
Swift v. **Gifford** (1872)	whale	open sea	No, Gifford (first to harpoon)
Durfee v. Jones (1877)[†]	$165	safe	Yes, Durfee
Bowen v. **Sullivan** (1878)[†]	two $50 bills	bale in facility	Yes, Bowen
Jackson v. **Steinberg** (1949)	several $100 bills	drawer in hotel room	Yes, Steinberg
Bridges v. Hawkesworth (1851)[†]	parcel	shop	Yes, Hawkesworth
McAvoy v. **Medina** (1866)	pocketbook	barbershop	Yes, Medina

[*] Bold indicates who the court ultimately ruled for.

[†] Wrongly decided on account of the general rule discovered in the chapter.

Flop: Ah, and did we pay for the lollipop?

Bing: Uh, no.

Flop: Oh, well . . . if we didn't pay for it, I'm afraid it must still belong to Padget.

Bing: Oh, can we keep it?

Flop: Well no, Bing, it's not yours.

Bing: Why not?

Flop: Well, if you take something without paying for it, that's not right, is it? It's called stealing.

Notice how naturally the show's writers assume a child will claim a thing first-in-hand. Preschool viewers identify with Bing, and no one teaches them to claim things they find as "Mine!" They do that all on their own. The lessons to be learned from their mentors are that created things like lollipops generally belong to someone and that taking something because "I want it" is not that same thing as being able to say, "It's mine."[12] What is right is that you must give in order to receive a created good.[13] One never forgets an actual lesson of what "Not Yours" means in the grocery store.

Especially If the Thing Is Your Creation

On the evening of April 6, 1869, Thomas Haslem instructed two employees to rake horse manure into piles off to the side of a public highway in Stamford, Connecticut.[14] After two hours of work, Haslem left the scene at 8:00 p.m., intending to cart the eighteen piles of manure to his land the next day. The next morning William Lockwood saw the manure and asked the borough warden if anyone had asked for permission to take the manure from the road. No one had asked. By noon Lockwood had removed the piles from the highway and applied them to his fields. Haslem asked to be compensated for the piles valued at $6 (roughly equivalent to $108 in 2017 U.S. dollars), but Lockwood refused.

---

[12] Neither J. E. Penner's nor Thomas Merrill and Henry Smith's theories of property in chapter 6 provide guidance on how people who do not have property in created goods (1) come to perceive such goods as something about which someone else can say, "This is mine" and (2) respect that property in them. We are taught by our mentors thusly. Karen Neary, Julia Van de Vondervoort, and Ori Friedman (2012) find that three-year-old children (1) expect created objects like toy trucks and forks to "belong to" someone and (2) do not expect naturally occurring things like leaves and seashells to "belong to" someone.

[13] Moreover, you must give something that the other person wants. When Flop and Bing return to the store, Bing offers to give Padget the carrot muffin in their wagon, but Padget explains that Flop has just paid for the lolly. Padget has that which she wants in exchange for the lolly.

[14] *Haslem v. Lockwood* (1871).

The trial court ruled in favor of Lockwood, saying that "the facts proved the plaintiff had not made out a sufficient interest in, or right of possession to," the piles of manure. The Connecticut Supreme Court, however, found in *Haslem v. Lockwood* (1871) that the lower court had erred. When the manure fell from the horses and the riders continued on their way, the manure is considered to be abandoned and Haslem should have been allowed a reasonable amount of time to return and cart away the manure.

There is no property in manure abandoned along a public road. When Haslem's employees raked the manure into piles, however, they created something no longer in the common state placed in nature. Manure doesn't fall in large tidy heaps. By ancient custom Haslem could thereby say, "These piles are mine." No one was present when Lockwood came by the unguarded, neat, and convenient piles, and like an American red squirrel, he made off with his adventitious find. Red squirrels, however, can't cognize external objects as creations, nor can they jointly attend to the heaper's end in creating the piles of manure. But humans like Lockwood and *Bing*'s preschool viewers can. By working so quickly, including a trip to the warden and back, Lockwood knew that the scheduling pattern of people who heap eighteen piles of manure for two hours included returning to the scene to collect them.[15] Arguing, as Lockwood did, that Haslem did not have property in the manure until it was removed from the public road was obviously self-serving. John Locke's barrage of questions seems appropriate here, for the moment of removal from the road is an arbitrary intermediate point in collecting the manure from the highway and depositing it on your field. The moment we create an object, it is first-in-hand (so to speak in the case of a pile of manure). When we create an object, we create the property in the object, provided, of course, that the creating act fits with the system of customs operating in the background.

But Also If the Thing Is in the Common State Placed by Nature

If there is a property case more widely discussed in law schools and legal scholarship than *Armory v. Delamirie*, it is the New York case of the fox that got away until it didn't, or *Pierson v. Post* (1805). Sometime between 1800 and 1803, Lodowick Post wounded a fox and was pursuing it on an unowned

---

[15] While obvious, it is not irrelevant to the custom that Lockwood knew that the piles wouldn't be exerting any natural liberty that day.

Long Island beach when Jesse Pierson, knowing that Post was in pursuit but without a clear line of sight, interloped, killed the fox, and took it with his very hands.[16] Two hundred years later, two undergraduates uncannily recreated the scene in my laboratory experiment in chapter 4 involving free-roving Atari-like circles instead of foxes.[17] Their verbal exchange went like this, with the litigants' names substituted for the experimental IDs:

Post: omg [Pierson]
Post: u saw i had that one
Post: [Pierson]
Post: that was mine
Pierson: u lost it so i have to get it

Post resented the outcome and sued Pierson. The justice of the peace ruled for Post, who argued that he was in hot pursuit with his hounds. By Locke's standard, he had mixed his labor with that fox and thought that he could therefore say, "That fox is mine." Moreover, Pierson was being just plain rude, disappointing him of what he expected. Pierson, though, thought another custom, also practiced from time immemorial, applied in this case: Only upon taking a wild animal's natural liberty by killing or trapping it can someone say, "This fox is mine." The court had to decide what the rule of property is for *ferae naturae* that lie free for any taker with a good line of sight, identifiable hot pursuit or first to have the varmint in hand.[18] In a majority opinion that went out of its way to cite Blackstone, Pufendorf, Grotius, and Justinian I, the New York Supreme Court reversed the decision and awarded the fox to Pierson.

Unlike a created composite object, a wild animal on a public beach is in the common state placed in nature. No one has property in a fox as it freely roams its home range. Moreover, its scheduling pattern regarding humans calls for evading anyone who attempts to put property via a bullet in it. Out of this additional cost of acquiring property in a thing emerged another of the uncountable customs that qualifies the Lockean custom of when someone can say, "This varmint is mine." Any labor is insufficient, and in particular, the pursuit of a fox is insufficient. Until you have actual physical control of the wild animal, you do not have property in it. When hunting wild animals

---

[16] Bethany Berger (2006).
[17] Bart Wilson, Taylor Jaworski, Karl Schurter, and Andrew Smyth (2012).
[18] Foxes were pests in the early nineteenth century and not the graceful creatures they are today.

on public land, the first person to deprive the animal of its natural liberty is the person who can say, "This animal is mine."

The participants in the open sea experiment platform in chapter 4 similarly have to settle on a rule of capture. They, however, had no recourse to courts to decide their dispute for them. My coauthors and I find that if civil-minded participants settle on a rule, they readily adopt the fast-fish-loose-fish rule with slow, easy-to-catch right whales (so named because they are the right whale to hunt).[19] We, however, do not replicably observe iron-holds-the-whale, even when the prey switched from right to sperm whales within a session. Mixing one's labor with pursuit plus, in the case of the experiment, sinking the cost of a colored line do not have the same regularizing effect. Why might that be? Adam Smith explains that "to be deprived of that which we are possessed of, is a greater evil than to be disappointed of what we have only the expectation."[20] The difference is that having a circle in hand creates positive harm when it is ripped from the hand, and Post's disappointment of expectations is just that, a disappointment. The former is emotionally hotter and hence easier to mutually empathize with when agreeing to a rule.

That's not to say that Post cannot get emotionally hot with disappointed expectations. The rumor is that the parties each spent £1,000 in 1805 on lawyer fees (a tidy fortune at the time).[21] When new circumstances of time and place bring to the foreground a conflict in expectations, "the task of rules of [property] can only thus be to tell people which expectations they can count on and which not" going forward.[22] The court decided that someone can say, "That fox is mine" once he has it in hand and such a clear rule prevents more confusion. I would add that the clarity of the rule coincides with how we cognize property, for once the prey is in hand it becomes more closely connected with the "I" in a body.

The Custom May Evolve to First-to-Work-Upon, If Costs Are High

Sometime in the mid-nineteenth century, the crew of the American whaling ship *Rainbow*, managed by Gifford, harpooned a finback whale in the Sea

---

[19] Bart Wilson, Taylor Jaworski, Karl Schurter, and Andrew Smyth (2012).
[20] Adam Smith (1759, p. 84).
[21] Angela Fernandez (2009).
[22] Friedrich Hayek (1973, p. 102).

of Okhotsk, located east of Siberia and north of Japan.[23] The line was originally attached to the ship, but somehow the whale escaped with the iron and the line still fastened in it. Gifford continued to pursue the whale, but the crew of the *Hercules*, owned by Swift, did not see the *Rainbow* in pursuit. The *Hercules* shot, killed, and captured the whale but had not yet cut into it when Gifford appeared on the scene. The two ships, both based out of the whaling capital of New Bedford, Massachusetts, established that one of Gifford's harpoons was indeed in the whale. Following the American whaling custom of iron-holds-the-whale, Swift then relinquished the physical control of the whale to Gifford.[24] The iron-holds-the-whale custom was that as long as a ship remained in pursuit of a harpooned whale, the pursuer maintained property in the whale provided the original marked harpoon remained in the whale and the claim was made before the subsequent ship had begun rendering the whale.

Upon returning home, Swift sued Gifford to reclaim the whale. Citing *Pierson v. Post*, among other cases, he argued "that the rule of law is, that wild animals become property only when fully and actually taken into possession." Moreover, the iron-holds-the-whale custom was "in contravention of this rule of law," "not universal," and "unreasonable." While Swift did not make this argument, eighteenth-century British whalers (who hunted right whales off the coast of Greenland) adhered to fast-fish-loose-fish.[25] If a harpooned whale was held fast to the ship, the harpooner maintained property in the whale. But if, for whatever reason, the ship no longer maintained its attachment to the whale, the loose fish was fair game for any other ship. The whale hunters of Lamalera have been using the same rule in Indonesia for hundreds of years.[26]

The court held in *Swift v. Gifford* (1872) that the iron-holds-the-whale custom was reasonable and applicable to this dispute. The different decisions in *Pierson v. Post* and *Swift v. Gifford* illustrate the critical importance of scheduling patterns in understanding how property works. In Coke's language of property ("She has property in the swan"), the relationships between the hunters and property, and the prey and property both loom large. There's more at play than the relationship between the hunters and their prey than the physical facts of who delivered the mortal blow and assumed physical

---

[23] *Swift v. Gifford* (1872).
[24] Robert Ellickson (1989).
[25] Ibid.
[26] Will Millard (2015).

control of the animal. Pierson has property in the fox because over the course of human history the ancient custom of fast-varmint-loose-varmint emerged to reduce the transaction costs of hunting land mammals. The custom of projectile-holds-the-varmint or pursuit-holds-the-varmint could have emerged, but neither did because they didn't fit the scheduling patterns of the hunters, their prey, and the hunters regarding their prey. American whalers inherited the English rule of first-fish-loose-fish, but when it didn't fit the scheduling patterns of their new prey, they increasingly adopted a new custom that reduced the transaction costs of hunting a mammal that was far too large and too far at sea for humans to ever hunt in ancient times.[27] Gifford has property in the whale because humans, armed with some new technology, adapted a new scheduling pattern to a new kind of prey.

A feature common to all these cases is that the contextual custom contains an element of firstness, first in hand (created or not) or first worked upon with intent to finish the job. Why is firstness important? Because another feature common to all these cases is that the thing in question is itself not contained in something about which someone can say, "This is mine." Except for *Armory*, which is silent on the issue, the person acquires property in the thing in a location about which no one can say, "This space is mine." How important is firstness when the thing in question is contained in something about which someone can say, "This is mine"? For judges, it's rather important, if not decisive; for us, it's immaterial, literally and figuratively.

Firstness Doesn't Matter If Location Priorly Matters

In April 1874, Herbert Durfee purchased an old safe and directed an agent to resell it. The agent offered to sell the safe to Orrin Jones, but Jones declined. The agent then left the safe with Jones, "authorizing him to keep his books in it until it was sold or reclaimed."[28] Jones found a roll of banknotes worth $165 in the lining of the inside wall of the safe, informed the agent of the money he had found, and offered to give the money to the agent to give to Durfee. The agent said that the money was not his or Durfee's and advised Jones to

---

[27] Robert Ellickson (1989). See also Bart Wilson, Taylor Jaworski, Karl Schurter, and Andrew Smyth (2012), who document how changing prey from "right whales" to "sperm whales" in a laboratory experiment increases the conflict among virtual whalers who endogenously follow a fast-fish-loose-fish rule.

[28] *Durfee v. Jones* (1877).

deposit the funds, "drawing interest until the rightful owner appeared."[29] When Durfee learned about the money from his agent, he first asked for the money from Jones, and when Jones refused him, Durfee "demanded the return of the safe and its contents, precisely as they existed when placed in [Jones's] hands. [Jones] promptly gave up the safe, but retained the money."[30]

Who has property in the banknotes found inside the wall of the safe? The bailee who finds the money in the walls of the safe or the bailor who has property in the safe itself? The Rhode Island Supreme Court ruled in *Durfee v. Jones* (1877) that "the general rule undoubtedly is, that the finder of lost property is entitled to it as against all the world except the real owner, and that ordinarily the place where it is found does not make any difference."[31]

I have my doubts. First, the place where one finds swans and foxes ordinarily matters. Lady Young has property in the swans . . . in her waters. The queen has property in the swans . . . in her waters. Post would have property in the fox had it been . . . in his woods. Second, if the court has *Armory* in mind, the location where Armory found the ring is unstated and irrelevant because the case was not between Armory and the owner of the building in which the ring was found.

By appending that location does not matter, the court tacitly acknowledges in *Durfee* that no custom stands independent of other customs, and the custom of first-in-hand for lost items is no different. Judges may accept that location does not matter as a matter of law, but everyday people do not. The psychologists Peter DeScioli and Rachel Karpoff asked fifty-nine people to read a synopsis of the *Durfee* case and then report who they thought owned the item. Forty-seven people (80 percent) chose Durfee, citing what? The location of the money *in* the safe.[32] It does not matter that the money was lost. It does not matter that Durfee was unaware of the money in the safe. And it does not matter that the money was never "in the protection of the safe as *his* safe, or so as to affect him with any responsibility for them."[33] If Durfee has property in the safe—not "property," the physical object, but property, the universal and uniquely human custom by which Durfee can say, "This safe is mine"—then Durfee has property in the money in the safe. Where the safe goes, so goes the property, and so goes the money in the lining. Because the

---

[29] Ibid.
[30] Ibid.
[31] Ibid.
[32] Peter DeScioli and Rachel Karpoff (2015).
[33] *Durfee v. Jones* (1877).

safe contains both the property and the money, we cognize Durfee as having property in the money in the safe.[34]

If You Have Property in *Y* and *X* Is in *Y*, You Have Property in *X* in *Y*

One year later *Durfee* serves as "the case more nearly in point than any other which has fallen under our observation," which is to say that Durfee's equivalent, Abner T. Bowen, also didn't think that first-in-hand applies to something found inside something he has property in, triply so.[35] Bowen and his partners owned a paper mill in Carroll County, Indiana, and had purchased a bale of rags and paper in Kansas to be sorted in their facility near Delphi. In May 1876, sixteen-year-old Ellen Quinn went to the paper mill in which her guardian and half-sister Anna Sullivan worked. (The litigants disputed whether Quinn also worked at the mill at the time of the incident.) Among the paper and rags loose and scattered on the floor, Quinn found a clean unmarked envelope inside of which were two $50 bills (roughly equivalent to $2,249 in 2017 U.S. dollars). She asked the floor supervisor to determine if the money was real and then to return it. The supervisor took the money to Bowen, who confirmed it was genuine. When Quinn asked for the money back from Bowen, he refused and instead offered her $10.

Who has property in the banknotes found in an envelope from inside a bale of paper and rags, the person who finds the money in the envelope or the person who has property in the bale inside his mill? The first case that the Indiana Supreme Court cites in *Bowen v. Sullivan* (1878) is *Armory v. Delamirie*:

> Ever since the case of *Armory v. Delamirie,* 1 Strange, 505, in which a chimney-sweeper's boy, having found a jewel, left it with a goldsmith to ascertain what it was, was held entitled to recover it, the law has been steady and uniform that the finder of lost property has a right to retain it against all persons except the true owner.[36]

---

[34] Note how this also applies to the *Haslem* case. Haslem does not have property in manure strewn along road. However, if Haslem, by custom, has property in the pile he creates, then he has property in the manure (contained) in the pile. Yes, the pile literally is manure, and the safe is not literally the money, but all abstract thought is metaphor, not literality. See Steven Pinker (2007).

[35] *Bowen v. Sullivan* (1878).

[36] Ibid.

This is where Lord Chief Justice Pratt's imprecise statement becomes consequential. Bowen is not the "true owner," but that's neither here nor there. The question is whether Bowen or Quinn has a better claim to say, "This money is mine." *Armory* may affirm the first-in-hand custom for subsequent graspers of the one ring, but that does not make the custom independent of context to rule all subsequent cases as precedent.

That location is irrelevant in *Armory* does not make location irrelevant here (or everywhere), which is why the Indiana Supreme Court considers *Durfee* to be the case more nearly in point. If the place where something is found ordinarily does not make any difference, then the prior court can hold "that, as the purchase was of the safe, not the safe and its contents, the money was not embraced in the purchase."[37] But wait. Didn't Bowen "purchas[e] the envelope containing the bills by weight [thereby] purchas[ing] the bank-bills in question"?[38] Also, aren't bills made of paper? To which the court replied, in effect, so what? "Their existence was unknown when the envelope was purchased, and their weight was so infinitesimally small, compared with their value, that we do not concur in this proposition. It is unreasonable."[39]

If Bowen has property in the bale in his mill, then Bowen has property in the money in the envelope in the bale in his mill. Where the bale goes, so goes the property, and so goes the money in the envelope. Not only does it not matter that Bowen was unaware of the money in the bale, but it also adds but another fact for a judge and jury to decide. Not only does it not matter that the money was lost, but it also adds but another fact for a judge and jury to divine. And not only does it not matter that the weight of the money is infinitesimally small, but it will also become but another fact for a future court to determine what is and is not reasonably small.[40] Because we cognize property as being contained in something with a well-defined boundary, an interior, and an exterior, perhaps we can use such clear physical demarcations to clarify and simplify the general rule of who can say, "This is mine." If person A has property in a thing Y and another thing X is in Y, then A has property in X in Y. Notice that the proposition nicely encapsulates the principle of accession in chattels like cattle. If I have property in a pregnant cow, then I too have property in the calf before and after its birth.

---

[37] Ibid.
[38] Ibid.
[39] Ibid.
[40] *Durfee v. Jones* (1877).

Such a general abstract rule questions the conclusions that Jeremy Waldron and Robert Nozick draw in their objections to Locke's labor mixing metaphor. Waldron's analogy goes like this:

> Suppose there is a vat of wet cement lying about which belongs to nobody in particular, and I drop my ham sandwich into it. Before I retrieve the sandwich, the cement hardens into a concrete block. (Or, better still: as in Locke's case, the cement is lying about and I *intend* to drop my sandwich into it, not wanting to retrieve it.) Can I now claim the concrete block in order to protect my entitlement to the sandwich? Can I object, when someone takes the block out of my control, that he is violating my entitlement to the sandwich?[41]

First, I might note, vats of wet cement are created goods and generally don't lie about without someone who can say, "This is mine." But this is a thought experiment; facts of the natural world do not necessarily apply. So let's suppose that a vat of wet cement exists in the common state of nature, and no one can say, "This vat of cement is mine." After dropping my sandwich into the vat, can I say, "This vat is mine" because I can say, "That sandwich is mine"? No, such an act does not make the vat mine. Waldron's conclusion that it does not is correct, but not because "the labour is to all intents and purposes lost in the object."[42] The conclusion follows because the property in the sandwich doesn't extend *out* into the cement. The rule isn't whatever touches what is mine is mine, for if it were, the world would be awash in conflicting claims. The general abstract rule is, if I have property in Y and X is in Y, then I have property in X in Y.

Nozick's analogy would, at first blush, appear to remedy such a problem because when I pour radioactive tomato juice, by design it would "mingle evenly throughout the sea."[43] But do our minds perceive the ocean as a bounded container? I think not. Oceans don't have well-defined boundaries. Locke's examples of property work, not because of labor mixing per se, but because his examples are bounded containers. If people went around eye-dropping food coloring into vials of water (found in the common state of nature, of course), the boundaries of the vial would indeed demarcate the limits to which someone could say, "This water is mine," and, moreover, people could know that what they say is true. Locke's labor mixing metaphor

---

[41] Jeremy Waldron (1983, p. 43, original italics).
[42] Ibid. (p. 43).
[43] Robert Nozick (1974, p. 175).

is a crude way of intuiting that when we work on something, by custom our minds emphysicalize property as being contained in the thing.

The General Rule Is That Simple

Such a rule, if courts were to adopt it, would make cases like *Jackson v. Steinberg* (1949) easier to decide. Laura Jackson worked as a chambermaid for Karl Steinberg doing business as Arthur Hotel in Oregon. In the course of her duties, she found several $100 bills "concealed carefully under [a] paper lining of [a] dresser drawer in [a] guest room."[44] When Steinberg was unable to find the original owner, Jackson asked Steinberg to return the money to her, but he refused.

Jackson argued that the money should be considered treasure trove. If something is treasure trove, then by another ancient custom someone who does not have property in the place where the treasure is found can say, "This treasure is mine." *The American and English Encyclopedia of Law* explains that "treasure trove, under law, must be hidden or concealed so long as to indicate that its owner, in all probability, is dead or unknown."[45] This was important to Jackson's appeal to the Oregon Supreme Court because "there is no question" the scheduling pattern/duty of hotel cleaning staff is "to seek for and find valuable property left behind in guest rooms by guests, and to deliver such property to [Steinberg]."[46] Determining whether this found money is treasure trove, which is straightforwardly not the case here, could easily be a nontrivial fact to discern. What does it mean to be hidden or concealed? How long is so long? What is the probability that the owner is dead or unknown? Instead of asking and answering a barrage of questions, the sole question to ask is, who has property in the drawer in the hotel in which the money was found? Steinberg or Jackson? The end. Next case. Or better, there's no case to begin with because the rule is that clear to avoid litigation altogether.

The other key feature of this case for the court to determine was whether the money was lost or mislaid, because as every first-year law student in the United States learns, the subtle difference matters. If the money was mislaid, precedent would award the money to Steinberg. But if the money was lost, it would go to Jackson. The origins of this split hair lie in our last two cases, which precede all of the aforementioned cases but *Armory* and *Pierson*.

---

[44] *Jackson v. Steinberg* (1949).
[45] Charles Williams (1894, p. 537).
[46] *Jackson v. Steinberg* (1949).

A Difficult Case Indicates How to Test the General Rule

In October 1847, Bridges called on, as the British say, the shop of Messrs. Byfield & Hawkesworth.[47] As he was leaving, he found a small parcel on the floor, which he opened up with the attending clerk. Inside was £65 (approximately $6,926 in 2017 U.S. dollars). Bridges gave the money to Hawkesworth to keep until the owner claimed it. After three years elapsed, during which time Hawkesworth advertised in *The Times* that the banknotes had been found, no one claimed the money. Bridges then requested the money be returned to him, which Hawkesworth refused.

Who has property in the banknotes found in the parcel in the shop? The shopkeeper who has property in the shop or the customer who found the parcel in the shop? The County Court of Westminster ruled for Hawkesworth, but Bridges appealed to the Court of the Queen's Bench, who reversed the decision. As we shall see, *Bridges v. Hawkesworth* (1851) is a difficult case that demonstrates the limits of the synthesis and analysis in this book. It is precisely because of such limits, however, that *Bridges* is, with hindsight, a poor case to serve as precedent for the aforementioned cases that would follow and appeal to it.

The Queen's Bench first reiterates the rule espoused in *Armory*:

> The general right of the finder to any article which has been lost, as against all the world, except the true owner, was established in the case of *Armory v. Delamirie*, which has never been disputed. *This right would clearly have accrued to the plaintiff had the notes been picked up by him outside the shop of the defendant*" (italics added).[48]

The case, moreover,

> resolves itself into the single point on which it appears that the learned judge decided it, namely, whether the circumstance of the notes being found inside the defendant's shop gives him, the defendant, the right to have them as against the plaintiff, who found them. There is no authority in our law to be found directly on point.[49]

---

[47] *Bridges v. Hawkesworth* (1851).
[48] Ibid.
[49] Ibid.

The court also noted that Hawkesworth was not aware of the parcel and hence, unlike an innkeeper, "the notes were never in the custody of the defendant, nor within the protection of his house." Nor were the notes intentionally placed with Hawkesworth. They appeared to be lost.

> We find, therefore, no circumstances in this case to take it out of the general rule of law, that the finder of a lost article is entitled to it as against all persons except the real owner, and we think that that rule must prevail, and that the learned judge was mistaken in holding that the place in which they were found makes any legal difference.[50]

Hawkesworth disputed *Armory* precisely on the basis that the parcel was found *in* his store. As the court specifically noted, if Bridges had picked up the parcel outside the shop, Hawkesworth clearly could not say, "Those notes are mine." The court appears to question why a mere few yards should matter. A mere few yards matter decisively in the *Case of the Swans*, which has the added difficulty that the object in question exercises natural liberty concerning the border in question. As noted in chapter 5, the mind does the marvelous work of instantaneously replacing the queen's notion of MINE with Lady Young's whether or not Lady Young knows a swan is in her waters or not. The Keeper of the Queen's Swans cannot find swans in Lady Young's private waters precisely because the boundary matters.

So why does the boundary *not* matter for the Queen's Bench but matter for the learned judge of the county court? Perhaps because the spatial container that the context conveys to the mind is less clear, less defined for the judges of the Queen's Bench than for the learned judge. If one perceives the parcel as located on a regularly traversed thoroughfare, more akin to a Long Island beach or Stamford, Connecticut, highway, then first-in-hand would appear to be the controlling custom. But if one perceives the parcel as contained within the well-defined boundaries of the shop, one would so qualify the first-in-hand custom.

DeScioli and Karpoff find that people agree with the Queen's Bench. Of the sixty people who read the *Bridges v. Hawkesworth* scenario, forty-five (75 percent) side with Bridges.[51] And therein lies the problem with *Bridges* setting a precedent for Jones, Quinn/Sullivan, Jackson, and their respective

---

[50] Ibid.
[51] Peter DeScioli and Rachel Karpoff (2015).

courts to argue that location is plainly irrelevant to where the item is found. The safe, the bale in the mill, and the drawer in the hotel are more readily perceived as contextually containing property and the thing in question than a path toward the exit of a store.

This may then explain why the original judge in *McAvoy v. Medina* went out of his way to justify awarding the found item to the proprietor (John Medina) and not the customer-finder (David McAvoy), thereby annoying American law students ever since with the fine distinction of lost versus mislaid items.[52] In this case, the plaintiff customer found a pocketbook on a table in the defendant's barbershop.

The Massachusetts Supreme Judicial Court opens its reasoning in *McAvoy* citing *Bridges*, bound by "the settled law that the finder of lost property has a valid claim to the same against all the world except the true owner, generally that the place in which it is found creates no exception to this rule."[53] It would seem quite easy for the judge in *McAvoy* to apply *Bridges* and be done with the case, but the physical context doesn't have the same feel. The pocketbook was not on the ground on a path on the way to an exit (note the prepositions), but on a table inside the barbershop. The in-ness is more salient for a table in a shop than a path on the floor of a shop. But the boundary in *Bridges* wasn't modestly ruled as a gray area but as explicitly irrelevant. So to get out from underneath of *Bridges*, the judge in *McAvoy* had to differentiate the case, not on the stark physical facts of the location, but on the intentions of the unknown person who lost the pocketbook as divined from the physical facts of the location. And so, the pocketbook is not "to be treated as lost property in that sense in which a finder has a valid claim to hold the same until called for by the true owner," but rather as mislaid, a term not used by the supreme court but one that would be subsequently and broadly adopted to distinguish *McAvoy* from *Bridges*.

McAvoy consequently raises the possibility to postdict how DeScioli and Karpoff's volunteers would decide this case. If, as I argue, there is more in-ness, more defined containment of the item in *McAvoy* than *Bridges*, then a higher percentage of people would choose Medina than Hawkesworth, which is 25 percent and statistically less likely than a flip of a coin. Furthermore, if there is less in-ness, less defined containment of the item in *McAvoy* than in *Durfee*, then we would also postdict that fewer people would side with Medina

---

[52] *McAvoy v. Medina* (1866).
[53] Ibid.

than Durfee, which is 80 percent and statistically more likely than a flip of a coin. What do we find? Voilà! The results fall neatly in between. Of the fifty-nine people surveyed, twenty-six (44 percent) choose Medina, which is statistically not different from flipping a coin.[54] As Ellickson says of the evidence in favor of his whaling norm hypothesis, "any ex post explanation risks being too pat, and this one is no exception."[55] But it does lead us to the following testable proposition for an ex ante laboratory experiment.[56] The more defined the containment of X in Y, the more people will adhere to the proposition that if A has property in Y and X is in Y, then A has property in X in Y.

In an alternate timeline if *Durfee* and *McAvoy* with clearer boundaries had preceded *Bridges*, we might have precedents that more closely coincide with how ordinary people cognize property. And even if the Queen's Bench had upheld the lower court in *Bridges*, despite conflicting with how a supermajority of people think about that case, we would still have a clearer general rule consistent with how our species cognizes the meaning of the custom.

The law and economics reader will judge the abstract rule by its incentives to generate value in excess of the costs forgone. By awarding X to the person who has property in Y, it looks as if the rule disincentivizes finders from bringing lost items to the light of day, to say nothing of decreasing the chances of returning X to the prior person who can say, "It's mine." The goodness of the finder's heart is not enough of an incentive, it is supposed, to bend over and pick up something on the floor or to stretch out an arm and pick up something on the counter. Why look behind the wall of a safe or under the lining of a dresser drawer if you don't have property in the safe or dresser to begin with? The answer doesn't have to be all or nothing. We can propose to split the baby and not come off as a monster. Bowen's immediate response was to offer Quinn 10 percent of the money in the envelope. The custom of New England whalers was to pay a finder's fee to the person who found a dead whale on the beach (with an identifying mark on the bomb-lance).[57] Sounds like a good, neighborly incentivizing addition to the general rule as part of the custom of settling disputes.

---

[54] Peter DeScioli and Rachel Karpoff (2015).
[55] Robert Ellickson (1989, p. 95).
[56] See also Bart Wilson, Taylor Jaworski, Karl Schurter, and Andrew Smyth (2012).
[57] Robert Ellickson (1989, p. 202).

8

The Results of a Test Are Agreeable
to the Prediction

The best part about being an experimental economist, the moment that
carries me through the sometimes years-long process of writing and publishing a journal article, is the nervous feeling I get when I look through
the one-way glass and I have no idea what the participants are going to do.
Sure, I have formal hypotheses and some educated guesses about what could
happen, but when it comes down to it, I would not bet a dollar on what
the participants will actually do in the first few sessions. Even though I have
been running laboratory experiments for twenty-five years, I never feel
like I know what will come next. Such a feeling is simultaneously thrilling
and nerve-wracking. What will the story be for this paper? Or will there
even be a story to tell? The one thing I have learned from nearly every economic experiment I have conducted is that whatever expectations I may
have about the project, I am inevitably surprised about something and almost as surely wrong about something else. Designing and conducting economic experiments is, as Ludwig Wittgenstein says of philosophy, "really
more a working on oneself. On one's own interpretation. On one's way of
seeing things. (And what one expects of them)."[1] When I build a virtual economic terrarium, I choose every detail of it to learn something particular
about my fellow human beings, and the way I learn is by comparing what the
participants actually do to what I expected of them and how I saw the world
before the experiment.

As I write (September 2018), I have conducted three of the four treatment
conditions that I originally planned to report in this chapter. I begin running the fourth, and hopefully final, treatment in three days. I say "hopefully" because I thought the third treatment would wrap up the story, but it
turns out the participants did not see their task as I saw it when I designed the

---

[1] Ludwig Wittgenstein (1980, p. 16e).

The Property Species. Bart J. Wilson. Oxford University Press (2020) © Oxford University Press.
DOI: 10.1093/oso/9780190936785.001.0001

experiment. So we shall see if the fourth treatment is indeed a suitable place to close this first test of our expectations.

Sometimes the starting point for designing a new experiment is obvious. For the homestead experiment in the prologue and chapter 4, it was the simple two-person, two-good exchange economy that every student of intermediate microeconomics learns.[2] One lesson we learned from designing that open-ended experiment, not grounded in anything more in the world than a standard textbook model, is that it is difficult to construct solutions to solve other people's problems.[3] Chaos ruled the unstable disconnections between people and things in our virtual world, and every tool we came up with only made their problems worse. As a direct result, one reason I was initially interested in testing whaling norms in the open sea experiment of chapter 4 was that we at least had history as a target for identifying success in a different experimental platform. If we couldn't replicate a fast-fish-loose-fish rule of capture, then we knew our experimental economic history was missing something important from the world.[4]

For this project, the disputes in chapter 7 seem like a natural point of departure. See Table 8.1 for a summary list of the cases. Not only do court cases provide specific examples of the connections people make between themselves and things, but also even more relevant to an empirical test is that the litigants have built-in conflicting expectations—that is, competing hypotheses—about how property should work in such circumstances. A second reason for designing an experiment around one of the court cases is that we have some prior findings from a psychology survey to guide our expectations of the test.[5] As an economist, however, and an experimental economist to boot, I have been trained, or maybe it is in my genes, to be wary of the responses people give for no or trivial amounts of money. So while I report with gusto the results of Peter Descioli and Rachel Karpoff in chapter 7, deep down I felt I needed something more to hang my hat on than the responses of fifty-nine people who were paid a mere 20 cents to

---

[2] Google Edgeworth box.
[3] Erik Kimbrough, Vernon Smith, and Bart Wilson (2010).
[4] Bart Wilson, Taylor Jaworski, Karl Schurter, and Andrew Smyth (2012, pp. 637–639, 653).
[5] Peter DeScioli and Rachel Karpoff (2015).

Table 8.1. Who Has Property in *X*, Which Is in *Y*, if Neither Person Had Property in *X* before *X* Was Acquired?

Case[*]	*X*	*Y*	Did someone have property in *Y*? If not, who has firstness in *X*?
Queen Elizabeth v. Young (1592)	swans	public river	Yes, Queen Elizabeth
Armory v. Delamirie (1722)	jewel	unknown	No, Armory (first in hand)
Pierson v. Post (1805)	fox	public beach	No, Pierson (first in hand)
Bridges v. Hawkesworth (1851)	parcel	shop	Yes, Hawkesworth
McAvoy v. **Medina** (1866)	pocketbook	barbershop	Yes, Medina
Haslem v. Lockwood (1871)	manure in piles	public highway	No, Haslem (first in the creation)
Swift v. **Gifford** (1872)	whale	open sea	No, Gifford (first to harpoon)
Durfee v. **Jones** (1877)	$165	safe	Yes, Durfee
Bowen v. **Sullivan** (1878)	two $50 bills	bale in facility	Yes, Bowen
Jackson v. **Steinberg** (1949)	several $100 bills	drawer in hotel room	Yes, Steinberg

[*] Bold indicates who the court ultimately ruled for.

answer a simple question: Durfee or Jones? McAvoy or Medina? Bridges or Hawkesworth?

Another reason to reexamine the psychology study is that the authors don't probe the counterfactual. They don't construct hypothetical cases to so-licit what could have been the responses of their participants if conditions of the actual case had been different. They ask what is, but not what is not the case. Durfee or Jones, if Jones owned the safe purchased from Durfee? Counterfactual conditionals are one way to establish social scientific causes. As improbable as it might seem that people would still choose Durfee if Jones owned the safe, we can't find an unexpected result if we don't conduct the test.

The next major decision is, which case? As I have already alluded, *Durfee v. Jones* seems like the obvious choice. The in-ness of finding money inside a wall inside a safe fits just too nicely with my explanation of how humans cog-nize property. If I build an experiment around *Durfee* and the participants routinely fail to pick out Durfee as the person who can say, "This money is mine," all of our expectations about the case itself and the choices in de-signing the experiment are up for interrogation. If the participants do indeed robustly award the item to Durfee, then the plan is to systematically alter the conditions of the experiment so as to reverse the result. If the results fall in the middle, then everything is up for reconsideration.

When researchers simply ask you to choose who you think should get the money found in the safe, there are no consequences in the world. There are no real live Durfees or Joneses to disappoint, and no reason to ponder whether you have indeed made the right choice to disappoint this person or the other. We also do not know how likely it is that people in the positions of Durfee and Jones would find themselves in a dispute over the money. Maybe *Durfee v. Jones* is a special case. Maybe most Durfees and most Joneses would never dispute the other's claim to the money.

Such considerations guide the design of the experiment. In the course of the session, two people—let's call them Red and Blue—unexpectedly find themselves in a position motivated by *Durfee*. Each is asked whether they claim a found item. Three other people, the Observers, who are watching the entire session, are tasked, after the item is found, with deciding whether the item is Red's or Blue's. A majority of the three Observers decides who receives the item worth $25 (cash) without discussion or knowing whom each has privately chosen. Observers in the majority receive $20 and those in the minority nothing. Economists call such an incentive system a beauty contest because the contestants cannot simply express their own preferred outcome without considering how the other two Observers might reason who should receive the item. Judges in actual court cases are presumably not imposing their own preferred outcomes but, rather, deciding on a rule that fits with the community's custom of what is right, which conforms to the expectations people in general have about the appropriate responses to the circumstances and events in a case.

A new consideration for this project is the display of the virtual world. All of my prior virtual worlds were programmed in two dimensions because, well, why not program the experiment in two dimensions? That's how the software engineer programs laboratory experiments. The prominence of three dimensions in the semantics of the preposition *in* and the in-ness of the testable rule from chapter 7, however, give us some pause and speak for designing the experiment in three dimensions and with a first-person point of view. As opposed to the participants looking at a two-dimensional world from outside of it (see, e.g., Figures 4.1 and 4.2), the participants in this experiment are *in* the virtual world. They see the world from within the world.

Figure 8.1 displays the three-dimensional world from the experimenter's third-person point of view. Figure 8.2 displays page 5 of the instructions from the participants' first-person view of the experiment. The instructions to the participants are as follows:

Welcome (page 1)

This is an experiment in the economics of decision making. The instructions are simple, and if you follow them carefully and make good decisions you can earn a considerable amount of money which will be paid to you in CASH at the end of the experiment.

In this experiment people navigate in a 3-D virtual world with a first-person point of view. You can move around the environment by using the arrow keys: ←, →, ↑, and ↓. Hit each key once.

To change your view of the world, move your mouse back to look down and forward to look up. Do this now.

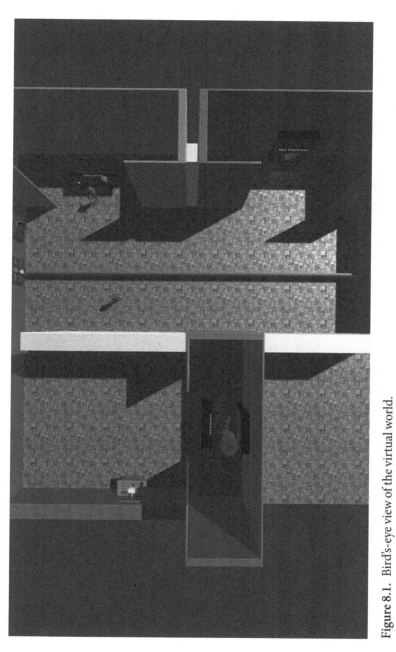

Figure 8.1. Bird's-eye view of the virtual world.

Figure 8.2. Participants' view of page 5 of the instructions.

If you have any questions at any point in the instructions, please raise your hand.

Press the "i" key to show and hide the mouse cursor to continue to the next page of instructions.

Player Types (page 2)

There are three types of participants in this experiment: a Red person, a Blue person, and 3 Observers. Everyone will go through the instructions as both a Red person and a Blue person.

Box Dispenser (page 3)

Red's task is to go to their box dispenser, pick up a box, empty its contents, and redeem the box's contents for money. Use the arrows to walk up to the box dispenser. When you are close enough, a box will appear in your hands. Slightly move your mouse back to see the box in your hands. Then move your mouse forward to straight ahead.

Press the "i" key to show and hide the mouse cursor to continue to the next page of instructions.

Sorting Station (page 4)

Now walk towards the sorting station table. When you walk up next to the table, you will automatically lay the box down on the table. Tokens will then roll out of the box onto the table.

Sorting Station Continued (page 5)

Look down to see if you are holding a token. If you are not holding a token, walk up to the table to automatically pick up a token.

If you are holding a yellow token, walk over to the yellow token bin and deposit the token in it. Each yellow token that Red deposits generates $0.50 in earnings for Red.

If you are holding a black token, put it in the trash; it is worth nothing. You must deposit the black tokens in the trash chute to advance the experiment.

Even though they are not shown here, a box may contain purple tokens. Each purple token that is deposited in the purple token bin generates $25.00 in earnings.

Once all the tokens have been deposited, go back to the bench and pick up the box.

Transfer Box (page 6)

Red will then give their box to Blue on the other side of the wall. Blue's job is to clean and sell the box for Red. Blue will receive a portion of the proceeds for selling the box and will then return the rest of the proceeds to Red.

Blue Person (page 7)

You are now going through the experiment from Blue's point of view. Your task is to clean Red's box for them and to sell it for money. Take the box over to the wash station now.

Once the box is clean, take the box over to the cleaned box table to sell it to the computerized robot. The robot will buy the cleaned box from you.

Money (page 8)

The robot will put money down on the table. Pick up the money. $0.50 is for Red. Blue can keep $1.50 for cleaning and selling the box for Red. Walk over to Red now to split the money.

Summary (page 9)

Red now starts the process over.

In this experiment, you are the Red person [Blue person/an Observer]. Observers will earn money later in the experiment. Their [their/your] task right now is to observe Red and Blue.

[Red and Blue only] To help you get your bearings in the virtual world, the monitor on your right displays a bird's eye view of your avatar. [Red, however, is blocked from seeing anything on the other side of the wall.]

This is the end of the instructions. If you have any questions, please raise your hand and a monitor will come by to answer them. If you are finished with the instructions, please click the Start button. The instructions will remain on your screen until the experiment begins. We need everyone to click the Start button before we can begin the experiment.

Each session consists of five periods of token sorting and box selling that generates $7.50 in earnings for Red and Blue. The sixth period proceeds like the previous five except that when Blue gives the cleaned box to the robot, the

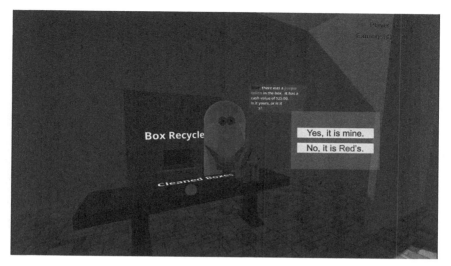

Figure 8.3. Blue finds a purple token that was in the box.

box is laid on the bench and a purple token rolls out from inside.[6] By design, Red is not present when the purple token is found. The robot says, "Blue, there was a purple token in the box. It has a cash value of $25.00. Is it yours, or is it Red's?"[7] As Figure 8.3 displays, the Blue participant is prompted to reply with either "Yes, it is mine" or "No, it is Red's." Once Blue makes a decision, the robot takes the purple token over to Red and correspondingly says, "Red, there was a purple token in the box. It has a cash value of $25.00. Is it yours, or is it Blue's?" In Figure 8.4, the Red participant is likewise prompted to reply with either "Yes, it is mine" or "No, it is Blue's." Regardless of how Red and Blue answer the question, the Observers must then decide to whom to award the purple token. Their decision is final.

The complete instructions for the Observers are displayed in Figure 8.5, and a demonstration of the "Red's Box" treatment is available at https://www.youtube.com/watch?v=wo0yreinUDQ.

Over the course of four days in September 2017, my lab coordinator, software engineer, and I conducted ten sessions with two groups of five participants in each session. These 100 participants were recruited from the

---

[6] In *Durfee*, Jones finds the money inside the wall inside the safe. The in-ness in our experiment is weaker in that the purple token is simply inside the box, not inside the wall inside the box.

[7] Blue participants are familiar with interacting with the robot as it always asks whether the box is clean and ready for recycling. Blue must click "Yes" before the robot lays the money on the table.

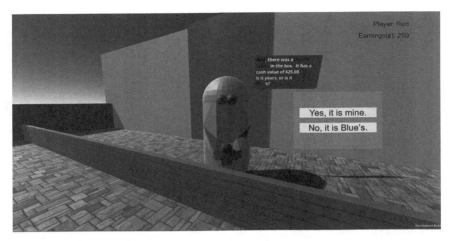

Figure 8.4. The robot inquires about the purple token with Red.

Figure 8.5. The Observers' task regarding the purple token.

general student body of Chapman University. No subject participated twice, and all had participated in at least one prior experiment of some kind in the same laboratory. They were randomly recruited via an electronic email system to participate in a one-hour session and were paid $7 for showing up on time. When they arrived at the laboratory, five women and five men were randomly seated at visually isolated computer terminals where they privately read through self-paced instructions. The participants were free to ask questions during the instructions and throughout the experiment. Not including the show-up payment, Observers earned either $20 or $0; Reds earned either $33.50 or $8.50, depending on the decisions of the Observers; and Blues either $7.50 or $32.50. All participants were paid privately at the conclusion of the session, which lasted approximately twenty to twenty-five minutes, including the instructions and the time to privately pay the participants.

After conducting these ten sessions, I made a small change to the robot's question with the intention to test its sensitivity. Instead of saying, "Blue [Red], there was a purple token in the box. It has a cash value of $25.00," the robot simply says, "Blue [Red], there was a purple token in Red's box." The question was whether reinforcing the owner of the box mattered to Red and Blue. (In making the change, I forgot to retain the statement regarding the cash value of the purple token, so there is also an unintentional second change.) We again over three days conducted ten sessions with two groups of five participants and equal numbers of men and women. Figure 8.6 reports the results for the two treatment conditions. The solid bars represent the first treatment condition and the hatched bars the second. The data fall into four different categories, represented by four different quadrants. For example, in the top-left

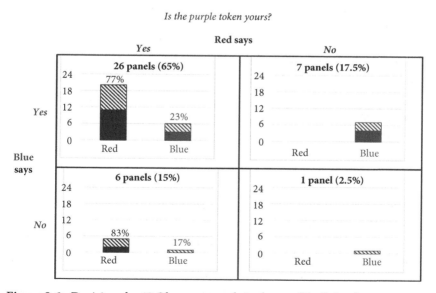

Figure 8.6. Decisions by 40 Observer panels in the two "Red's box" treatments.

corner both Red and Blue claim the purple token as "mine." Each observation is the final decision of an independent three-person Observer panel.

The first thing to notice in Figure 8.6 is that in two-thirds of the cases when Red and Blue both claim the purple token, the experimental test is, as Adam Smith would say, agreeable to the prediction 77 percent of the time. Of the seventy-eight Observers in the top-left corner, fifty-three choose Red and twenty-five Blue. In this case, an economist's suspicion about DeScioli and Karpoff's survey for trivial stakes is unwarranted. I find that nearly the same percentage of panels side with Durfee in a decision that impacts real people in the very room with them and for real salient stakes 100 times greater than DeScioli and Karpoff's. These two treatment conditions provide direct evidence that if A has property in Y and X is in Y, then people will say that A has property in X in Y.

The second thing to notice in Figure 8.6 is that in only two-thirds of the cases do Red and Blue both claim the purple token. When they both agree that one or the other can say that the purple token is "mine," there are as many Reds as Blues who claim it. Only one time out of thirteen does an Observer panel award the purple token to someone who doesn't claim it when the other person does. Such a result indicates that the Observers as a trio are unwilling to overrule the parties themselves. If Durfee doesn't want the purple token, then the Observers are not willing to give it to him anyway. The off-diagonal situations in the experiment provide information about property disputes that no study of court cases can, because the participants avoid such a dispute in the first place.

The last thing to notice in Figure 8.6 is that the two changes to the robot's dialogue have no impact on the participants. The solid and hatched boxes are nearly evenly split.

Our aim now shifts to exploring a counterfactual condition of *Durfee v. Jones*. What if, holding as much as we can constant, Jones owns the box? The actions of the participants are exactly the same. Red picks up the box, sorts its contents, and gives the box to Blue. Blue then washes the box, sells it to the robot, and gives some of the proceeds to Red. The only difference is that Red is sorting the tokens for Blue, who owns the box, and the partial payment from Blue is for sorting the tokens. The software works exactly the same way as it does in the prior two treatment conditions except that the instructions explain that Blue is the owner of the box and the robot says, "Blue [Red], there was a purple token in Blue's box."

If the results in the upper-left corner of Figure 8.6 swing the other way so that something like 77 percent of the panels award the purple token to Blue, we have strong corroborating evidence that if A has property in Y and X is in Y, then people say that A has property in X in Y.

The subjects have spoken in ten sessions of two 5-person groups, and, no, we do not have strong corroborating evidence for the testable prediction. As Figure 8.7 reports, we find quite the opposite. We find that even if Blue owns the box and there is a dispute, the Observers award the purple token to Red 70 percent of the time. Nineteen of the Observers chose Red and eleven Blue. I didn't conduct the "Blue's box" treatment condition expecting to be wrong, but here I am, squarely rejected. Such is the life of an experimental economist, rebuffed by my subjects.

At such a juncture, I am faced with the Duhem-Quine problem: The empirical evaluation of my hypothesis about property is a composite test of several interconnected auxiliary assumptions or hypotheses.[8] Does the disconfirming evidence in Figure 8.7 speak against my hypothesis or against some subsidiary assumption in my implementation of the empirical test? The results of the first two "Red's box" treatments point to the latter, but we don't know unless we conduct another treatment condition, or two, deliberately designed to isolate the source of the disconfirming evidence.[9]

With an Unexpected but Consistent-with-the-Prediction Proviso

Two observations on how I saw the world prior to the results in Figure 8.7 guide the design of the fourth treatment condition. First, I assumed that because I told the participants that Blue was the owner of the box, the Observers would act as I hypothesized them to act and award the purple token to Blue. The "Blue's box" treatment seems to call that subsidiary assumption into question. The Observer panels appear to treat Red as the owner of the box no

[8] See Sandra Harding (1976).
[9] See Vernon Smith (1994).

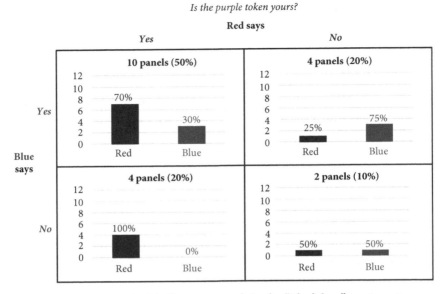

Figure 8.7. Decisions by 20 Observer panels in the "Blue's box" treatment.

matter what instructions I give them. Second, I assumed that the Observers would not interpret the scripted actions for Red and Blue as a basis for Red to say, "This box is mine." (Notice how I am continuing to rely on the assumption that the first two treatments confirm my major hypothesis for the reasons I hypothesize.) So, what could Red be doing such that the Observers would think that Red is the owner of the box? Red only does two things: pick up the box from the dispenser and sort the tokens in it. Hard-core Lockeans may see the sorting task as the source of Red's ownership over the tokens, but I am inclined to think that Red may represent Marc Armory, as well as Herbert Durfee, the moment he grasps the created object from the dispenser. The results from a postexperiment survey also seem to bolster this reading of the experiment. Of the 157 participants who said that Red should have received the purple token, 34 (22 percent) gave reasons like "[Red] pulled the box out of the sorting station" and included words like *originally, first,* and *retrieved* (see Appendix A).

To test such an interpretation of the experiment, I redesigned the software so that Red continues to sort the tokens but Blue is the person who picks up the box from the dispenser. The instructions remain the same as in the previous "Blue's box" treatment; that is, the instructions and robot still

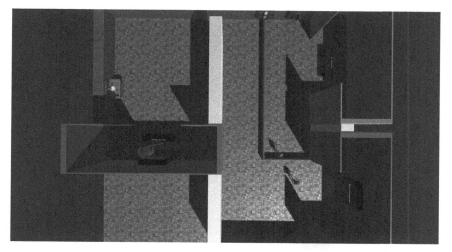

Figure 8.8. Bird's-eye view of the "Blue's box from Blue's dispenser" treatment.

say that the box is Blue's, but I rearrange the sequence of events so that Blue maintains her physical connection to the box for more than a few seconds before handing it over to Red to sort for her. Thus, in this "Blue's box from Blue's dispenser" treatment, Blue goes to the other side of the wall to wash the box before giving it to Red to sort. (Appendix B reports the instructions for this treatment.) The period ends like in every other treatment with Blue selling the box to the robot and giving Red the same amount of money. Figure 8.8 displays Blue's access to the dispenser, which now glows blue instead of red.

Figure 8.9 reports the decisions by twenty Observer panels in the "Blue's box from Blue's dispenser" treatment.[10] Just like in the "Blue's box" treatment, half of the Red-Blue pairs mutually disagree. But unlike the prior treatment, giving Blue the task of picking up the box completely shifts the decisions of the Observer panels to Blue's favor. If Blue says that the box is "mine," 100 percent of the panels award the purple token to Blue. Not half of the panels, or a quarter of the panels, but every single three-person panel awards the purple token to Blue. We have gone from 30 percent of the panels in Blue's favor in the "Blue's box" treatment to 100 percent in this treatment. As a whole, twenty-five Observers chose Blue, and only five chose Red.

[10] This brings the total number of participants to 400 (240 Observers, 80 Reds, and 80 Blues).

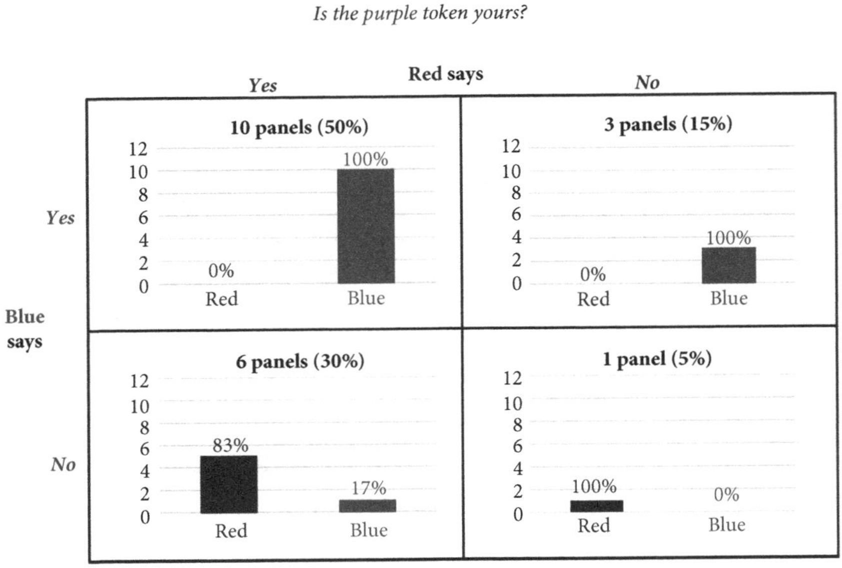

Figure 8.9. Decisions by 20 Observer panels in the "Blue's box from Blue's dispenser" treatment.

The last treatment condition provides further evidence that third parties settle actual disputes by adhering to the rule that if A has property in Y and X is in Y, then A has property in X in Y. The proviso, which the last two treatment conditions add, is that it matters how A comes to have property in Y. The circumstances of the physical world must fit the assertion in words (from the experimenter on high) that A indeed has property in Y. Over the course of four treatment conditions, the participants robustly award X, which is in Y, to the person who first grasps Y.

Appendix A

Coding Results of Postexperiment Survey for the "Red's Box" and "Blue's Box" Treatment Conditions

Each participant filled out a short postexperiment survey while the experiment monitor prepared to pay the participants. The survey consisted of three questions: (1) "Who should have received the purple token?" (2) "Why did you answer (1) the way you did?"

(3) "Why do you think others would answer (1) the way they did?" I presented the raw data to five undergraduates after they went through the experiment themselves and asked them to analyze the responses to the first two questions. Each of the coders individually created their own set of categories to summarize the responses to the second question. The coders categorized the responses for a subset of ten to fifteen 5-person groups. The first cycle of coding generated the following categories:

Coder 1:

- Possession of box
- Level of work
- Accuracy of work
- Description of work
- Claim of ownership
- Other

Coder 2:

- Possession of box
- Finder of box
- Efficiency in work
- Amount of work
- Fair
- Money driven
- Other

Coder 3:

- Token sorter
- Fairness
- Benevolence: Wanting to do something nice
- Profit maximizing
- Possession
- Box ownership
- No dispute
- Other/none

Coder 4:

- Origin: Where box came from
- Last touched: Who last possessed token
- Perceived efficiency
- Perceived workload
- Unfair distribution/equality
- Wording/instructions
- Influenced by players
- Teamwork
- Personal bias
- Other

Coder 5:

- Ownership:
  a. Blue to Blue (Blue said he should receive the purple token)
  b. Blue not (Blue made a decision that was irrational)
  c. Blue to Red (Blue said the purple token should go to Red)
  d. Observer to Blue (Observer said Blue should receive the purple token)
  e. Observer to Red (Observer said Red should receive the purple token)
  f. Red to Red (Red said he should receive the purple token)
  g. Red not (Blue made a decision that was irrational)
  h. Red to Blue (Red said the purple token should go to Blue)
- Work:
  a. Blue to Blue (Blue said he should receive the purple token)
  b. Blue not (Blue made a decision that was irrational)
  c. Blue to Red (Blue said the purple token should go to Red)
  d. Observer to Blue (Observer said Blue should receive the purple token)
  e. Observer to Red (Observer said Red should receive the purple token)
  f. Red to Red (Red said he should receive the purple token)
  g. Red not (Blue made a decision that was irrational)
  h. Red to Blue (Red said the purple token should go to Blue)
- Efficiency:
  a. Blue to Blue (Blue said he should receive the purple token)
  b. Blue not (Blue made a decision that was irrational)
  c. Blue to Red (Blue said the purple token should go to Red)
  d. Observer to Blue (Observer said Blue should receive the purple token)
  e. Observer to Red (Observer said Red should receive the purple token)
  f. Red to Red (Red said he should receive the purple token)
  g. Red not (Blue made a decision that was irrational)
  h. Red to Blue (Red said the purple token should go to Blue)

The five coders then met as a group to determine the emergent codes. The similarities allowed them to unanimously agree on a list of nine category labels:

- DISPENSER
  - Originally had box
  - Inclusive terms: *originally, first, retrieved, red's*
  - Best-fit example: "[Red] pulled the box out of the sorting station."
  - Loose-fit example: "Because red was the one receiving the box, it was in there possession"
- POSSESSOR
  - Had box after transfer
  - Inclusive terms: *after, discovery, received, finders keepers*
  - Best-fit example: "The box was in [Blue's] possession and the Red person gave [Blue] the box to have."
  - Loose-fit example: "Because there wasn't a purple token when Red first poured it out, therefore, it is mine"
- TASK
  - Who is responsible
  - Inclusive terms: *responsible, job, instructions, supposed to, red sorts tokens*

- Best-fit example: "I believe that since it was Red's job to take the tokens out, they are his. Blue's only job it to clean the boxes, not take tokens."
- Loose-fit example: "I answered this way because of what is fair. The red player was being paid accordingly to do his job, and likewise to the blue player. The purple ball should never be an option for the blue player, had the red player done his job right."
- AMOUNT
  - Workload
  - Inclusive terms: *most of work, less work, heavy lifting*
  - Best-fit example: "Red was doing more work than Blue so Red should have gotten it."
  - Loose-fit example: "I answered the way I did based on the effort exerted per character based on the pay we respectfully received. Red did much more and was paid 1/3 less per box. Because red picked up the box and opened it and threw away the trash to get it all ready."
- MORAL
  - Fairness/inequality
  - Inclusive terms: *split, fair, honesty, nice, moral obligation*
  - Best-fit example: "Because people are jerks, share the love baby."
  - Loose-fit example: "Because Blue earns more from cleaning & selling boxes. And all the earning from inside the box should go to Red."
- CLAIM
  - Who claimed token
  - Inclusive terms: *both, agreed, agreement*
  - Best-fit example: "Blue said the token was theirs, and Red also said the token was Blue's."
  - Loose-fit example: "Because red deserved the purple token, not blue. Because they also believed red deserved the token"
- QUALITY
  - Better/worse job
  - Inclusive terms: *faster, efficient, superior, longer to complete, effort*
  - Best-fit example: "Because blue was faster and more effective"
  - Loose-fit example: "Because blue was far superior to red"
- SELF
  - Personal gain (money)
  - Inclusive terms: *wanted, selfish, paid, reward, award*
  - Best-fit example: "cause we tryna get paid and that's $25"
  - Loose-fit example: "I don't trust the other player since it's an anonymous game and there's no social reward for being generous."
- OWNER
  - Whose box? (given by instructions)
  - Inclusive terms: *The robot said, i wanted to know*
  - Best-fit example: "The robot did not say blue's box, therefore it's reds."
- OTHER
  - Inclusive terms: *I assume, I don't know*

The five coders met as a group and placed each of the 280 survey responses in a category. (The first two sessions of ten people did not receive the survey.) Figure 8.10 reports the counts of the categories stratified by their answers to the first survey question, "Who

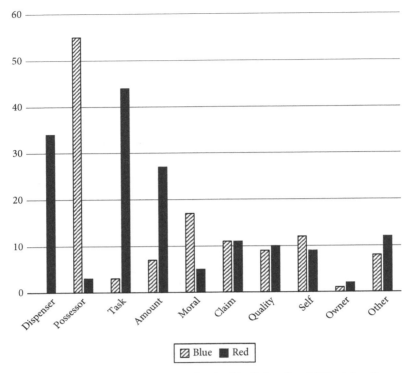

Figure 8.10. Frequency distribution for the "Red's box" and "Blue's box" treatments.

should have received the purple token?" Because the frequency of the reasons given do not vary across the three treatment conditions, all 280 responses are displayed in one figure.

Participants said that Red should get the purple token because Red originally retrieves the box (*dispenser*), is responsible for sorting the tokens (*task*), and does most of the work (*amount*). Not surprisingly, when participants said that Blue should get the purple token, it is because Blue has possession of the box when the token was found (*possessor*).

Appendix B

Experiment Instructions and Survey Results for the "Blue's Box from Blue's Dispenser" Treatment

Welcome (page 1)

This is an experiment in the economics of decision making. The instructions are simple, and if you follow them carefully and make good decisions you can earn a considerable amount of money which will be paid to you in CASH at the end of the experiment.

In this experiment people navigate in a 3-D virtual world with a first-person point of view. You can move around the environment by using the arrow keys: ←, →, ↑, and ↓. Hit each key once.

To change your view of the world, move your mouse back to look down and forward to look up. Do this now.

If you have any questions at any point in the instructions, please raise your hand.

Press the "i" key to show and hide the mouse cursor to continue to the next page of instructions.

Player Types (page 2)

There are three types of participants in this experiment: a Red person, a Blue person, and 3 Observers. Everyone will go through the instructions as both a Red person and a Blue person.

Box Dispenser (page 3)

Blue's task is to go to their box dispenser, pick up a box, clean the box, and then hand it to Red for sorting. Use the arrows to walk up to the box dispenser. When you are close enough, a box will appear in your hands. Slightly move your mouse back to see the box in your hands. Then move your mouse forward to straight ahead.

Press the "i" key to show and hide the mouse cursor to continue to the next page of instructions.

Cleaning (page 4)

Now walk towards the wash station on the other side of the wall. Once the box is clean, return to this side of the wall and hand the cleaned box to Red.

Red Person (page 5)

You are now going through the experiment from Red's point of view. Your task is to sort and redeem the tokens as partial payment from Blue.

Now walk towards the sorting station table. When you walk up next to the table, you will automatically lay the box down on the table. Tokens will then roll out of the box onto the table.

Sorting Station (page 6)

Look down to see if you are holding a token. If you are not holding a token, walk up to the table to automatically pick up a token.

If you are holding a yellow token, walk over to the yellow token bin and deposit the token in it. Each yellow token that Red deposits generates $0.50 as partial compensation for Red.

If you are holding a black token, put it in the trash; it is worth nothing. You must deposit the black tokens in the trash chute to advance the experiment.

Even though they are not shown here, a box may contain purple tokens. Each purple token that is deposited in the purple token bin generates $25.00 in earnings.

Once all the tokens have been deposited, go back to the bench and pick up the box.

Transfer Box (page 7)

Red will give Blue's box to Blue on the other side of the wall. Blue will sell the box, receive a portion of the proceeds for selling it, and then give the rest of the proceeds to Red.

Blue Person (page 8)

You are now going through the experiment from Blue's point of view.

Take the box to the cleaned box table, on the other side of the wall, to sell it to the computerized robot. The robot will buy the cleaned box from you.

The robot will put money down on the table. Pick up the money. Blue receives $1.50 for selling their box. Red also receives $0.50 for sorting the contents of the box for Blue. Walk over to Red now to split the money.

Summary (page 9)

Blue now starts the process over.

In this experiment, you are the Red person [Blue person/an Observer]. Observers will earn money later in the experiment. Their [their/your] task right now is to observe Red and Blue.

[Red and Blue only] To help you get your bearings in the virtual world, the monitor on your right displays a bird's eye view of your avatar.

This is the end of the instructions. If you have any questions, please raise your hand and a monitor will come by to answer them. If you are finished with the instructions, please click the Start button. The instructions will remain on your screen until the experiment begins. We need everyone to click the Start button before we can begin the experiment.

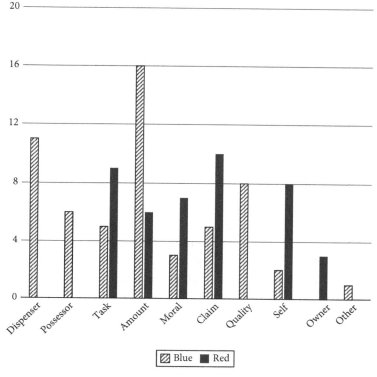

Figure 8.11. Frequency distribution for "Blue's box from Blue's dispenser" treatment.

Figure 8.11 reports the counts of the categories stratified by their answers to the first survey question for the "Blue's box from Blue's dispenser" treatment. Two of the original five coders were joined by three new coders to assess the responses for this treatment condition.

Participants said that Blue should get the purple token because Blue does most of the work (*amount*) and originally retrieves the box (*dispenser*). Interestingly, possession is no longer the overwhelming reason for Blue to receive the purple token. Only Observers say that whoever claims the token should get it (*claim*). Red then gets the purple token when the Observer's reason is, for example, that "both blue and red said that the purple token was red's so therefore the token went to red, even if I felt it should have gone to blue."

9

Economics Is Founded Upon Property, Not Property Rights

Any study of how *Homo sapiens* "manages its scarce resources" or "produc[es], distribut[es], and consum[es] . . . goods and services" would be incomplete without property and the concept MINE.[1] That is my claim. "Way to go out on a limb," some will surely say. "Who would disagree with that?" others will rhetorically ask. But my claim is not about the importance of property rights as nearly every economist would read into my statement, but about property. There is a difference. Are we merely talking about semantics? No, because as chapter 2 makes clear, there is no "merely" about meaning. Semantics isn't simple, and, consequently, neither is property nor economics.

Almost every modern principle of economics textbooks contains some discussion of property rights in an introductory chapter. For N. Gregory Mankiw, "property rights are the ability of an individual to own and exercise control over scarce resources."[2] For the Nobel Laureate Paul Krugman and Robin Wells, "property rights are the rights of owners of valuable items, whether resources or goods, to dispose of those items as they choose."[3] Property rights are important, because, as Mankiw explains:

> Market economies need institutions to enforce property rights so individuals can own and control scarce resources. A farmer won't grow food if she expects her crop to be stolen; a restaurant won't serve meals unless it is assured that customers will pay before they leave; and an entertainment

---

[1] N. Gregory Mankiw (2015, p. 4) and Paul Krugman and Robin Wells (2009, p. 2).
[2] N. Gregory Mankiw (2015, p. 12). An "ability" is a weak anchor for such an important definition, but it is the same consequentialist one that Yoram Barzel (1997) uses (see chapter 4).
[3] Paul Krugman and Robin Wells (2009, p. 111). Note the circularity of the definition discussed in chapter 4.

The Property Species. Bart J. Wilson. Oxford University Press (2020) © Oxford University Press.
DOI: 10.1093/oso/9780190936785.001.0001

company won't produce DVDs if too many potential customers avoid paying by making illegal copies. We all rely on government-provided police and courts to enforce our rights over the things we produce—and the invisible hand counts on our ability to enforce our rights.[4]

Krugman and Wells explain that "property rights are what make the mutually beneficial transactions in the used-textbook market, or any market, possible."[5] They also tack on, perhaps unsurprisingly, that "markets generally fail due to incomplete property rights."[6] But apart from these few sentences, property rights largely go unmentioned in introductions to the study of economics until a much later chapter on public goods and common-pool resources (with literally one sentence in between on patents as a property right to encourage invention).[7] When things go awry in the world, like with toxic effluents in rivers and rhinoceroses on the verge of extinction, then property rights become important in economics. But until then, not much needs to be discussed about property rights in teaching the Principles of Economics.[8]

Such brief but ubiquitous references to property rights in modern economics textbooks reflect the important influence of Armen Alchian and Harold Demsetz, who first provided a framework for diagnosing problems and proffering solutions that economists historically could not satisfactorily account for. Demsetz, for example, famously discusses how the Montagnes on the Labrador Peninsula organized themselves before and after a market for beaver pelts developed.[9] When the benefits change relative to the costs, property rights emerge to constrain the individual. But over the last fifty years, economists have not really done much more with Alchian and Demsetz's groundbreaking lead than report how different patterns of property rights lead to different patterns of behavior. We continue to frame the persistent problems and the property rights solutions in terms of the external world imposing itself on the individual.

---

[4] N. Gregory Mankiw (2015, p. 12).

[5] Paul Krugman and Robin Wells (2009, pp. 111–112).

[6] Ibid. (p. 112).

[7] Seriously, one sentence in between. See Paul Krugman and Robin Wells (2009) and N. Gregory Mankiw (2015).

[8] Tyler Cowen and Alex Tabarrok (2018) are a notable exception. They do not specifically define the term for students, nor introduce it in an early chapter. But unlike most introductory texts, they spend an entire page and a half discussing property rights as one of five "key institutions" for understanding chapter 27 on "The Wealth of Nations and Economic Growth" (p. 539). "Institutions," Cowen and Tabarrok explain, "are the 'rules of the game' that structure economic incentives."

[9] Harold Demsetz (1967).

Take, for instance, Alchian and Demsetz's disturbing example.[10] They argue that property rights are important because we have to find a way to constrain the Canadian hunters who crush baby seals' skulls with heavy clubs and skin them alive. Why yes, a set of rules that fails to exclude others from using a resource can lead to "barbaric and cruel" conduct.[11] But something critical is missing from economics if what we say about the first-come, first-served system is that it "forces persons to behave in ways that are thought to be immoral."[12] We can do better than blaming the rules for "encouraging" immoral behavior than saying, in essence, the costs and benefits made them do it. We have fifty years of examples identifying the relative costs and benefits of when property rights do and do not emerge. How do the rules of property integrate, or fail to integrate, with other customs to form a sense of how to conduct ourselves efficiently *and* rightly? Imagine the conversations we could have with our friends in the humanities about property and economics.[13]

Mankiw similarly argues that property rights are important because human moral failings have economic consequences; that is, we must constrain the thieves that dine and dash and steal crops. Why yes, we must and we do. But is the enforcement of property rights by police and courts the reason that children follow their parents' example and don't steal?[14] No, you may concede, that's not why children don't steal. They learn, like Bing learns from Flop, about what it means to give into an impulse of I WANT THIS and take a lolly in a grocery store. *That's not right, is it? It's called stealing.* The consummate consequentialist still must ask: Don't parents refrain from stealing because of the police and courts? Well, yes, some people explicitly weigh the costs of punishment against the benefits of stealing before making the decision. We call them con artists and sociopaths. But most of us, that is, 96 percent of the population, have well-functioning internal moral self-governance.[15] Even if such self-governance isn't broadly a local custom regarding some things in a particular community, we humans have the capacity for it. We self-contemplate our deeds and our character. We follow moral scheduling patterns, as Vernon Smith and I put it, out of "a sense of duty socialized to and accountable for living life with a large number of other

---

[10] Armen Alchian and Harold Demsetz (1973).

[11] Ibid. (p. 20).

[12] Ibid.

[13] Or, just imagine having conversations with friends in the humanities.

[14] Rhetorical question for legal centralists. See Edward Stringham (2015), especially chapter 9. His book is literally dedicated to you.

[15] Martha Stout (2005).

members of its kind."[16] Property is much more than an external check on aberrant, antisocial thievery. It comes from within as much as from without, part of an ongoing dialogue between the individual and their community. Rules of property emerged in *Homo sapiens* to eliminate real and positive hurt of the mischievous acts regarding things that would threaten to dissolve the bonds of a community. We contemplate our actions for the sake of contemplating them, not merely to restrain, as Adam Smith so eloquently says, "the arrogance of our self-love," but to socialize our conduct to something that our fellow human beings "can go along with."[17] We care what other people think of us. Human sociability shapes our character and conduct concerning the connections we make, and refrain from making, with things.

Bear with me as I continue nitpicking on Mankiw. He refreshingly puts in print what most economists are only willing to argue informally in conversation. The hypothetical syllogism economists employ, however, isn't valid, and it goes like this. If the government enforces property rights (R), then people will not steal (not-S). The second conditional statement is inferred, namely that, if people generally will not steal (not-S), then a farmer does not expect other people to specifically steal her crops (not-P). The conclusion is, therefore, if the government enforces property rights (R), then a farmer does not expect other people to steal her crops (not-P). Mankiw then attempts a second syllogism with the conclusion being, therefore, if the government enforces property rights (R), then the farmer will grow crops (Q). But Mankiw doesn't argue if not-P then Q so that he can say, therefore, if R then Q. He says the inverse: If a farmer expects other people to steal her crops (P), then she won't grow crops (not-Q), which is not logically equivalent to if not-P then Q.[18]

The point of such an observation is not that it blows a hole in Mankiw's excellent and widely adopted introduction to economics. He could have easily said, "Market economies need institutions to enforce property rights so individuals can own and control scarce resources. A farmer will grow more crops than she can personally use if she does not expect her crop to be stolen." My

---

[16] Vernon Smith and Bart Wilson (2019, p. 74).

[17] Adam Smith (1759, p. 83): "Though it may be true, therefore, that every individual, in his own breast, naturally prefers himself to all mankind, yet he dares not look mankind in the face, and avow that he acts according to this principle. . . . He must . . . humble the arrogance of his self-love, and bring it down to something which other men can go along with." See also Vernon Smith and Bart Wilson (2019, chs. 1, 5, and 13).

[18] *Mankiw's argument entails by* modus tollens *that if the farmer will grow crops (Q), then the farmer does not expect other people to specifically steal her crops (not-P).* But how does one get from R (the government enforces property rights) to Q (the farmer will grow crops)?

point is that the reason Mankiw's argument about property rights appears to work, even though a conditional statement and its inverse are not logically equivalent, is that the meaning of property does not unidirectionally point from the external world to the individual. Rather, our intersubjective moral reasoning makes property and markets possible. While hypothetical syllogisms proceed strictly from left to right, the meaning of property also points in the reverse direction: from the mind of the individual to the external world. If, by custom, a farmer can say, "This crop is mine," other people can know this is true, and if other people cannot say, "This crop is mine," the farmer may grow extra crops for other people.[19] If the farmer cannot say, "This crop is mine," and other people can say, "This crop is mine," she may *not* grow crops for other people. Both statements convey meaning regarding crop production in a particular context in which *the other could occur but does not*. Like with the Pleistocene boojum in chapter 2, property is symbolic, simultaneously meaning both what is the case and what is not the case but could have been if conditions of the world had been different.

A key question for students of economics is—or, to be prescriptive, a key question should be—why indeed is property prosocial and the expected norm for farmers, restaurateurs, and entertainment companies? Why is it the case that a restaurateur can say, "This meal is mine," and other people cannot say, "This meal is mine" when the opposite could occur but doesn't? The answer would seem important to answering the question of why someone goes to the time, effort, and expense of making meals for complete strangers who may never visit their establishment again. How does property make it possible for people to do good things for people they do not personally know? Imagine the work that could be done to document and explain how MINE promotes the social good that enables people to live better, more comfortable lives.

The Language of "Property Rights" Contains a Tacit Assumption

The stumbling block to overcome is to accept that property is not just an external restraint imposed upon the individual, but that property socializes the individual's conduct to fit with the external world, to fit with what is right.

---

[19] I am using *can* and *cannot* in the semantically primitive, universally translatable senses that evoke "social rules" and "reflect the fundamental human experiences of constraint and freedom from constraint" (Anna Wierzbicka 1996, pp. 104–105).

Moreover, we have to be open to the possibility that commerce may be an integral part of that socializing and ethicizing process.[20] One fear is that if we acknowledge that we actively accept property as a custom taught by our authoritative mentors, its rules will tend to appear arbitrary. We can overcome this fear if we treat property as a custom, because as a custom, property is dialogic. Every action regarding property is a two-way dialogue among those who practice the custom. The highly abstract and probably universal human custom of "Thou shalt not steal" keeps customary rules like first-in-hand active, and the application of the rule reaffirms the abstract custom, as in *Pierson v. Post*. But the current application of the rule also modifies the custom by amalgamating into the background all of the nuances of its application. For example, the costs of hunting a fox were not such that Post had a case for a rule of projectile-holds-the-varmint. Change the prey to finback whales, however, and *Swift v. Gifford* illustrates how the custom of "Thou shalt not steal" keeps the rule of first-in-hand active *except* for situations in which a new customary rule has emerged in response to new technologies and new costs of a new kind of prey. Property is neither an exterior monologue, as Swift maintained, nor an interior monologue, as Post seemed to wish.[21]

The language of economics reveals that economists think property rights work as an external restraint, a one-way causal mechanism. Krugman and Wells say property rights are "rights . . . to dispose of items." Alchian defines property rights as "the rights of individuals to the use of resources."[22] When Alchian and Demsetz ask, "What consequences for social interaction flow from a particular structure of property rights?," they are asking about how consequences flow from a particular structure of property rights to social interactions.[23] The word *rights* doesn't stand by itself. In each instance another little word follows, to wit, *to*. Whether as a preposition or an infinitive particle, the word *to* points in the direction of what comes next, a noun or a verb. In English, a right doesn't stand alone; it points to something like free speech, due process, a speedy trial, and so forth.

What this means is that economic discourse relies subsidiarily on a particular type of spatial-geometric representation for the conception of property

---

[20] Deirdre McCloskey (2006).

[21] As I mentioned in chapter 7, one of Swift's arguments was that the iron-holds-the-whale rule was "in contravention" to the rule of law. Swift was treating the rule of law as externally given, not dynamically applied to the fluctuating circumstances of time and place.

[22] Armen Alchian (1965).

[23] Armen Alchian and Harold Demsetz (1973, p. 17).

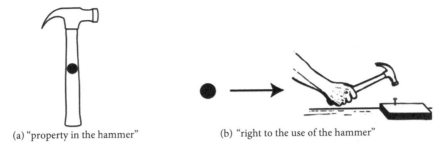

(a) "property in the hammer"   (b) "right to the use of the hammer"

Figure 9.1. Mental Representations of *in* and *to* after Andrea Tyler and Vyvyan Evans

rights. In Alchian and Demsetz's metaphor, consequences "flow from" the structure of property rights *to* social interactions. Note the explicit movement in their metaphor. Alchian's general form of a property right is "Person *A* has the right to the use of *Y*." The preposition *to* is doing some heavy important work. Recall the example of *He ran to the hills* from chapter 5.[24] The runner is physically located away from the hills but headed in that direction. What is important is where the preposition is pointing, namely, the hills. In economics we represent a property right as something external to an action involving a thing. A property right points toward an action involving *Y*. What is important is the action involving *Y*. Figures 9.1a and 9.1b compare that mental representation with the hypothesis that people cognize property as located in *Y*.

Let's drill down on what the representations convey. In panel (a) the dot represents the compound abstract concept PROPERTY. Property is a substantive inside the hammer. There is no person. There is no human action. There is no use. There is just a physical thing with property contained in it. The property is not in motion. It is firmly established in the hammer, part of the very thing itself. A characteristic of the hammer itself is that there is property in it. Where the hammer goes, so goes the property in it. If we remove the dot, the scene merely represents a hammer.

In panel (b) the dot represents the compound abstract concept RIGHT. If we remove the dot, the scene merely represents someone using a hammer. While the words represented are *the use of the hammer*, hammers don't use

---

[24] The Latin preposition for *to, ad,* takes the accusative case, which connotes motion toward something.

themselves. For a hammer to be in use, there must be someone to use it. That someone is a person, not any animal. Using a hammer also involves using other things like nails and wood.

A right in panel (b) is a substantive that hangs in the air. It cleaves to nothing; it's just out there. The right is not part of the physical scene of a person using a hammer. It is disembodied from the person using a hammer and, pardon the neologism, disemphysicalized from the hammer. The right is being imposed on the scene from outside the scene; the right is moving toward the person using the hammer. Where the use of the hammer goes, does the right so follow? The mental representation is unclear. Maybe the right whizzes right on by.

Such a difference between *in* and *to* meant something to the early seventeenth-century Jesuit priest and philosopher Francisco Suárez. As James Tully explains, Suárez distinguished a right in a thing (*ius in re*) from a right to a thing (*ius ad rem*).[25] The choice of preposition and case meant either the claim is already established—located as it were in the thing—or the claim is due or owed a person but yet to be established—located as it were outside the thing but in motion toward the thing.

Consider, further, representations of the noun phrases in Figure 9.1 but prepended with "She has": "She has property in the hammer" and "She has a right to the use of the hammer." The English transitive word *have* is durative of Proto-Germanic from the Proto-Indo-European *keh_2p-, meaning to take, seize, catch, that is, to grasp with one's hands.[26] Figures 9.2a and 9.2b contrast a literal representation of these two sentences.

The physicality of "She has property in the hammer" remains in panel (a). To grasp the property in the hammer, the woman grasps the hammer that contains the property. The property is literally within her grasp. (That's how easy it is to synecdochize the custom.) We cognize the abstract features of the physical world such that property is within her grasp. From the beginning tools were experienced as inside out, in common with others and thus with shared agreement and external acceptance. To grasp "a right to the use of the hammer," however, the woman in panel (b) grasps an amorphous concept. With an outside-in representation, something else must give it form.

The first point of this graphical excursion is to reiterate from chapter 1 that the conception of property rights as "the right to the use of Y" is too

---

[25] James Tully (1980, p. 67).
[26] See https://en.wiktionary.org/wiki/have. Last accessed August 17, 2016.

(a) "She has property in the hammer."   (b) "She has a right to the use of the hammer."

Figure 9.2. Mental Representations of "She has ... "

modern, too complex, and possibly too Anglo to explain how humans cognize property. We can't escape the modernity of how of our minds work, and I'm not discounting the value of the contemporary notion of property rights to explain the world. So let me be clear. The property right paradigm is a significant advancement in the study of economics, dare I say a Nobel Prize–worthy contribution by Alchian and Demsetz. But the conceptual complexity of this explanation inverts the simplicity with which property works in practice. More to the point, such conceptual complexity introduces a masked assumption about how property works. What I am proposing are the micro- and meso-level foundations for how people, from the Pleistocene plain to seventeenth-century Quebec and the modern world today, cognize property in things.

Property Effects Property Rights

The custom of property is knowing from experience, from physiological memory, when you can say about certain things, "This thing is mine." Such a claim under such circumstances is not the end of property. If it were, then property would be as purely subjective as I WANT THIS is. Rather, property is intersubjective in that people other than me can know from experience, from physiological memory, that what I say under such circumstances is *true*. Finally, property also involves an element of singularity. If under such circumstances I can say about certain things, "This is mine," then other people cannot say, "This is mine" about the very same things. Only I can use the singular atomic concept MINE to predicate a first-person claim on something that I have property in. Everyone else must use the compound concept YOURS when second-personally referring to my first-person claim. Mine and thine are intertwined. I rely on the concept of yours when I want others to acknowledge my claim that something is mine.

Such abstractions compose the moral custom of property and make possible other secondary scheduling patterns involving things. The primacy of property, rooted in the abstract concept MINE, explains other sets of expectations about what a person will do or won't do, the circumstances and probable effects of those actions, and the appropriate responses to what happens.[27] For example, my expectations as someone who can say, "This hammer is mine" are that:

1) I have exclusive physical control over the hammer;
2) I can personally use and enjoy the hammer;
3) I can decide how and by whom the hammer shall be used;
4) I can enjoy the fruits, rents, and profits arising from my personal use of the hammer;
5) I can alienate the hammer and waste or destroy the hammer;
6) I will have property in the hammer indefinitely if I choose and if I remain solvent;
7) I can transfer the property in the hammer to another person;
8) I am entitled to the property in the hammer for a duration of time;
9) I cannot use the hammer in ways that cause harm to others; and
10) I am liable to have the property in the hammer dissolved or transferred in case of debt or insolvency.[28]

[27] The general principle of the section follows F. A. Hayek (1952, 1978).
[28] See note 19.

Other people's expectations are also such that (1) through (10) are true. They say to me, "That hammer is yours."

Honoré's incidents from chapter 6 are secondary expectations that form because I have property in the hammer, because (1) I can say about the hammer: "It is mine"; (2) people can know that what I say is true; and (3) other people cannot say, "It is mine" about the hammer. Honoré's incidents are not the content of what it means to have property in things. Of course, I cannot use the hammer in any possible way that I imagine, like indiscriminately as a weapon, but that's not a constraint on the custom by which I can say, "This hammer is mine." Property does not constrain my use of the hammer as a weapon; other abstract customs in the social system, like "Thou shalt not murder," proscribe such uses of hammers.

Another expectation from having property in the hammer is that I can exclude you from using the hammer, and excluding you from using the hammer is likewise not the content of what it means to say, "This hammer is mine." An appropriate response by others, if I have property in the hammer and can say, "This is mine," is that they cannot say, "This hammer is mine." Another appropriate response is that others cannot use the hammer without my permission. I can say, "No!"[29] Like with expectations, such responses, however, are not the content of what it means to have property in the hammer. "This thing is mine" means "this thing is mine" in every language and cannot be deconstructed into any more primitive concepts. This conceptual and normative singularity serves as the core of property. The custom *in practice* constitutes a set of living expectations and appropriate responses to people's actions.

Compare this with how Alchian and Demsetz introduce "The Structure of Rights" in their seminal 1973 article entitled "The Property Right Paradigm":

> In common speech, we frequently speak of someone owning this land, that house, or these bonds. This conversational style undoubtedly is economical from the viewpoint of quick communication, but it masks the variety and complexity of the ownership relationship. What is owned are *rights* to *use* resources, including one's body and mind, and these rights are always circumscribed, often by the prohibition of certain actions. To "own land" usually means to have the right to till (or not to till) the soil, to mine the soil, to *offer* those rights for sale, etc., but not to have the right to throw soil at a

---

[29] David Schmidtz (2012).

passerby, to use it to change the course of a stream, or to *force* someone to buy it. What are owned are socially recognized rights of action. . . . It is not the resource itself which is owned; it is a bundle, or a portion, of rights to use a resource that is owned.[30]

Notice that Alchian and Demsetz de-thingify property in things in the tradition of legal realism. Property is not about things. Property is a bundle of incorporeal rights, that is, moral/legal/"socially recognized" relations between people. They don't define property rights in terms of what people can do, say, know, think, and feel about property in things, but in terms of the external effects, the consequences of what people do, say, know, think, and feel about the property in things. If the consequences, not how people think about things, are what matter, the things themselves become superfluous. Whereas property transcends the disjunction between the mind and the external world, the conception of property rights fixates on the external world to the exclusion of the internal mind. Mankiw doesn't mention any internal ethic against stealing, that we don't steal for the sake of not stealing, only that "we all rely on government-provided police and courts" to externally keep (other) bad people in line.[31]

When Alchian and Demsetz define "what is owned" by the expectations that follow from practicing the custom of property, it is, *pace* Alchian and Demsetz, the past participle *owned* that masks. Who verbs what? And why? In the active voice, the legal realist would say, "She owns a right to mine the soil." That sounds a little awkward, but okay, let's go with it for the moment. Why can she say, "A right to mine the soil is mine," and why can other people not say, "A right to mine the soil is mine"? Not because the woman "owns" the soil, because that "would mask the variety and complexity of the ownership relationship." What does such a right have to do with the woman, the soil, and the mining thereon? The language of a right is external to the woman, the soil, and the mining thereon. A right to mine the soil is disembodied from the woman and disemphysicalized from the soil.

The right is furthermore imposed on the scene from outside the scene. A right, though, isn't a "thing" in the physical world that imposes itself, so who imposes it? An assigner of rights? And how is the right imposed on the scene? Alchian and Demsetz continue their explanation of the structure of rights:

---

[30] Armen Alchian and Harold Demsetz (1973, p. 17, original italics).
[31] N. Gregory Mankiw (2015, p. 12).

The strength with which rights are owned can be defined by the extent to which an owner's decision about how a resource will be used actually determines the use. If the probability is "1" that an owner's choice of how a particular right should be exercised actually dominates the decision process that governs actual use, then that owner can be said to own absolutely the particular right under consideration. For example, a person may have an absolute right to pick apples off a tree, but not to prune the tree.[32]

The language of rights and the focal attention on the use of a resource unnecessarily muddy the problem. The important economic question is not, "Which property rights exist?," as if rights "exist" like a hammer physically exists.[33] Rather, the important economic question is, what is the human scheduling pattern regarding the tree and the apple? What do people do, say, know, think, and feel about property in the tree and the apple? The irony is that the language of rights cannot escape the physical world. Legal realists physicalize abstract rights with the metaphor of a bundle of sticks, which they then talk about as "existing" in the physical world like an actual stick exists in the physical world.[34] *Physicalizing the unphysical and dispensing with physical things is the inverse, I submit, of how human beings cognize property. We start with the thing and abstract the physical.*

If the thing is a cow, our symbolic minds cognize the property as in the cow, which means that property is also in the milk, calf, and hide of the cow. It makes no difference whether the use is consumption at home, alienation domestically or for export, nor that the hooves might someday be useful. The property in the thing indirectly refers to the use of the thing in the external world through the people and thing involved in the custom, like the word *cow* indirectly refers to the object 🐄 through the ideas conveyed in a sentence. Our minds use custom to pick out the reference in the world. *The woman has property in the swan.* With three substantives—person, property, thing—there are three pairwise relationships among them to pick out what property in a thing refers to in the external world. The problem with doing away with things is that without the constraints of the physical world of people and things, legal realists are free to imagine what they can design about something they can know rather little, particularly about the future.

---

[32] Armen Alchian and Harold Demsetz (1973, p. 17).
[33] Ibid. (p. 18).
[34] For detailed discussion of the bundle-of-rights metaphor of property, pro and con, see Symposium (2011).

Moreover, their designs may very well not fit with what people can do, say, know, think, and feel about property in things. Exhibit A: *Durfee*. Exhibit B: *Bowen*. Exhibit C: Lost versus mislaid items. Exhibit D: Employees as slaves.

If I have property in a tree, (1) I can say, "This tree is mine"; (2) other people know that what I say is true; and (3) other people cannot say, "This tree is mine." MINE is the singular atomic core of property. Just like with a pregnant cow, I have property in the apple before and after my tree produces it. One expectation that follows from having property in the tree is that I can prune the tree, and another is that you cannot prune it. I also have the expectation that I can sell the apple or grant you permission to pick the apple. Such are the secondary scheduling patterns of humans regarding apple trees. There is no need, at the meso-level, to invoke the amorphous concept of "a right" to use the thing and introduce the *qualitas occulta* of some assigner who imposes the right on the scene. Nor do we need to define the problem in terms of the use of the apple, the consequences of property. If I can say, "This tree is mine," I can sell you the apple or grant you permission to pick the apple. If I do either, implicitly by custom I am saying, "This apple is not mine; it is yours." The content of property is in what you and I do, say, know, think, and feel about property in the tree and the apple, at the singular center of which is the universal human concept MINE.

Because the concrete specifics regarding the connections between people and things can widely vary and countlessly so, not all of Honoré's incidents necessarily follow from the primary abstraction of property. Hammers don't seem to reproduce on their own, and the bank is unlikely to take the time and effort to seize it if I declare bankruptcy. So, Secondary Scheduling Patterns #4 (fruits provision) and #10 don't seem to apply to hammers.[35] But cows get pregnant and give birth to calves, and a Lexus is valuable enough to repossess and offset my deficiency balance. So, Secondary Scheduling Pattern #4 would apply to cattle and #10 to cars. The abstraction, the symbolic thought, common to hammers, cows, and cars is that by custom (1) I can say about the hammer, cow, or car: "This is mine"; (2) people can know that what I say is true; and (3) other people cannot say, "This is mine" about the hammer, cow, and car. The specific secondary scheduling patterns that follow depend on specific circumstances of time, place, people, and things. Our minds are a

---

[35] Another custom recorded in the Torah and Mishnah could also limit the application of Secondary Scheduling Pattern #10 to hammers. The tools of the trade exemption codified in U.S. bankruptcy law protects an insolvent debtor's livelihood.

system of abstract rules that classify and produce the "concrete particulars" of time and place.[36] *For the same reason that our minds operate in such a way that the abstract effects the particular, property effects property rights.*

The reason Honoré does not and could not assert his standard incidents to be a strict definition of the necessary-and-sufficient conditions of property is not because, as legal realists and bundle-of-sticks theorists assert, there is no strict essence of property, no prior concept of property. Their failure to articulate a universal concrete list of incidents to property does not imply, however, that there is no prior normative conception guiding the connections that humans make between themselves and things. Legal realists are wrong about this fact. "This is mine" is indeed prior, normative, and, moreover, universal to humankind. Property is an abstraction of a symbolic species that imposes only certain attributes, certain secondary scheduling patterns, on particular groups of people regarding certain things.

Some peoples, for example, those who live in common and civil law systems, use Secondary Scheduling Patterns #1, #2, and #5 as a foundation for legally settling disputes. Secondary scheduling patterns are secondary because property, on my account, is a pattern of human action cognitively and temporally prior to, in the words of Richard Epstein, "the rights of ownership . . . with three separate incidents: possession, use, and disposition."[37] The ancient Roman jurists appealed, respectively, to general rights of *ius possendi, ius utendi,* and *ius abutendi* to adjudicate competing first- and second-person claims of who can say, "*Hoc est meum.*" Such third-party adjudicators discovered what was indeed right and true regarding the circumstances of time and place surrounding a concrete particular dispute. Over time a "trinity of rights" emerged as part of the customary way of settling what are necessarily backward-looking cases.[38] Property effects rights of ownership, for as Hayek explains, "the task of the judge [is] to tell [disputants] what ought to have guided their expectations . . . because this was the established custom which they ought to have known."[39]

People unwilling to yield the primacy of rights to the primacy of property will no doubt object: *Saying "This is mine" is ipso facto a right. To say "This is mine!" is to talk of rights and wrongs. If someone says, "This tree is mine," it is wrong for someone else to chop it down and take the wood. It is wrong to*

[36] F. A. Hayek (1978, pp. 36–37).
[37] Richard Epstein (1985, pp. 59–60).
[38] Ibid. (p. 60).
[39] Friedrich Hayek (1973, p. 87).

carve one's initials into the trunk. It is wrong to even prune the tree. The rights of the tree owner correlatively define the duties of the nonowners. To which I reply, our minds mediate the ipso facto and any such right and correlative duty. Our symbolic minds form a connecting link between acts in the physical world and our sensing, our interpretation, of such acts as social facts and of any moral imperatives that follow from such acts.

Rights are secondary scheduling patterns because they only make sense with symbolic reference from the conception of property, namely that someone can say, "This tree is mine"; other people can know what they say is true; and other people cannot say, "This tree is mine." The abstract custom of property that operates in our minds classifies and produces particular concrete rights for the circumstances of time and place in question. I am not doing away with rights with respect to property. I am putting them in their rightful place, subordinate to a primeval human custom and our mediating symbolic minds.

Property Is a Fundamental Principle of Economics

Krugman and Wells note in passing that property rights make mutually beneficial transactions in markets possible. How does property make mutually beneficial exchange possible if, as I argue, property means more than restraining the thief in all of us just itching to get out? Parents don't teach their children the word for MINE; they learn it all on their own. Parents also don't teach their children the following rules of MINE:

- if I like it, it's mine;
- if I see it, it's mine;
- if it's in my hand, it's mine;
- if it looks like mine, it's mine;
- if I can take it from you, it's mine; and
- if I had it a little while ago, it's mine.[40]

Yet no human parent in any age or community lets these untaught rules of MINE stand unchecked, even for children raised by pirates.[41] Every generation

---

[40] See Google image search for "Kid's Property Laws," authors unknown.
[41] Peter Leeson (2009).

of parents socially transmits to their children the rules of how *not* to acquire something. In the modern world we create television programs to assist with the uptake. Parents teach and their children learn the rules of when they by practice can say, "This is mine," and reciprocally, the rules of when someone else by practice can say, "This is mine." As arbitrary as they may initially appear, children accept the authority of these rules because they accept their parent as an authority on how to conduct themselves. They follow the rule for the sake of following the rule, and they learn with age to follow the rule for its bearing on their character.

The problem is not that humans aren't taught the rules of when by custom they can say, "This is mine" and "That is yours." The problem is who is included in the reciprocal set of those to whom I respect and say, "That is yours." If only the personally known members of the small group or tribe count as those to whom I say, "That is yours," then historically everyone else is in the set of strangers who can be plundered.[42] Actually, the problem is primevally much worse than that. Alien primates, including humans for all but a tiny fraction of our history, are an instant homicidal threat. If five male chimpanzees happen upon a sixth not from their tribe, four each grab a limb while the fifth attacks the most vulnerable parts of the anatomy, beginning with the genitals. The conspecific need not be an actual physical threat. Chimpanzees will devour a foreign baby chimpanzee deserted by its mother (who so feared for her life that she somehow left her progeny behind).[43] Or, if you would like the authentic *Homo sapiens* experience, cross paths sometime with a pair of tribesmen in a Bolivian jungle so that you can feel the reciprocal instinctual fear of encountering strangers alone in the wild.[44] It was a remarkable event in human history when the first person—Ridley speculates in all likelihood that it was a woman—proposed exchanging one thing for another thing with an alien enemy.[45] We are the only species that regularly does this. As Ridley discusses at length, any old primate can exchange favors, like backscratching and sex, for food, but only humans routinely truck, barter, and exchange one thing for another with people we do not personally know.[46]

---

[42] See Bart Wilson (2015) and references therein.
[43] Thank you, Elizabeth Lonsdorf and Crickette Sanz, for sharing that truly horrifying video.
[44] Personal conversation with the field anthropologist Hillard Kaplan, who experienced just that.
[45] Matt Ridley (2010).
[46] Ibid.

To make exchange work between instinctual homicidal enemies, it would seem that the conspecifics would necessarily (1) need symbolic thought and (2) share a core set of primitive concepts.[47] Exchange for mutual benefit requires a mind that can think outside the here and now. Suppose Eve has eggs and happens upon Hava who has hemp. Eve thinks, "I want hemp" and wonders whether this person wants something like eggs. To exchange, Eve must imagine a future state of the world in which she has hemp and Hava eggs. To propose an exchange, Eve communicates the thoughts in her head to Hava. Setting the eggs in front of Hava, she asks, "Do you want this?" Then, pointing to the hemp, she says, "I want that." To do this, Eve must hold several symbols of the present in her mind: (1) a future Hava (2) who sets in front of her in the future (3) some future hemp (4) to a future herself. The future Hava points to the Hava in front of Eve, but it is symbolic because the future Hava does not directly refer to the Hava standing in front of Eve. Eve could have chosen *not* to set the eggs in front of Hava (something Hava could likewise imagine outside the here and now).

Jointly attending to Eve's goal, which is no simple ordinary thing in the animal kingdom, Hava could respond in many ways. She could, while pointing at the eggs, say, "I don't want that." Or she could attempt to take the eggs and run. Why would Hava need to run? Because Eve would still say, "That [basket] is mine." It would be bad for Eve to have no eggs and no hemp, and so she would respond accordingly to that harm.

Or, Hava could set the hemp down in front of Eve and say, "This is not mine; this is yours." At that very moment the physical world has not changed, but how Eve and Hava now think about the world has. They perceive the same neurophysical inputs differently. Up until that moment Eve could pick up the eggs and leave. Unless Hava had ill intentions all along, she would simply turn around and leave. But once Hava says, "This is not mine; this is yours" about the hemp, Hava cannot pick up the hemp, and Eve cannot touch the eggs without each responding to the discordant act. Of course, Hava could grab the hemp and run, but that is not Eve's expectation the moment Hava says, "This is not mine; this is yours."

The concepts MINE and YOURS (you can say about it: "This is mine") change how we think about things in the external world. Hava can at will think about and with MINE all she wants, but until she vocalizes the

---

[47] In what follows, see also Bart Wilson (2015). See Table 3.1 for a partial list of universal semantic primes, which includes, for our purposes: I, YOU, SOMETHING/THING, PERSON/PEOPLE, THIS, WANT, DON'T WANT, SAY, (IS) MINE, NOT, and CAN.

thought, until she says the words, "This is not mine; this is yours," MINE and YOURS do no work in the external world. Saying "This is not mine; this is yours" puts Eve's and Hava's minds in dialogue with each other and the external world. The words change the connections between people and things by changing how people perceive the physical objects themselves.

All voluntary exchanges in the physical human world rely on joint, reciprocal thoughts of "This is not mine; this is yours" whether they are explicitly voiced or not. While the concept MINE is at the constituent core of what makes exchanging things possible, it is the joint, reciprocal attention to the meaning of "This is not mine; this is yours" that makes exchanging things possible. As Adam Smith says, "Give me that which I want, and you shall have this which you want, is the meaning of every such offer."[48] The universal meaning of "This is not mine; this is yours" explains how *Homo sapiens* universally distributes and consumes goods in a way that no other animal does. In short, "This is not mine; this is yours" is a basic principle in the study of economics that makes possible an amazing feat of nature, the routine voluntary exchange of one thing for another thing.

What happens if the basic principle "This is not mine; this is yours" cannot be said of something, say, of rhinoceroses and elephants? If by government decree no one can say, "This ivory is mine," then no one can say freely in the open, "This ivory is not mine; this is yours." To call such a situation "market failure" means that we *expect* voluntary exchange to operate as it does for things like eggs and hemp. Why should we expect voluntary exchange to work the same for rhinoceroses and elephants when a basic principle is absent? Markets don't fail rhinoceroses and elephants. Let's place the blame where it squarely belongs and where economists never seem to put it: on people. People fail rhinoceroses and elephants. People are following a first-in-hand custom of hunting rhinoceroses and elephants in the common state of nature to the point that their populations are disappearing. Elephants are threatened because property is in the dead elephant and its ivory tusks, not in the live elephant. Such in-ness differentiates elephants from domestic cattle for which there curiously is no concern of extinction.

Why are rhinoceroses and elephants in the common state of nature? If people can say about swans in certain estuaries, "This swan is mine," why can't some people say about elephants in certain areas, "This elephant is

---

[48] Adam Smith (1776, p. 26).

mine"? If elephant populations were large and stable like swan populations, presumably people would be freely able to say, "This elephant is mine," because people, thinking beyond the here and now, care about conserving endangered species, not abundant species. If someone accidently or purposely destroyed all the elephants on his private lands but there were hundreds of thousands of every species elsewhere, we might cast aspersion on the person and punish him for his neglect or cruelty, but we wouldn't do so out of some concern for the survival of species. We would resent the person because he broke the moral customs against neglect or cruelty toward other living beings, not because he could say, "This elephant is mine." The potential for human neglect or cruelty toward elephants, however, doesn't seem to be much different than for any other wild grazing animal. People do not seem to be generally concerned that New Zealanders and Canadians fence in literally millions of white-tailed deer and call them "mine." So why can't Africans in some countries call some elephants "mine"? Elephants in many countries are in the common state of nature because some people do not want other people to be able to say, "This elephant is mine." Having heard stories about how some circus owners have maltreated elephants, we do not trust strangers to do right by the species. We harbor a fear that mine means something commercial, and commerce, we all know, corrupts us to do terrible things.[49] Or maybe MINE itself is the root of evil. Imagine what miseries and horrors will occur if we forget that the elephants of the world belong to all and the world to no one. Property in elephants is theft!

But with a little reflection I think we can say that MINE is not an inherently immoral concept. We must take care to distinguish an arrogant, chimpish notion of I WANT THIS masquerading as a claim of "This is mine." How we act on MINE can be repulsive, wasteful, and immoral when it doesn't adhere to a moral scheduling pattern of property, or it can be marvelous, prudent, and moral when it does. MINE is neither an economic panacea nor the Rousseauian font of all human misfortune and horror. MINE is a universal human concept, acted upon for good and for ill, but it only becomes the semantic core for property when people reciprocally and jointly recognize some things as mine and other things as yours to prevent conflict and avoid contention and injury.

---

[49] Washington Irving (1824), John Steinbeck (1939), Oliver Stone (1987), Neill Blomkamp (2009), Mohsin Hamid (2013), and so on and so on.

When some people are allowed to say, "This elephant is mine," they defend attacks against the elephant like they defend against attacks against their own person. In contrast, when government agents are tasked with defending elephants against attacks, they are not as effective—the evidence strongly suggests—in protecting elephants about which they cannot say, "These are mine."[50] Think about it natural-historically: Isn't it astonishing that people who can say, "This elephant is mine" will protect and defend the life of a distantly related fellow mammal against members of their own species who wish that distant relative harm? Isn't it furthermore prudent for such people to do so?[51] And isn't it then morally incumbent upon us to consider the possibility that property can save elephants from extinction?[52] Consider, for the moment, the beautiful and humane thoughts made possible by MINE.

Property Rights Are Unidirectional, but Human Action Is Bidirectional

Our conception of property is rooted *in* the external world; it doesn't hang in the air independent of the physical world. The legal realist assumes that the conception of a property right exists outside the physical world, which then, because humans think with such thoughts, can be articulated and applied at will to people in the physical world. And the legal centralist assumes that government enforcement is why ordinary people do not steal. The minds of the people, their scheduling patterns, and the things themselves are minor details. One consequence of thinking this way is that economists and political scientists—exemplified by such luminaries as Daron Acemoglu and James Robinson—tend to treat institutions as something to be added and stirred into human intercourse, to borrow Deirdre McCloskey's apt metaphor (see again Figure 9.1b).[53] If you merely change the "extractive institutions," Acemoglu and Robinson claim, economists can "engineer prosperity."[54] No, as McCloskey rightly argues in three lengthy volumes on the Bourgeois era, not if there's an "ethical failure" in the local scheduling pattern.[55] What the

---

[50] Michael McPherson and Michael Nieswiadomy (2007).
[51] Philosophers: Begin prescription.
[52] Philosophers: End prescription.
[53] Daron Acemoglu and James Robinson (2012) and Deirdre McCloskey (2016, ch. 15).
[54] Daron Acemoglu and James Robinson (2012, p. 450).
[55] See specifically Deirdre McCloskey (2016, p. 137).

external theory of property rights and macro-level institutions cannot explain is why the same institutions work with some groups of people and not with others, why different groups of people have different sets of expectations about what each other will or will not do and the appropriate responses to such actions. It cannot account for such different circumstances because it ignores the micro- and meso-foundations of property. It ignores the human mind and the community within which human minds reside.

People's conduct can be GOOD or BAD with respect to property. Property means both what is the case and what is not the case but contextually could have been. Certain abstract ideas like "I want to be a good person for the sake of being a good person and will respect commonly accepted claims of 'mine'" are what make the custom of property possible, and other abstract ideas like "I want this and I don't care what people think about me if I don't respect someone's commonly accepted claim of 'mine'" are what can make it impossible. There are no sufficient conditions for property and prosperity, only necessary ones.

The evidence I present critically calls the external theory of institutions into question for the case of property. The alternative I present situates the idea of property in a bidirectional relationship that extends to and from the minds of individuals and the moral scheduling pattern of their community. Humans cognize property as located in the thing, and we use the meaning of property to do work in the physical world by changing how we comprehend the very things themselves. Property is the custom by which we jointly and reciprocally think with the abstract concepts MINE and YOURS to perceive the physical world of things and people. One of the most consequential and marvelous things about thinking with property is that it makes the routine exchange of things possible, which is the hallmark of humanity and the very foundation of the study of economics.

Epilogue

The question of questions for economics, the problem that forms the basis of the discipline, to paraphrase the nineteenth-century biologist Thomas Henry Huxley, is the determination and discovery of humankind's relations to the universe of things. What are the limits of our power over things and of things' power over us are problems that present themselves, with great personal interest, to every human being born into the world.[1]

Almost without fail, the typical modern introduction to economics anchors the inquiry with the concept of allocating, specifically, allocating scarce resources among people with unlimited wants. Such a frame situates the problem in the mind's eye with a sense of motion (*al-*), of scanning the world to *locate* things as they move in time and space from point A to point B, but not point C. With a surer eye, Adam Smith makes clear that the core principle of the wealth of nations—today we might call it an axiom—is "the certain propensity in human nature . . . to truck, barter, and exchange one thing for another."[2] Things in a Smithian study of the world don't move in time and space by sheer forces of nature, like leaves on the wind or sticks in a river, but eyeball to eyeball, from Eve's grasp to Hava's, and reciprocally, from Hava's to Eve's. The human propensity regarding things, Smith astutely observes, is to exchange them by one's own accord. Human beings stand in the foreground of Smith's political economy, not in the shadows of the things themselves.

"Whether this propensity be one of those original principles in human nature, of which no further account can be given," Smith continues, "or whether, as seems more probable, it be the necessary consequence of the faculties of reason and speech, it belongs not to our present subject to inquire. It is common to all men, and to be found in no other race of animals." What Smith calls "the faculties of reason and speech," Terrence Deacon, Derek Bickerton, and I would call, not so simply, "symbolic thought and reference," and it can be found in one and only one species on the planet, ours. Confirming his genius, Smith unsurprisingly presages such an observation: "Nobody ever saw one animal by its gestures and natural cries signify to

---

[1] Thomas Henry Huxley (1863).
[2] Adam Smith (1776, p. 25).

The Property Species. Bart J. Wilson. Oxford University Press (2020) © Oxford University Press.
DOI: 10.1093/oso/9780190936785.001.0001

another, this is mine, that yours."[3] I have tried in the book to build on Adam Smith and explain his core axiom, to give more meaning to his almost surely carefully chosen words of *signify, mine,* and *yours,* which in haste we might be prone to read right over.

All animals make connections between themselves and certain things in their environment. Such connections to food and shelter, mates and off-spring, are necessary to keep our bodies alive and propagate the species. But humans have done more than simply propagate the species for 100,000 to 300,000 years. As recent as 10,000 years ago, every human being lived in extreme poverty, the modern equivalent of less than $1.90/day, and as recent as 300 years ago, the average human being lived on $1.90 to $3/day. As I write, the human career is approaching an amazing milestone. The extreme poverty rate is falling below 10 percent of the population and steadily approaching 5 percent.[4] Moreover, half of the world, according to a Brookings Institution estimate, is now living middle-class lives or better, on at least $11/day.[5] Let's let that sink in: half of the world. Extreme poverty is no longer the human condition. Since 1990, over 1 billion people have left extreme poverty.[6] That's 1 billion less in addition to 2.3 billion more total people living on the planet. The University of Oxford data visualizer Max Roser gives us some perspective: "Newspapers could have had the headline 'Number of people in extreme poverty fell by 137,000 since yesterday.' "[7] The life expectancy of 7.7 billion human beings is also increasing. In 1960, the world average was 52.6 years. Today, it is over 71.[8] No other species in the history of the planet is creating longer, healthier, more comfortable lives for itself. We do it by making and using tools to make and use tools. We do it by creating new objects. We do it by saying, in any language of the world, "This is mine," respectfully, "That is yours," and reciprocally, "This is not mine; this is yours."

In 1926, E. M. Forster wrote an essay that dealt with the psycho-ethical difficulties of property.[9] Feeling shameful as the new owner of a small grove, purchased with the royalties from Americans who wished to own personal copies of *A Passage to India,* Forster felt we should ask ourselves,

---

[3] Ibid. (p. 26).
[4] Max Roser and Esteban Ortiz-Ospina (2018).
[5] Homi Kharas and Kristofer Hamel (2018).
[6] Max Roser and Esteban Ortiz-Ospina (2018).
[7] https://twitter.com/MaxCRoser/status/919921745464905728. Last accessed December 28, 2018.
[8] World Bank Development Indicators.
[9] E. M. Forster (1926).

in accents that will vary in horror, this very important question: What is the effect of property upon the character? Don't let's touch economics; the effect of private ownership upon the community as a whole is another question—a more important question, perhaps, but another. Let's keep to psychology. If you own things, what's their effect on you? What's the effect on me of my wood?[10]

His answer: Owning the wood made him feel "enormously stout, endlessly avaricious, pseudo-creative, intensely selfish, . . . until those nasty Bolshies come and . . . thrust me aside into the outer darkness."[11] Forster lives, with a soft playful touch of irony, in the human tension of owning things. He wrote at a time when people would literally go on to murder millions who humanly dared to call things "Мой!" Yet notwithstanding such horrors, property weighs on Forster's spirit. It also weighs on the spirit of millions of people in nations today who, on average, live luxuriously on at least $130/day, but with little to no irony or playfulness.

If property does indeed bidirectionally extend to and from the minds of individuals and the moral scheduling pattern of their community, I think it right that we consider inverting Forster's question and ask ourselves, in accents that will vary in encouragement and wonder, this important question: What is the effect of character on property? Let's keep to biology and moral psychology. If you can say that something is "Mine!," what's the effect of your character on the socially transmitted practice of property? What's the effect on my local scheduling pattern of my character?

People in the arts and humanities are like economists, social scientists, lawyers, and ordinary people. They tend to think that the external world of things imposes itself upon us. I don't deny that it does. At any moment in time, four of the n dimensions of the physical world impose an interior, an exterior, and a boundary upon our minds. The tea is in the cup. But the relationship isn't one-way, as artists are acutely aware.[12] We humans with the spark of symbolic thought also impose ourselves, our minds, upon the world of things. Thus, much more mundanely than an artist's creation, the cow is represented to our minds as *in* heat. The woman has property *in* the swan.

---

[10] Ibid. (pp. 22–23).
[11] Ibid. (p. 26).
[12] Samuel Alexander (1933).

I can say, "This is mine," and other people can know that what I say is, in fact, true.

So when Forster says, and we re-cognize in ourselves, that owning something "makes me feel heavy" and "produces men of weight," it conveys meaning in a context in which owning something could make us feel light and produce people of buoyancy but didn't.[13] Why doesn't owning something make us feel light, fit, buoyant, and on a path through the eye of a needle into the Kingdom of Heaven? Why does our physiological memory convert the physiological impulses from a thing we call "Mine!" into a feeling of heaviness? It's not the physical thing itself. We're firmly in metaphorical territory here, except, of course, for the part that our physical bodies are indeed the store of our accumulated experiences. So why does the "I" in our body feel heavy when we can say about something, "This is mine"? We can remain ignorant in Nomanneslond as to whether it's a physical cause in our bodies or in our environment, or some combination of the two, that explains why we feel heavy. The point is, our moral psychology is embodied in the same physical container that we call "I." The physiological memory of our body may classify the neurophysical inputs it receives before presenting its representations to our mind, but it is the "I" in the body who feels and knows something about the world. It is the "I" in the body who feels that what I call mine "ought to be larger."[14] What I own doesn't unidirectionally make me feel heavy or avaricious or selfish. I feel, and I am responsible for how I act on how I feel.

Such responsibility is foisted upon me by our human sociality. I am socialized to and accountable for living with conspecifics in a number of different communities.[15] If I have a tendency to be avaricious or selfish, if I am disposed to act greedily or self-centeredly, my actions will adversely impact those whose paths I cross, and they will hold me responsible for how I act on my feelings. With symbolic thought, I evaluate my actions and how they fit, or fail to fit, with the scheduling patterns of the group. I self-contemplate my deeds and character. Through judicious responses to circumstances, I can cultivate my tendencies, my habits, to act as I would like to be thought of, by others, as acting.[16] I *can* feel light, fit, buoyant when I look out on Naboth's vineyard.

---

[13] E. M. Forster (1926, p. 23).
[14] Ibid.
[15] Vernon Smith and Bart Wilson (2019).
[16] Julia Annas (2011) and Adam Smith (1759).

Having Jezebel at my side, however, would make that more difficult than it already is. We rely on the people we surround ourselves with to serve as the mirror we need to think of our own character.[17] "[The mirror] is placed in the countenance and behavior," Adam Smith says, "of those [we] live with, which always mark when they enter into, and when they disapprove of [our] sentiments; and it is here that [we] first view the propriety and impropriety of [our] own passions, the beauty and deformity of [our] own mind[s]."[18]

Forster's essay exudes a sense of isolation. The discourse lives in the first-person singular with nary any first-person plural or third-person, singular or plural, physically present to serve as his mirror. His harsh diction—*enormously stout, endlessly avaricious, pseudo-creative, intensely selfish*—indicates the imperious demands of feeling to which his mind is subjected when he is alone.[19] Before the Bolshies arrive to wrap things up, such language feels discordantly punchy and a bit over the top for a new owner of a wood contemplating a bird and some blackberries. But it does fit Mary Shelley's Victor Frankenstein to a T. He sequesters himself from his professors, father, brother, and future wife to feverishly work on his grand creation, "to become greater than his nature will allow."[20] As we ponder the projects we wish to pursue, we must do the opposite of Frankenstein and surround ourselves with kith and kin, the loves of our lives.[21] We do bad things to people when we remove ourselves from the countenance of society.

Ahab, however, didn't murder Naboth and his sons. Jezebel is clearly, with a tinge of androcentrism, the villain of the story. But was not Ahab king over Israel? Was not Ahab the authority who could exhort what was right to the queen? A king with self-command would not sulk at Naboth's "unassailable" title.[22] But if he did, a king with cultivated self-awareness would contemplate his character and express some moral indignation at the queen's suggestion to kingly chimp up and take something if the alpha wants it. The uniquely human custom of property stood between Ahab and the vineyard to protect Naboth from those who had a stronger hand to challenge his grasp. Ahab's character failed Naboth and Jezebel, and everyone who practiced the custom and depended on it for their protection.

---

17 Adam Smith (1759, part III).
18 Ibid. (p. 110).
19 See Vernon Smith and Bart Wilson (2019, pp. 22–23).
20 Mary Shelley (1818, p. 35).
21 Jan Osborn, Bart Wilson, Mitchell Briggs, Alison Lee, and Alec Moss (2018).
22 Francis Andersen (1966, p. 47).

Exceedingly fit, mindfully temperate, and jointly attentive, an ethical character can restrain our unlimited thoughts of "I want this" with a cultivated respect for "This is mine" and "That is yours." The ancient custom of property affords a humane peace for us to pursue creative projects that make it entirely possible for the second half of humanity to also become middle class and wealthier.

Cases Cited

Armory v. Delamirie, 1 Strange 505 (1722), *The English Reports* (1378–1865) 93.

Bowen v. Sullivan, 62 (Indiana 1878) 281.

Bridges v. Hawkesworth, 21 (*Law Journal, Queen's Bench* 1851) 75, 15 *The Jurist* 1079.

Durfee v. Jones, 11 (Rhode Island 1877) 588.

Haslem v. Lockwood, 37 (Connecticut 1871) 500.

Jackson v. Steinberg, 186 (Oregon 1949) 129.

McAvoy v. Medina, 11 Allen (Massachusetts 1866) 548.

Pierson v. Post, 3 Cai. R. 175 (New York Supreme Court 1805).

Swift v. Gifford, 23 Federal Cases 558 (D. Massachusetts 1872) (No. 13,696).

References

Acemoglu, Daron, and James Robinson. 2012. *Why Nations Fail: The Origins of Power, Prosperity, and Poverty*. New York, NY: Crown Business.

Alchian, Armen A. 1965 [2006]. "Some Economics of Property Rights," *Il Politico* 30: 816–829. Reprinted in *The Collected Works of Armen A. Alchian: Volume 2: Property Rights and Economic Behavior*. Indianapolis, IN: Liberty Fund.

Alchian, Armen A., and Harold Demsetz. 1973. "The Property Rights Paradigm," *Journal of Economic History* 33, 16–27.

Alexander, Samuel. 1933 [1968]. *Beauty and Other Forms of Value*. New York, NY: Crowell Company.

Allen, Douglas W. 1991. "What Are Transaction Costs?," *Research in Law and Economics* 14, 1–18.

Almain, Jacques. Died 1515 [1706]. *Expositio, Circa Decisiones Magistri Guillielmi Occam, Super Potestate Summi Pontificis, De Potestate Ecclesiastica & Laica*, in Johannes Gerson's *Opera Omnia*, 1013–1120.

Ambrose, Stanley H. 2001. "Paleolithic Technology and Human Evolution," *Science* 291, 1748–1753.

Ambrose, Stanley H. 2010. "Coevolution of Composite-Tool Technology, Constructive Memory, and Language: Implications for the Evolution of Modern Human Behavior," *Current Anthropology* 51(S1), 135–147.

Ames, James B. 1913. *Lectures on Legal History*. Cambridge, MA: Harvard University Press.

Andersen, Francis I. 1966. "The Socio-Juridical Background of the Naboth Incident," *Journal of Biblical Literature* 85(1), 46–57.

Anderson, Terry L., and Laura E. Huggins. 2003. *Property Rights: A Practical Guide to Freedom and Prosperity*. Stanford, CA: Hoover Institution Press.

Annas, Julia. 2011. *Intelligent Virtue*. New York, NY: Oxford University Press.

Austin, J. L. 1975. *How to Do Things with Words*. Cambridge, MA: Harvard University Press.

Aylmer, G. E. 1980. "The Meaning and Definition of 'Property' in Seventeenth-Century England," *Past and Present* 86, 87–97.

Bacon, Francis. Died 1626 [1838]. *The Works of Lord Bacon*, Volume I. London, UK: William Ball, Paternoster Row.

Bakhtin, M. M. 1982. *The Dialogic Imagination: Four Essays*. Edited by Michael Holquist and translated by Michael Holquist and Caryl Emerson. Austin, TX: University of Texas Press.

Banner, Stuart. 2011. *American Property: A History of How, Why, and What We Own*. Cambridge, MA: Harvard University Press.

Barzel, Yoram. 1997. *Economic Analysis of Property Rights*. New York, NY: Cambridge University Press.

Beck, Benjamin B. 1980. *Animal Tool Behavior*. New York, NY: Garland Press.

Bell, Duran. 1998. "The Social Relations of Property and Efficiency," in *Property in Economic Context*, 29–45. Edited by Robert C. Hunt and Antonio Gilman. Lanham, MD: University Press of America.

Berger, Bethany R. 2006. "It's Not about the Fox: The Untold History of *Pierson v. Post*," *Duke Law Journal* 55(6), 1089–1143.

Berry, Christopher. 1982. *Hume, Hegel and Human Nature*. Boston, MA: Martinus Nijhoff Publishers.

Bickerton, Derek. 2009. *Adam's Tongue: How Humans Made Language, How Language Made Humans*. New York, NY: Hill and Wang.

Bing. 2015. "Not Yours," Episode 71. Produced by Mikael Shields. Based on Ted Dewan's original *Bing* books. London, UK: StudioCanal.

Birks, Peter. 2000. *English Private Law*. New York, NY: Oxford University Press.

Biro, Dora, Noriko Inoue-Nakamura, Rikako Tonooka, Gen Yamakoshi, Claudia Sousa, and Tetsuro Matsuzawa. 2003. "Cultural Innovation and Transmission of Tool Use in Wild Chimpanzees: Evidence from Field Experiments," *Animal Cognition* 6, 213–223.

Blackstone, Sir William. 1765 [2003]. *Commentaries on the Laws of England in Four Books*, Volume I, Book II. Clark, NJ: Lawbook Exchange.

Blackstone, Sir William A. 1803. *Commentaries on the Laws of England*. London, UK: Strahan.

Blomkamp, Neill (Director, Film). 2009. *District 9*. Wingnut Films.

Boehm, Christopher. 2012. *Moral Origins: The Evolution of Virtue, Altruism, and Shame*. New York, NY: Basic Books.

Boesch, Christophe. 2013. "Ecology and Cognition of Tool Use in Chimpanzees," in *Tool Use in Animals: Cognition and Ecology*, 21–47. Edited by Crickette M. Sanz, Josep Call, and Christophe Boesch. New York, NY: Cambridge University Press.

Brosnan, Sarah F. 2011. "Property in Nonhuman Primates," *Origins of Ownership of Property: New Directions for Child and Adolescent Development* 132, 9–22.

Brosnan, Sarah F., and Frans B. M. de Waal. 2002. "A Proximate Perspective on Reciprocal Altruism," *Human Nature* 13(1), 129–152.

Brown, Donald E. 1991. *Human Universals*. New York, NY: McGraw-Hill.

Brownell, Celia A., Stephanie S. Iesue, Sara R. Nichols, and Margarita Svetlova. 2013. "Mine or Yours? Development of Sharing in Toddlers in Relation to Ownership Understanding," *Child Development* 84, 906–920.

Buchanan, Joy A., and Bart J. Wilson. 2014. "An Experiment on Protecting Intellectual Property," *Experimental Economics* 17(4), 691–716.

Buckle, Stephen. 1991. *Natural Law and the Theory of Property: Grotius to Hume*. New York, NY: Oxford University Press.

Burke, Kenneth. 1966. *Language as Symbolic Action: Essays on Life, Literature, and Method*. Berkeley, CA: University of California Press.

Burt, William H. 1943. "Territoriality and the Home Range Concepts as Applied to Mammals," *Journal of Mammalogy* 24, 346–352.

Call, Josep, Malinda Carpenter, and Michael Tomasello. 2005. "Copying Results and Copying Actions in the Process of Social Learning: Chimpanzees (*Pan troglodytes*) and Human Children (*Homo sapiens*)," *Animal Cognition* 8, 151–163.

Carbaugh, Donal. 1988. *Talking American: Cultural Discourses on Donahue*. Norwood, NJ: Ablex.

Carvalho, Susana, Tetsuro Matsuzawa, and William C. McGrew. 2013. "From Pounding to Knapping: How Chimpanzees Can Help Us Model Hominin Lithics," in *Tool Use in*

Animals: Cognition and Ecology, 225–241. Edited by Crickette M. Sanz, Josep Call, and Christophe Boesch. New York, NY: Cambridge University Press.

Chang, Yun-chien, and Henry E. Smith. 2015. "The *Numerus Clausus* Principle, Property Customs, and the Emergence of New Property Forms," *Iowa Law Review* 100(6), 2275–2308.

Cheung, Steven N. S. 1969. *A Theory of Share Tenancy*. Chicago, IL: University of Chicago Press.

Claeys, Eric R. 2012. "Exclusion and Private Law Theory: A Comment on 'Property as the Law of Things,'" *Harvard Law Review Forum* 125, 133–150.

Claeys, Eric R. 2013. "Productive Use in Acquisition, Accession, and Labour Theory," in *Philosophical Foundations of Property Law*, 13–46. Edited by James Penner and Henry E. Smith. New York, NY: Oxford University Press.

Clark, Eve V. 1983. "Meanings and Concepts," in *Handbook of Child Psychology*, 4th Edition, Volume 3: *Cognitive Development*, 787–840. Edited by John H. Flavell and Ellen M. Markman (Paul H. Mussen, General Editor). New York, NY: Wiley.

Coase, Ronald. 1960. "The Problem of Social Cost," *Journal of Law and Economics* 3, 1–44.

Coke, Sir Edward. 1600 [2003]. *Selected Writings and Speeches of Sir Edward Coke*, Volume 1. Edited by Steve Sheppard. Indianapolis: Liberty Fund.

Coke, Sir Edward. 1628. *The First Part of the Institutes of the Lawes of England*. London, UK: Adam Islip for the Society of Stationers.

Coke, Sir Edward. 1642. *The Second Part of the Institute of the Lawes of England*. London, UK: Miles Flesher and Robert Young for Ephraim Dawson, Richard Meighen, William Lee, and Daniel Pakeman.

Cole, Daniel H., and Peter Z. Grossman. 2002. "The Meaning of Property Rights: Law versus Economics?," *Land Economics* 78(3), 317–330.

Cowen, Tyler, and Alex Tabarrok. 2018. *Modern Principles of Economics*, 4th Edition. New York, NY: Worth Publishers.

Crockett, Sean, Vernon L. Smith, and Bart J. Wilson. 2009. "Exchange and Specialisation as a Discovery Process," *Economic Journal* 119(539), 1162–1188.

Dawkins, Richard. 1976. *The Selfish Gene*. New York, NY: Oxford University Press.

Deacon, Terrence W. 1998. *The Symbolic Species: The Co-evolution of Language and the Brain*. New York, NY: W. W. Norton & Company.

Demsetz, Harold. 1967. "Toward a Theory of Property Rights," *American Economic Review* (*Papers & Proceedings*) 57, 347–359.

d'Errico, Francesco, Christopher S. Henshilwood, and Peter Nilssen. 2001. "An Engraved Bone Fragment from c. 70,000-Year-Old Middle Stone Age Levels at Blombos Cave, South Africa: Implications for the Origin of Symbolism and Language," *Antiquity* 75, 309–318.

d'Errico, Francesco, and Marian Vanhaeren. 2016. "Upper Paleolithic Mortuary Practices: Reflection of Ethnic Affiliation, Social Complexity, and Cultural Turnover," in *Death Rituals, Social Order and the Archaeology of Immortality in the Ancient World: "Death Shall Have No Dominion*," 45–62. Edited by Colin Renfrew, Michael J. Boyd, and Iain Morley. New York, NY: Cambridge University Press.

DeScioli, Peter, and Rachel Karpoff. 2015. "People's Judgments about Classic Property Law Cases," *Human Nature* 26(2), 184–209.

DeScioli, Peter, and Bart J. Wilson. 2011. "The Territorial Foundations of Human Property," *Evolution and Human Behavior* 32, 297–304.

Dixon, Thomas. 2008. *The Invention of Altruism: Making Moral Meanings in Victorian Britain*. New York, NY: Oxford University Press.

Domínguez-Rodrigo, Manuel, and Travis Rayne Pickering. 2003. "Early Hominid Hunting and Scavenging: A Zooarcheological Review," *Evolutionary Anthropology: Issues, News, and Reviews* 12(6), 275–282.

Dutton, Denis. 2010. *The Art Instinct: Beauty, Pleasure, and Human Evolution*. New York, NY: Bloomsbury Press.

Ellickson, Robert C. 1989. "A Hypothesis of Wealth-Maximizing Norms: Evidence from the Whaling Industry," *Journal of Law, Economics and Organization* 5, 83–97.

Ellickson, Robert C. 1994. *Order without Law: How Neighbors Settle Disputes*. Cambridge, MA: Harvard University Press.

Emery, Nathan J., and Nicola S. Clayton. 2004. "The Mentality of Crows: Convergent Evolution of Intelligence in Corvids and Apes," *Science* 306, 1903–1907.

Epstein, Richard A. 1985. *Takings: Private Property and the Power of Eminent Domain*. Cambridge, MA: Harvard University Press.

Epstein, Richard A. 1998. "Possession," in *The New Palgrave Dictionary of Economics and the Law*, Volume 3, 1462–1468. Edited by Peter Newman. New York, NY: Palgrave Macmillan.

Ferguson, Adam. 1767 [1782]. *An Essay on the History of Civil Society*, 5th Edition. London, UK: T. Cadell.

Fernandez, Angela. 2009. "The Lost Record of 'Pierson v Post,' the Famous Fox Case," *Law and History Review* 27(1), 149–178.

Fisher, Irving. 1906. *The Nature of Capital and Income*. New York, NY: Macmillan Company.

Forster, E. M. 1926 [1936]. "My Wood," in *Abinger Harvest*, 22–26. New York, NY: Harcourt, Brace and Company.

Fragaszy, Dorothy M., and Susan Perry. 2008. *The Biology of Traditions: Models and Evidence*. New York, NY: Cambridge University Press.

Frege, Gottlieb. 1879 [1970]. *Begriffsshcrift, a Formula Language Modeled on That of Arithmetic, for Pure Thought*. English translation in *Frege and Gödel: Two Fundamental Texts in Mathematical Logic*, 1–82. Edited by Jean van Heijenoort. Cambridge, MA: Harvard University Press.

Friedman, Ori, and Karen R. Neary. 2008. "Determining Who Owns What: Do Children Infer Ownership from First Possession?," *Cognition* 107(3), 829–849.

Fuster, Joaquín M. 2003. *Cortex and Mind: Unifying Cognition*. New York, NY: Oxford University Press.

Gardenston(e), Lord. 1774. "Lords Opinions Concerning Literary Property," *Scots Magazine* 36, 14–17.

Gintis, Herbert. 2007. "The Evolution of Private Property," *Journal of Economic Behavior and Organization* 64, 1–16.

Goddard, Cliff. 2011. *Semantic Analysis: A Practical Introduction*, Revised 2nd Edition. New York, NY: Oxford University Press.

Goddard, Cliff. 2012. "Semantic Primes, Semantic Molecules, Semantic Templates: Key Concepts in the NSM Approach to Lexical Typology," *Linguistics* 50(3), 711–743.

Goddard, Cliff, and Anna Wierzbicka. 1994. *Semantic and Lexical Universals: Theory and Empirical Findings*. Amsterdam: John Benjamins.

Goddard, Cliff, and Anna Wierzbicka. 2002. *Meaning and Universal Grammar: Theory and Empirical Findings*, Volume 2. Philadelphia, PA: John Benjamins Publishing Company.

Goddard, Cliff, and Anna Wierzbicka. 2014. *Words and Meanings: Lexical Semantics across Domains, Languages, and Cultures*. New York, NY: Oxford University Press.

Goddard, Cliff, and Anna Wierzbicka. 2016. "'It's Mine!'. Re-thinking the Conceptual Semantics of 'Possession' through NSM," *Language Sciences* 56, 93–104.

Goddard, Cliff, Anna Wierzbicka, and Horacio Fabréga Jr. 2014. "Evolutionary Semantics: Using NSM to Model Stages in Human Cognitive Evolution," *Language Sciences* 42, 60–79.

Goethe, Johann Wolfgang von. 1981. *Goethes Werke, Naturwissenshaftliche Schriften 1* in *Hamburger Ausgabe*, 14 Volumes. Edited by Erich Trunz and Hans Joachim Schrimpf. München: Verlag C. H. Beck.

Gower, John. c.1393 [2013]. *Confessio Amantis*, Volume 2. Edited by Russell A. Peck and translated by Andrew Galloway. Kalamazoo, MI: Medieval Institute Publications. Available at http://d.lib.rochester.edu/teams/publication/peck-gower-confessio-amantis-volume-2. Last accessed April 1, 2016.

Grotius, Hugo. 1604 [1868]. *De Jure Praedae Commentarius*. Edited by H. G. Hamaker. Hagae Comitum: Martinus Nijoff.

Grotius, Hugo. 1604 [1995]. *De Iure Praedae Commentarius*, Volume I. Translated by Gwladys L. Williams and Walter H. Zeydel. Buffalo, NY: William S. Hein.

Grotius, Hugo. 1625 [1853]. *Rights of War and Peace, an Abridged Translation*. Translated by William Whewell. London, UK: Cambridge University Press.

Grotius, Hugo. 1625 [1913]. *De Iure Belli ac Pacis, Liber II*. Washington, DC: Carnegie Institution of Washington.

Grotius, Hugo. 1625 [1925]. *De Iure Belli ac Pacis, Liber II*. Translated by Francis W. Kelsey. London, UK: Clarendon Press.

Grotius, Hugo. 1625 [2005]. *The Rights of War and Peace, Book II*. Edited by Richard Tuck. Indianapolis: Liberty Fund.

Hallowell, A. Irving. 1943. "The Nature and Function of Property as a Social Institution," *Journal of Legal and Political Sociology* 1, 115–138.

Hamid, Mohsin. 2013. *How to Get Filthy Rich in Rising Asia: A Novel*. New York, NY: Riverhead Books.

Harding, Sandra G. (Editor). 1976. *Can Theories Be Refuted: Essays on the Duhem-Quine Thesis*. Dordrecht, Holland: D. Reidel Publishing Company.

Hayek, F. A. 1952. *The Sensory Order: An Inquiry into the Foundations of Theoretical Psychology*. Chicago, IL: University of Chicago Press.

Hayek, F. A. 1963. "Rules, Perception and Intelligibility," *Proceedings of the British Academy* 48, 321–344.

Hayek, Friedrich A. 1973. *Law, Legislation, and Liberty, Volume 1: Rules and Order*. Chicago, IL: University of Chicago Press.

Hayek, F. A. 1978. "The Primacy of the Abstract," in *New Studies in Philosophy, Politics, Economics, and the History of Ideas*, 35–56. London, UK: Routledge & Kegan Paul.

Hayek, F. A. 1988. *The Fatal Conceit: The Errors of Socialism*. Chicago, IL: University of Chicago Press.

Henrich, Joseph, Steven J. Heine, and Ara Norenzayan. 2010. "The Weirdest People in the World," *Behavioral and Brain Sciences* 33, 61–83.

Henshilwood, Christopher, Francesco d'Errico, Karen L. van Niekerk, Yvan Coquinot, Zenobia Jacobs, Stein-Erik Lauritzen, Michel Menu, and Renata García-Moreno. 2011. "A 100,000-Year-Old Ochre-Processing Workshop at Blombos Cave, South Africa," *Science* 334 (6053), 219–222.

Heylighen, Francis. 1999. "Advantages and Limitations of Formal Expression," *Foundations of Science* 4, 25–56.

Hickey, Robin. 2015. "*Armory v. Delamirie* (1722): Possession, Obligation, and the Evolution of Relative Title to Goods," in *Landmark Cases in Property Law*, 131–150. Edited by Simon Douglas, Robin Hickey, and Emma Waring. Portland, OR: Hart Publishing.

Hockett, C. F. 1973. *Man's Place in Nature*. New York, NY: McGraw-Hill.

Hodgson, Geoffrey M. 2015. "Much of the 'Economics of Property Rights' Devalues Property and Legal Rights," *Journal of Institutional Economics* 11, 683–709.

Hoffman, Elizabeth, Kevin McCabe, Keith Shachat, and Vernon Smith. 1994. "Preferences, Property Rights, and Anonymity in Bargaining Games," *Games and Economic Behavior* 7(3), 346–380.

Hohfeld, Wesley N. 1919. *Fundamental Legal Conceptions as Applied in Judicial Reasoning and Other Legal Essays*. New Haven, CT: Yale University Press.

Holmes, Oliver Wendell. 1881. *The Common Law*. Boston, MA: Little, Brown and Company.

Honoré, A. M. 1961. "Ownership," in *Oxford Essays in Jurisprudence*, 107–147. Edited by A. G. Guest. New York, NY: Oxford University Press.

Hume, David. 1740 [2000]. *A Treatise of Human Nature*. Edited by David Fate Norton and Mary J. Norton. New York, NY: Oxford University Press.

Hume, David. 1751 [1961]. *Enquiries Concerning the Human Understanding and Concerning the Principles of Morals*, 2nd Edition. Edited by L. A. Selby-Bigge. New York, NY: Oxford University Press.

Hunt, Gavin R., Russell D. Gray, and Alex H. Taylor. 2013. "Why Is Tool Use Rare in Animals?," in *Tool Use in Animals: Cognition and Ecology*, 89–118. Edited by Crickette M. Sanz, Josep Call, and Christophe Boesch. New York, NY: Cambridge University Press.

Huxley, Thomas Henry. 1863. *Evidence as to Man's Place in Nature*. London, UK: Williams & Norgate.

Irving, Washington. 1824 [1975]. "The Devil and Tom Walker," in *The Complete Tales of Washington Irving*, 437–448. Edited by Charles Neider. Garden City, NY: Doubleday & Company.

Jarman, Peter J., and Hans Kruuk. 1996. "Phylogeny and Spatial Organization in Mammals," in *Comparison of Marsupial and Placental Behaviour*, 80–101. Edited by David B. Croft and Udo Ganslosser. Fiirth, Germany: Filander Verlag.

Jaworski, Taylor, and Bart J. Wilson. 2013. "Go West Young Man: Self-Selection and Endogenous Property Rights," *Southern Economic Journal* 79, 886–904.

Jelbert, S. A., R. J. Hosking, A. H. Taylor, and R. D. Gray. 2018. "Mental Template Matching Is a Potential Cultural Transmission Mechanism for New Caledonian Crow Tool Manufacturing Traditions," *Nature Scientific Reports* 8, 8956.

Johnson, Allen W., and Timothy Earle. 2000. *The Evolution of Human Societies: From Foraging Group to Agrarian State*. Stanford, CA: Stanford University Press.

Kant, Immanuel. 1797 [1996]. *The Metaphysics of Morals*. Edited and translated by Mary Gregor. New York, NY: Cambridge University Press.

Kharas, Homi, and Kristofer Hamal. 2018. "A Global Tipping Point: Half the World Is Now Middle Class or Wealthier," Brookings Institution, September 27 Blog Post. Available at https://www.brookings.edu/blog/future-development/2018/09/27/a-global-tipping-point-half-the-world-is-now-middle-class-or-wealthier/. Last accessed November 6, 2018.

Kimbrough, Erik O. 2011. "Learning to Respect Property by Refashioning Theft into Trade," *Experimental Economics* 14(1), 84–109.

Kimbrough, Erik O., Vernon L. Smith, and Bart J. Wilson. 2008. "Historical Property Rights, Sociality, and the Emergence of Impersonal Exchange in Long-Distance Trade," *American Economic Review* 98(3), 1009–1039.

Kimbrough, Erik O., Vernon L. Smith, and Bart J. Wilson. 2010. "Exchange, Theft, and the Social Formation of Property," *Journal of Economic Behavior and Organization* 74(3), 206–229.

Kimbrough, Erik O., and Bart J. Wilson. 2013. "Insiders, Outsiders, and the Adaptability of Informal Rules to Ecological Shocks," *Ecological Economics* 90, 29–40.

Klein, Richard G. 2000. "Archeology and the Evolution of Human Behavior," *Evolutionary Anthropology* 9, 17–36.

Klugh, A. Brooker. 1927. "Ecology of the Red Squirrel," *Journal of Mammalogy* 8, 1–32.

Krugman, Paul, and Robin Wells. 2009. *Economics*, 2nd Edition. New York, NY: Worth Publishers.

Kuhn, Sherman M., and Hans Kurath. 1952. *Middle English Dictionary*, Volume 8. Ann Arbor, MI: University of Michigan Press.

Kummer, Hans, and Marina Cords. 1991. "Cues of Ownership in Long-Tailed Macaques, *Macaca fascicularis*," *Animal Behaviour* 42, 529–549.

Kummer, Hans, Wolfgang Götz, and W. Angst. 1974. "Triadic Differentiation: An Inhibitory Process Protecting Pair Bonds in Baboons," *Behaviour* 49, 62–87.

Leeson, Peter T. 2009. *The Invisible Hook: The Hidden Economics of Pirates*. Princeton, NJ: Princeton University Press.

Lewis, Charton T., and Charles Short (Editors). 1879. *A Latin Dictionary Founded on Andrews' Edition of Freund's Latin Dictionary*. Oxford, UK: Clarendon Press.

Linton, Ralph. 1952. "Universal Ethical Principles: An Anthropological View," in *Moral Principles of Action: Man's Ethical Imperative*, 645–660. Edited by Ruth Nanda Anshen. New York, NY: Harper & Brothers.

Locke, John. 1689 [1988]. *Two Treatises of Government*. Edited by Peter Laslett. New York, NY: Cambridge University Press.

Long, George. 1842. "Actio," in *A Dictionary of Greek and Roman Antiquities*, 7–11. Edited by William Smith. London, UK: Samuel Bentley.

Mackeldey, Ferdinand. 1883. *Handbook of the Roman Law*. Translated and edited by Moses A. Dropsie. Philadelphia, PA: T. & J. W. Johnson & Co.

Macleod, Henry Dunning. 1881. *The Elements of Economics*, Volume 1. New York, NY: D. Appleton & Co.

Madison, James. 1792. "Property," *National Gazette* 14 (March 29), 266–268. Available at http://press-pubs.uchicago.edu/founders/documents/v1ch16s23.html. Last accessed April 18, 2016.

Mair, John. Died 1550 [1706]. *Disputatio, De Statu & Potestate Ecclesiae*, in Johannes Gerson's *Opera Omnia*, 1121–1164.

Mäkinen, Virpi. 2001. *Property Rights in the Late Medieval Discussion on Franciscan Poverty*. Leuven, Belgium: Peeters.

Mankiw, N. Gregory. 2015. *Principles of Economics*, 7th Edition. Stamford, CT: Cengage Learning.

Matsuzawa, Tetsuro, Dora Biro, Tatyana Humle, Noriko Inoue-Nakamura, Rikako Tonooka, and Gen Yamakoshi. 2001. "Emergence of Culture in Wild Chimpanzees: Education by Master-Apprenticeship," in *Primate Origins of Human Cognition and Behavior*, 557–574. Edited by Tetsuro Matsuzawa. Tokyo, Japan: Springer.

Maynard Smith, John, and George R. Price. 1973. "The Logic of Animal Conflict," *Nature* 246(2), 15–18.

McCloskey, Deirdre N. 2006. *The Bourgeois Virtues: Ethics for an Age of Commerce.* Chicago, IL: University of Chicago Press.

McCloskey, Deirdre N. 2010. *Bourgeois Dignity: Why Economics Can't Explain the Modern World.* Chicago, IL: University of Chicago Press.

McCloskey, Deirdre N. 2016. *Bourgeois Equality: How Ideas, Not Capital or Institutions, Enriched the World.* Chicago, IL: University of Chicago Press.

McPherson, Michael A., and Michael L. Nieswiadomy. 2007. "African Elephants: The Effect of Property Rights and Political Stability," *Contemporary Economic Policy* 18(1), 14–26.

Merrill, Thomas W. 1998. "Property and the Right to Exclude," *Nebraska Law Review* 77, 730–755.

Merrill, Thomas W., and Henry E. Smith. 2000. "Optimal Standardization in the Law of Property: The *Numerus Clausus* Principle," *Yale Law Journal* 110, 1–70.

Merrill, Thomas W., and Henry E. Smith. 2001. "What Happened to Property in Law and Economics," *Yale Law Journal* 111, 357–398.

Merrill, Thomas W., and Henry E. Smith. 2007. "The Morality of Property," *William and Mary Law Review* 48, 1849–1887.

Millard, Will (Host, Series). 2015. "The Whale Hunters of Lamalera," Episode 1, in *Hunters of the South Seas.* London, UK: British Broadcasting Corporation.

Munzer, Stephen R. 2001. "Property as Social Relations," in *New Essays in the Legal and Political Theory of Property*, 36–75. Edited by Stephen R. Munzer. New York, NY: Cambridge University Press.

Murdock, George P. 1945. "The Common Denominator of Cultures," in *The Science of Man in the World Crisis*, 123–142. Edited by Ralph Linton. New York, NY: Columbia University Press.

Neale, Walter C. 1998. "Property: Law, Cotton-Pickin' Hands, and Implicit Cultural Imperialism," in *Property in Economic Context*, 47–64. Edited by Robert C. Hunt and Antonio Gilman. Lanham, MD: University Press of America.

Neary, Karen R., Julia W. Van de Vondervoort, and Ori Friedman. 2012. "Artifacts and Natural Kinds: Children's Judgments about Whether Objects Are Owned," *Developmental Psychology* 48(1), 149–158.

Nicholas, Barry. 1962. *An Introduction to Roman Law.* New York, NY: Oxford University Press.

North, Douglass C. 1992. *Transaction Costs, Institutions, and Economic Performance.* San Francisco, CA: ICS Press.

Nozick, Robert. 1974. *Anarchy, State, and Utopia.* New York, NY: Basic Books.

Olivecrona, Karl. 1974. "Locke's Theory of Appropriation," *Philosophical Quarterly* 24(96), 220–234.

Ortolan, Joseph Louis Elzéar. 1896. *The History of Roman Law*, 2nd Edition. Translated by Iltudus T. Prichard and David Nasmith. London, UK: Butterworth & Co.

Osborn, Jan, Bart J. Wilson, Mitchell Briggs, Alison Lee, and Alec Moss. 2018. "A Theory of Sociality, Morality, and Monsters: Adam Smith and Mary Shelley," Working paper, Smith Institute for Political Economy and Philosophy, Chapman University. Available at SSRN: https://ssrn.com/abstract=3206800 or http://dx.doi.org/10.2139/ssrn.3206800.

Pack, Spencer J., and Eric Schliesser. 2006. "Smith's Humean Criticism of Hume's Account of the Origin of Justice," *Journal of the History of Philosophy* 44(1), 47–63.

Pavlenko, Aneta. 2011. "Introduction: Bilingualism and Thought in the 20th Century," in *Thinking and Speaking in Two Languages*, 1–28. Edited by Aneta Pavelenko. Tonawanda, NY: Multilingual Matters.

Penner, J. E. 1997. *The Idea of Property in Law*. New York, NY: Oxford University Press.

Penner, James, and Henry E. Smith (Editors). 2013. *Philosophical Foundations of Property Law*. New York, NY: Oxford University Press.

Pierce, Jon L., Tatiana Kostova, and Kurt T. Dirks. 2003. "The State of Psychological Ownership: Integrating and Extending a Century of Research," *Review of General Psychology* 7(1), 84–107.

Pinker, Steven. 1999. *How the Mind Works*. New York, NY: W. W. Norton & Company.

Pinker, Steven. 2007. *The Stuff of Thought: Language as a Window into Human Nature*. New York, NY: Viking.

Pipes, Richard. 2000. *Property and Freedom*. New York, NY: Random House.

Plutarch. Died c. 120 CE [1874]. *Plutarch's Morals*. Translated from the Greek by several hands. Corrected and revised by William W. Goodwin. Boston, MA: Little, Brown, and Company.

Polanyi, Michael. 1958. *Personal Knowledge: Towards a Post-critical Philosophy*. Chicago, IL: University of Chicago Press.

Pollock, Sir Frederick, and Frederic W. Maitland. 1895. *The History of English Law before the Time of Edward I*, Volume II. Boston, MA: Little, Brown, & Company.

Posner, Richard A. 2000. "Savigny, Holmes, and the Law and Economics of Possession," *Virginia Law Review* 86, 535–67.

Proudhon, Pierre-Joseph. 1840 [2011]. *Property Is Theft!: A Pierre-Joseph Proudhon Anthology*. Edited by Iain McKay. Oakland, CA: AK Press.

Pufendorf, Samuel. 1672 [2005]. *Of the Law of Nature and Nations: Eight Books*. Clark, NJ: Lawbook Exchange.

Rasmussen, Douglas B., and Douglas J. Den Uyl. 2005. *Norms of Liberty*. University Park, PA: Pennsylvania State University Press.

Ridley, Matt. 2004. *The Agile Gene: How Nature Turns on Nurture*. New York, NY: Harper.

Ridley, Matt. 2010. *The Rational Optimist: How Prosperity Evolves*. New York, NY: Harper.

Ripstein, Arthur. 2009. *Force and Freedom: Kant's Legal and Political Philosophy*. Cambridge, MA: Harvard University Press.

Ripstein, Arthur. 2013. "Possession and Use," in *Philosophical Foundations of Property Law*, 156–181. Edited by James Penner and Henry E. Smith. New York, NY: Oxford University Press.

Roberts, Simon. 1982. "More Lost Than Found," *Modern Law Review* 45, 683–689.

Robinson, Jonathan. 2013. *William of Ockham's Early Theory of Property Rights in Context*. Boston, MA: Brill.

Rose, Carol M. 1985. "Possession as the Origin of Property," *University of Chicago Law Review* 52, 73–88.

Rose, Carol M. 1994. *Property and Persuasion: Essays on the History, Theory, and Rhetoric of Ownership*. Boulder, CO: Westview Press.

Rose, Carol M. 2013. "Psychologies of Property (and Why Property Is Not a Hawk/Dove Game)," in *Philosophical Foundations of Property Law*, 272–288. Edited by James Penner and Henry E. Smith. New York, NY: Oxford University Press.

Roser, Max, and Esteban Ortiz-Ospina. 2018. "Global Extreme Poverty," Published online at *OurWorldInData.org*. Retrieved from https://ourworldindata.org/extreme-poverty. Last accessed October 30, 2018.

Rousseau, Jean-Jacques. 1754 [2005]. *On the Origin of the Inequality*. Translated by G. D. H. Cole. New York, NY: Cosimo.

Ruiz, April, and Laurie R. Santos. 2013. "Understanding Differences in the Way Human and Non-human Primates Represent Tools: The Role of Teleological-Intentional Information," in *Tool Use in Animals: Cognition and Ecology*, 119–133. Edited by Crickette M. Sanz, Josep Call, and Christophe Boesch. New York, NY: Cambridge University Press.

Rutz, Christian, Barbara C. Klump, Lisa Komarczyk, Rosanna Leighton, Joshua Kramer, Saskia Wischnewski, Shoko Sugasawa, Michael B. Morrisey, Richard James, James St. Clair, Richard A. Switzer, and Bryce M. Masuda. 2016. "Discovery of Species-Wide Tool Use in the Hawaiian Crow," *Nature* 537, 403–407.

Salmond, John W. 1907. *Jurisprudence, or, the Theory of Law*, 2nd Edition. London, UK: Stevens and Haynes.

Sanz, Crickette M., Caspar Schöning, and David B. Morgan. 2010. "Chimpanzees Prey on Army Ants with Specialized Tool Set," *American Journal of Primatology* 72, 17–24.

Scarre, Christopher, and Brian M. Fagan. 2008. *Ancient Civilizations*, 3rd Edition. New York, NY: Routledge.

Schmidtz, David. 2012. "The Institution of Property." Mimeo. Revised from "The Institution of Property," *Social Philosophy and Policy* 11 (1994), 42–62.

Schulz, Fritz. 1951. *Classical Roman Law*. New York, NY: Oxford University Press.

Seipp, David J. 1994. "The Concept of Property in the Early Common Law," *Law and History Review* 12, 29–91.

Sened, Itai. 1997. *The Political Institution of Private Property*. New York, NY: Cambridge University Press, 1997.

Seyfarth, Robert, Dorothy Cheney, and Peter Marler. 1980. "Monkey Responses to Three Different Alarm Calls: Evidence of Predator Classifications and Semantic Communication," *Science* 210, 801–803.

Shelley, Mary. 1818 [2008]. *Frankenstein, or, The Modern Prometheus*. Edited by Marilyn Butler. New York, NY: Oxford University Press.

Shriver, Lionel. 2018. *Property: Stories between Two Novellas*. New York, NY: Harper.

Shumaker, Robert W., Kristina R. Walkup, and Benjamin B. Beck. 2011. *Animal Tool Behavior: The Use and Manufacture of Tools by Animals*. Baltimore, MD: Johns Hopkins University Press.

Sigg, Hans, and Jost Falett. 1985. "Experiments on Respect of Possession and Property in Hamadryas Baboons (*Papio hamadryas*)," *Animal Behaviour* 33, 978–984.

Smith, Adam. 1759 [1982]. *The Theory of Moral Sentiments*. Indianapolis, IN: Liberty Fund.

Smith, Adam. 1776 [1982]. *An Inquiry into the Nature and Causes of the Wealth of Nations*, Volume I. Indianapolis, IN: Liberty Fund.

Smith, Adam C., David Skarbek, and Bart J. Wilson. 2012. "Anarchy, Groups, and Conflict: An Experiment on the Emergence of Protective Associations," *Social Choice and Welfare* 38(2), 325–353.

Smith, Henry E. 2009. "Community and Custom in Property," *Theoretical Inquiries in Law* 10(1), 5–41.

Smith, Henry E. 2012. "Property as the Law of Things," *Harvard Law Review* 125, 1691–1726.

Smith, Vernon L. 1994. "Economics in the Laboratory," *Journal of Economic Perspectives* 8(1), 113–131.

Smith, Vernon L., and Bart J. Wilson. 2019. *Humanomics: Moral Sentiments and the Wealth of Nations for the Twenty-First Century*. New York, NY: Cambridge University Press.

Stake, Jeffrey E. 2004. "The Property 'Instinct,'" *Philosophical Transactions of the Royal Society of London, UK: Biological Sciences* 359, 1763–1774.

Steinbeck, John. 1939 [2006]. *The Grapes of Wrath*. New York, NY: Penguin Classics.

Strassman, Joan E., and David C. Quellar. 2014. "Privatization and Property in Biology," *Animal Behaviour* 92, 305–311.

Stone, Oliver (Director, Film). 1987. *Wall Street*. Twentieth Century Fox Film Corporation.

Stout, Martha. 2005. *The Sociopath Next Door—The Ruthless versus the Rest of Us*. New York, NY: Broadway Books.

Stringham, Edward P. 2015. *Private Governance: Creating Order in Economics and Social Life*. New York, NY: Oxford University Press.

Sugden, Robert. 1986 [2005]. *The Economics of Rights, Cooperation and Welfare*, 2nd Edition. New York, NY: Palgrave Macmillan.

Swadling, William. 2008. "Ignorance and Unjust Enrichment," *Oxford Journal of Legal Studies* 28(4), 627–658.

Symposium. 2011. "Property: A Bundle of Rights?," *Econ Journal Watch* 8(3), 193–291.

Tattersall, Ian. 2012. *Masters of the Planet: The Search for Our Human Origins*. New York, NY: Palgrave Macmillan.

Thieme, Harmut. 1997. "Lower Palaeolithic Hunting Spears from Germany," *Nature* 385, 807–810.

Thorpe, W. H. 1963. *Learning and Instinct in Animals*. Cambridge, MA: Harvard University Press.

Thrasher, John. 2019. "Self-Ownership as Personal Sovereignty," *Social Philosophy and Policy* 36(2), 116–133.

Tomasello, Michael. 2014. *A Natural History of Human Thinking*. Cambridge, MA: Harvard University Press.

Tully, James. 1980. *A Discourse on Property: John Locke and His Adversaries*. New York, NY: Cambridge University Press.

Tuomela, Raimo. 2010. *The Philosophy of Sociality: The Shared Point of View*. New York, NY: Oxford University Press.

Tyler, Andrea, and Vyvyan Evans. 2003. *The Semantics of English Prepositions*. New York, NY: Cambridge University Press.

Underkuffler, Laura S. 2003. *The Idea of Property: Its Meaning and Power*. New York, NY: Oxford University Press.

van Dijk, Conrad. 2013. *John Gower and the Limits of Law*. New York, NY: Boydell and Brewer.

von Bayern, A. M. P., S. Daniel, A. M. I. Auersperg, B. Mioduszewska, and A. Kacelnik. 2018. "Compound Tool Construction by New Caledonian Crows," *Nature Scientific Reports* 8, 15676.

Visalberghi, Elisabetta, and Dorothy Fragaszy. 2013. "The Etho-*Cebus* Project: Stone-Tool Use by Wild Capuchin Monkeys," in *Tool Use in Animals: Cognition and Ecology*, 203–222. Edited by Crickette M. Sanz, Josep Call, and Christophe Boesch. New York, NY: Cambridge University Press.

Wadley, Lyn, Tamaryn Hodgkiss, and Michael Grant. 2009. "Implications for Complex Cognition from the Hafting of Tools with Compound Adhesives in the Middle Stone Age, South Africa," *Proceedings of the National Academy of Sciences* 106, 9590–9594.

Waldron, Jeremy. 1983. "Two Worries about Mixing One's Labour," *Philosophical Quarterly* 33(130), 37–44.

Waldron, Jeremy. 1988. *The Right to Private Property*. New York, NY: Oxford University Press.

Warneken, Felix, and Michael Tomasello. 2009. "Varieties of Altruism in Children and Chimpanzees," *Trends in Cognitive Science* 13, 397–402.

Weinar, Leif. 2015. "Rights," *The Stanford Encyclopedia of Philosophy*. Edited by Edward N. Zalta, http://plato.stanford.edu/archives/fall2015/entries/rights/. Last accessed November 17, 2015.

Wierzbicka, Anna. 1972. *Semantic Primitives*. Frankfurt, Germany: Athenäum Verlag.

Wierzbicka, Anna. 1987. *English Speech Act Verbs*. New York, NY: Academic Press.

Wierzbicka, Anna. 1996. *Semantics: Primes and Universals*. New York, NY: Oxford University Press.

Wierzbicka, Anna. 2006. *English: Meaning and Culture*. New York, NY: Oxford University Press.

Wierzbicka, Anna. 2010. *Experience, Evidence, and Sense: The Hidden Cultural Legacy of English*. New York, NY: Oxford University Press.

Wierzbicka, Anna. 2014. *Imprisoned by English: The Hazards of English as a Default Language*. New York, NY: Oxford University Press.

Wilkins, Jayne, Benjamin J. Schoville, Kyle S. Brown, and Michael Chazan. 2012. "Evidence for Early Hafted Hunting Technology," *Science* 338(6109), 942–946.

Williams, Charles F. (Supervisor). 1894. *The American and English Encyclopedia of Law*, Volume 26. New York, NY: Edward Thompson Company.

Williamson, Oliver. 1993. "Contested Exchange versus the Governance of Contractual Relations," *Journal of Economic Perspectives* 7, 103–108.

Williamson, Oliver. 1996. *The Mechanisms of Governance*. New York, NY: Oxford University Press.

Wilson, Bart J. 2015. "Humankind in Civilization's Extended Order: A Tragedy, the First Part," *Supreme Court Economic Review* 23(1), 35–58.

Wilson, Bart J., Taylor Jaworski, Karl Schurter, and Andrew Smyth. 2012. "The Ecological and Civil Mainsprings of Property: An Experimental Economic History of Whalers' Rules of Capture," *Journal of Law, Economics and Organization* 28(4), 617–656.

Wittgenstein, Ludwig. 1953. *Philosophical Investigations*. Translated by G. E. M. Anscombe. Malden, MA: Blackwell Publishing.

Wittgenstein, Ludwig. 1958. *The Blue and Brown Books*. New York, NY: Harper & Row.

Wittgenstein, Ludwig. 1980. *Culture and Value*. Translated by Peter Wench. Edited by G. H. von Wright and H. Nyman. Chicago, IL: University of Chicago Press.

Wrangham, Richard. 2009. *Catching Fire: How Cooking Made Us Human*. New York, NY: Basic Books.

Wycliffe, John. Died 1384. *Two Short Treatises, against the Orders of the Begging Friars*. Available at http://quod.lib.umich.edu/e/eebo/A15298.0001.001/1:5?rgn=div1;view=fulltext. Last accessed October 19, 2019.

Index

Note: Tables and figures are indicated by *t* and *f* following the page number. Small caps indicate the concept

For the benefit of digital users, indexed terms that span two pages (e.g., 52–53) may, on occasion, appear on only one of those pages.

Printed in the USA/Agawam, MA
February 11, 2022

788251.005